Praise for MALCO

About the Author

As wine correspondent of the *Guardian*, Malcolm Gluck has been finding wine bargains for readers of the Saturday edition for seven years – through the medium of his weekly *Superplonk* column. He is also consultant wine editor of *Sainsbury's Magazine* – an independent publication, not a ragbag of public relations puffery. His BBC-2 series on wine, *Gluck! Gluck!! Gluck!!!* will be transmitted this autumn and a book of the series will be published simultaneously.

Superplonk 1997

Malcolm Gluck

CORONET BOOKS
Hodder and Stoughton

Copyright © 1996 by Malcolm Gluck

First published in Great Britain as
a Coronet paperback original in 1996

The right of Malcolm Gluck to be identified as the Author of
this Work has been asserted by him in accordance with the
Copyright, Designs and Patents Act 1988.

10 9 8 7 6 5 4 3 2

British Library Cataloguing in Publication Data

Gluck, Malcolm
Superplonk 1997
1. Wine and wine making – Great Britain – Guidebooks
I. Title
641.2′2′0296′41

ISBN 0 340 66676 5

Typeset by Palimpsest Book Production Limited,
Polmont, Stirlingshire
Printed and bound in Great Britain by
Mackays of Chatham PLC, Chatham, Kent

Hodder and Stoughton
A division of Hodder Headline PLC
338 Euston Road
London NW1 3BH

To Felicity Rubinstein, for providing an ever-ready ear
and an ever-resourceful mind

'Sir, more than kisses, letters mingle souls.'

John Donne

CONTENTS

INTRODUCTION

I confess to drinking every wine in this book but not to spitting out every word. My readers have written this introduction, just as they have compiled the introductions to each individual retailer. Over the past seven years I have received letters on every conceivable aspect of wine, though many have a common theme, and the time has come to expose these missives in all their glory. Not only because they provide an entertaining and instructive exposé of wine drinkers' concerns and interests but also because they offer useful clues to the business style of the supermarkets about whom many of these letters complain and compliment.

My postbag is such that there are times when I spend more time a week replying to correspondents than I do writing my weekly *Guardian* column. I do not begrudge this time spent – though I must admit to wondering whether the newspaper will ever feel moved to recompense me for these covert labours – and I often look enviously upon those other columnists who lock the letterbox by suffixing their outpourings with 'It is regretted that the author cannot enter into correspondence'. But my envy is not genuine. I would feel imprisoned if readers did not feel free to bludgeon me with my boobs and congratulate me on my coups. And I would feel I was not doing my job properly if they were forced to consider themselves not at liberty to open their hearts on anything to do with the wine fever which has gripped the nation now that so much inexpensive, deliciously fruity wine is so widely available.

Whether in response to the *Superplonk* column in the *Weekend Guardian* magazine or the guides, readers' letters cover a vast range of subjects from corks and cellaring to religion and politics, and even the formation of Gluck Associations. I have been asked questions about which wines are most likely to give the drinker headaches, the relative merits of organic wines and where to buy vegan wines. I have also received letters from former acquaintances, wondering whether I am one and the same person they knew in a former life. One such reader was struck while reading a write-up of mine for a Montepulciano d'Abruzzo in *Superplonk 1993* by the thought, 'Blimey, could the author be the hairy, thin young fart I knew in Watford? Probably not. The Malcolm Gluck in the Class of '63 was not a great chorizo scoffer and the only foreign words he knew were *"double entendre"'*.

Many of the letters are amusing, some include poetry, and some are amazing for their length and detail. In contrast, one or two betray a staggering lack of attention to detail, particularly those which, despite my name appearing either above or below the column for all those years, have been addressed variously to Martin Gluck, Malcolm Cluck, Simon Gluck and Malcolm Glug, among other epithets. Several correspondents have taken to addressing me as Superplonker which I accept must be deliberate but resolutely believe is meant as a term of affection.

This introduction and the prefaces to each retailer section, which are based on letters concerning the specific supermarkets, can only give a fleeting taste of the huge range and variety of the letters and their authors. But while the subject matter ranges widely, there are one or two subjects which come up time and time again. A high proportion of letters are from readers who have for any number of reasons been unable to buy a wine reviewed in the column or the book. Most commonly, the wines have been out of stock, discontinued or only available in a limited number of stores. As the raison d'etre of *Superplonk* is the pursuit of value for money, it is no surprise that readers are at their most vociferous if prices are higher in the shops than those stated in the reviews. In these instances, I always pass on readers' letters to the retailers concerned and it is pleasing to hear that they have received apologies, free bottles of wine, or gift vouchers from contrite supermarkets. As these letters refer to specific retailers, I have generally included them in the relevant retailer sections. For that reason, there are actually few examples here of the kind of letters I receive most often.

Whatever the precise reasons for the letters, I have to say that the overwhelming majority are appreciative of what I attempt to do with *Superplonk* – which is consistently to find terrific bargains, be they £1.99 or £10.99. This convinces me I am doing the right thing and I find it immensely gratifying. For my part in de-mystifying wine and taking some of the angst out of wine-buying, readers appear to be genuinely grateful. Among them, Anne Jones of Reading who wrote charmingly in January 1996:

> Since I was given a copy of *Superplonk 1995* last Christmas, and also began to read your column with more attention, my life, as the old advertisements say, has been transformed. Before our daughter got married in April, my husband and I had a most enjoyable time trying out lots of wines from various sources, before settling on three that were not only extremely good but also much cheaper than those the caterer was offering. I estimate you saved us several hundred pounds, for which many thanks!

While I cannot claim that all readers' letters wax so effusively about life transformations, a great majority are extremely positive. And while letters may go on to gripe about an inaccuracy in the column or the unaccountable disappearance of a recommended wine, most begin or end with a pat on the back. Such is the change in some readers that I receive letters not from them, but from their nearest and dearest – like Polly Fairbairns of Brighton:

> My other half is totally obsessed with your column. I get desperate messages from him at work on a Saturday,

pleading with me to rush out to supermarkets near and far to acquire the latest recommendations.

From my position I see him as a poor helpless soul almost completely under your control and it was on August 20th that you got what you wanted. He was at fever pitch when he read out 17, 18, 18.5, and 19 points. He has been maniacally phoning our local Marks and Spencer's ever since. I think he's past the point of no return.

He is approaching 50 fast. Any chance of sending him a birthday card for a laugh?

It is particularly touching to receive poems from readers such as this one from Mrs Win Webster of Sheffield which landed on my doormat in May 1994:

BACCHUS OF YOU

Dear Malcolm Gluck, I'd like to say
What you have done for me.
I don't know much about good wine -
I really prefer tea.

My husband is disabled, so
I have to do the driving.
I always end up with fruit juice,
No chance of me imbibing.

So my delight is wine at home,
But which ones do I choose?
Red or white, or sweet or dry,
I've got so much to lose.

Fifteen pounds a bottle is a lot,
You must agree,
And three pounds must be just *too* cheap;
But that's where you help me.

Your column tells me what is best
In supermarket wine.
I try them all, and I must say,
Your choice just suits me fine.

Before I read you, you must know,
The wine shelves were my curse.
Now there's no doubt, you really are
The *Guardian* of my purse.

Superplonk has not only been the inspiration for poetry. I received a letter in June 1996 from Ms Silba Knight of Crouch End, north London. Her letter asked if she could lift a few sentences from one of my reviews to use in a short story she was writing.

I like your column a great deal, and even since I had to stop drinking – alas, because of illness – I still enjoy your weekly piece in the *Guardian*.

In fact, so much do I think of your very clear appreciation of wine, I have included a brief excerpt of last week's article in a short story I am writing. I clearly attributed it to you.

I used a couple of your phrases, clearly quoted, where my main character was sharing an empathy with you over a particular wine. I hope you think this is OK. Please can you give me your permission to do so if you think it necessary?

I was most happy to grant her request. Ms Knight is not the first person to write to me who has been forced to give up drinking wine but still enjoys reading the column. That too is most gratifying to hear.

Readers' letters have been enormously helpful in shaping the column, giving me new ideas and feedback on how I was approaching the subject, and I have been able to act on many of the suggestions which have been made over the years. At times, I feel like some kind of vinous ombudsman. It is as a result of readers' vigilance that many a bad batch of wine has been spotted and reported on, I have alerted the retailer concerned, and action has been taken. In one notable instance (see Kwik Save), a wine was totally removed from the shelves and delisted. Another very recent correspondent, Mr G. Foster of London W4, was quick to suss that Sainsbury's had changed its supplier of Sicilian Red and perhaps the wine was not as thrilling as it had been. I am investigating this matter as this book goes to press, but so far, I must say the wine seems okay to me, though one of the bottles I sampled was horrifically corked. But then corked wines are anathema as far as I am concerned and I often wonder, following my published enthusiasm for a particular wine, how many of my readers will end up with tainted bottles and instead of suspecting the contents of being faulty (since the fruit is merely dull and inexpressive rather than patently disgusting and malodorous) conjecture that perhaps old Superplonker simply lost his judgemental marbles on this one. The laws of statistical probability say that around one reader in twenty will buy a bottle contaminated, to a greater or lesser degree, by cork taint. The letters I have received on this subject have, as regular readers will know only too well, made me campaign vigorously for the abolition of natural cork and its replacement by screwcaps or synthetic corks.

Letters have ranged from the sensible and practical, such as Mr Tibor Z. Gold's exhortation to include the addresses and contact numbers for all the retailers in my wine shop guide, to the original and off-the-wall. In May 1994, Paul Bovett of Taunton wrote to me with a brilliant suggestion:

> In a recent article you said a Penfolds Cabernet Sauvignon would get to 19/20 points in 2008. I would welcome your advice re what wine to lay down now (costing say £10 to £15) to drink in celebration of the year 2000 – perhaps you could do this in your weekly column?

In 1974 our local Dominic's manager recommended a 1961 Smith Haut Lafite and a 1962 Chateau Climens for the year 1991. The red was slightly over but the Climens was a wow (20 points for sure). However a Climens now is too dear for us.

The AD 2000 series which I introduced to the weekly column later that year proved very popular and I thank Mr Bovett for the idea (but he must share the inspiration for it with the *Guardian* sub-editor who also suggested wines for the millennium). I also received enquiries about laying-down wines from Mrs Campbell of Haywards Heath in January 1992 who wanted some suggestions of wines she could lay down for her grandchildren's coming-of-age. I also received a 'laying-down' enquiry from Mrs Diana Singer of Bishop's Stortford in March 1993. Mrs Singer is another correspondent who has had to cope with a *Superplonk*-obsessed spouse.

First of all, I have to tell you that my husband is an absolute fan and it has been known for us – en route to the supermarket – to have to return home because he hasn't got your book with him!

I realise I've left it a bit late, but he is retiring on June 1st, his sixty-fifth birthday, and I am wondering if you would be kind enough to let me have your recommendation for some pretty special wines which I could give him to lay down or whatever. I promise not to take the credit for it! Many thanks.

In my reply, I gave Mrs Singer some ideas for wines that could be laid down for drinking over the next few years, along with some general advice on ageing wines – which wines were suitable for laying-down and for how long. Her letter prompted me to devote a whole article to this subject. In order to store wine properly you need a cool, dark place with a fairly even temperature, such as a coal-hole. I later heard from Mrs Singer that they did not have a coal-hole or a cellar, but were blessed with a WW2 air raid shelter in their back garden. A Grade II listed building perhaps now?

Another area where I have received useful feedback from readers is food and wine pairing. One of the key elements in any wine review is to give the reader an idea of what food would be appropriate to eat with the wine. While I often include such suggestions in my column, some of the world's rarer delicacies never receive a mention in this regard, which prompted Ms Sandy MacDonald of Braunston near Daventry, to write in 1991:

> I realise you can't make individual replies but would you recommend a wine to go with haggis in your column? I have just come back from a holiday in Scotland with an award-winning haggis and apart from whisky I can't think of a suitable drink to serve with it. I am going to try Valpolicella but perhaps you could come up with something better?

I was able to suggest the Marks & Spencer Jeunes Vignes to drink with the haggis, though I was later informed by Ms MacDonald that she had already finished the haggis by the time she had tracked down the appropriate wine. But she told me that the Jeunes Vignes was very fine – even without the intestinal accompaniment. If you have been wondering why Marks & Spencer stocks up on Jeunes Vignes around the time of Burns Night, perhaps this correspondence may have something to do with it.

Brian Seager of Pirbright in Surrey suggested in September 1994 that the title *Superplonk* was something of a misnomer.

> I'm a regular reader of *Superplonk*, but I was disappointed with your offering last Saturday. Your quoted prices were £2.99, £3.49, £6.99, £4.99, £4.99, £6.49, £8.99, £12.99.

Apart from the Tradition Coteaux de Languedoc, super they may be, but plonk they most definitely are not. Time to change the title of the column?

Clearly I was writing about some expensive wines at that time because I also received the following letter from Philip Rea of St Albans in July 1994.

Plonk, to my mind, is a low-quality, low-cost wine which is just drinkable; it is one step above a cheap and nasty wine which would still be undrinkable at half the price. Even in 1994, I would not expect to pay more than £3.00 for a bottle of plonk.

'Superplonk' I would define as a better-quality wine at a slightly higher price but, if pushed, I would set a maximum retail price of £4.00 a bottle. By no stretch of the imagination would I describe an Australian white, selling at £4.99 and rated 16 points by Mr Cluck (sic) as superplonk or any other form of plonk. I would describe it as a very good wine at a reasonable price.

Anyone who pays £14.99 for a bottle of superplonk must surely qualify for the title 'Superplonker of the Year'.

In a similar vein, Mr K. McLachlan of Shirley Warren, Southampton, wrote in July 1994:

I used to be a big fan of *Superplonk* which has either saved me much money in recent years, or allowed me to drink more wine than I'd otherwise have been able to, I'm not sure which.

Alas, you seem to have moved upmarket since the start of the column. For example, on 16th July you appear to describe wines at £3.49 and above as immensely cheap! Not when you live on my income, £2.50 is about the top line except for very special occasions. I live with students who are worse off than myself so please believe me that there's plenty of us povs. out here who'd appreciate a little guidance through the wide selection of Bulgarian country plonks that are available.

All these letters gave me food for thought. However catchy the title of my book and *Guardian* column, I had to agree with Mr Seager when I replied to his letter that the word 'plonk' was inappropriate. I have never written employing plonk in the pejorative sense of the term, I have only ever applied it to terrific wine at whatever the price *as long as that price represents wonderful value for money.* Above all, I am interested in bargains and bargains can be found at both £1.99 and £12.99.

Interestingly enough, I would say that many readers are quite interested in more expensive wines because they rather like to splash out on special occasions and I am committed to writing for all the readership, a broad church surely, and not just those who are interested in extremely cheap bargains. I wrote to Mr Rea:

Your letter amused me greatly and what you say about the word 'Superplonk' is certainly interesting. However, I hope that by now the use of the word to front a column like mine over the last five years has changed one's notion of what plonk is. I always think plonk is just inexpensive wine which is terrific value for money.

Often I stretch 'inexpensive' to something which represents quite a sum, say £15, but I always take value into account when I rate such a wine and at that price I'd probably rate it on the basis of comparing it with extremely prestigious, highly expensive wines costing £30 or £40.

We certainly don't have any plans to change the name of my column, or the way I write, or the way I approach the rating of wines!

I have, over the years, had a few run-ins with gentlemen of the cloth. Apart from the time when I inadvertently embarrassed a Methodist minister from Yorkshire responsible for the pastoral care of 300 churches (by printing his name in the column as an avid reader and imbiber), I also received this letter from the Rev D.J. Dermott of Hinderwell near Saltburn in September 1994:

> I wonder if anyone else took exception to the headline and first paragraph of your *Weekend Guardian* piece a couple of weeks ago? I did feel that it was less than thoughtful or considerate of the feelings of those who take the Gospel seriously. Senor Puelles would probably be embarrassed, as well. Nor did the wine have anything in common with water; it scored 20 points, and more! See John 3:10.
>
> You will need to be more careful in making any reference to Islamic matters or you may be the first wine writer under a fatwa!
>
> In spite of all this I shall continue to take your column as gospel – small 'g' – and to look out for your more modest selections.

I might usefully explain here, for those readers not possessed of elephantine memories, that the Senor Puelles referred to is a Spanish wine-maker whose first name – about which I ventured a small joke – is Jesus. As it happens, I met Jesus Puelles some time later and discovered he thought the article most amusing. He even keeps it handy in his office to demonstrate to visitors that the English do possess a sense of humour after all.

But no humour was in evidence, from certain readers, where General Pinochet and a nuclear bomb test-mad France were concerned. I got ticked off for writing about Chilean wine – even though the plebescite which restored democracy to that country encouraged me to feel my personal boycott was no longer necessary – and the French came in for an extensive verbal bashing in 1995 from correspondents, some of whom urged me to bar French wine from the column completely. Peter and Christine Hodgkinson from Charcombe in Oxfordshire wrote to ask for suggestions to avoid, as they put it, a 'Chirac-contaminated Christmas'. I was happy to point out that my column regularly listed bargains from many countries other than the one the beastly bellicose Frogs inhabit.

Another subject which became an issue of conscience both in the column and in my correspondence was South Africa. It came as a surprise to me, even as someone who had been an active anti-apartheid sloganeer for many years, that writing about South African wines after Mr Nelson Mandela was released would still be considered by many to be politically unacceptable. It evoked a response from readers and I was fascinated to hear the views expressed. The letters, in sum, suggested that my writing about the wines legitimised buying them and was an attempt de-politicise what was still a highly emotive subject even though, as it seemed to me, Mr Mandela's political interests were better served by making Cape wines once again an acceptable part of the UK wine scene. Phyllis Rodinsky of Greenwich wrote in December 1992:

> Just to say how much I enjoy your *Superplonk* columns as well as the book – I've learned a lot from them (and my local Safeway has benefited too!).
>
> I wish, tho, you wouldn't even mention South African wines. I realize that we aren't compelled to buy them, but even a mention has the sense of a tacit endorsement and since I assume that you read 'The G' as well as writing for it, you'll know how the wine-growers' workforce is treated; Well, you know all the arguments.

In September 1993 an article I wrote for the newspaper, but which was not a *Superplonk* column, bore the headline 'Hospitality and Fine Wine while the blacks sweat'. This headline was not mine but a sub-editor's. It elicited a considerable amount of correspondence, from South Africa as well as in this country. In particular it inspired Pam Tommy of Southwark to send me a poem she had written while out in South Africa. My article, she wrote, had 'brought back vivid, painful memories of my drives through those lush winelands of the Western Cape. Thank you for honouring those voiceless unfortunates.'

In response to the same article, Mr A.F. Slee of Pensby in The Wirral took a rather different stance, suggesting that I should not have brought politics into wine at all. This underlines how differently people can react to the same subject. When the dust died down, my feelings were largely unchanged. I do not accept that I introduced politics into the situation, for surely apartheid did that long before I got to see a Cape vineyard, and I was only prepared to lift my embargo, self-imposed, on writing about wines from that country once I was convinced that it was no longer in the interests of the new South Africa to maintain it.

I have often wondered why it is that people who have written in with reservations or complaints about my reviews, often extremely frustrated by not finding what they were looking for on the shelves, generally adopt such a positive attitude to my work. A singularly simple explanation for this, however, was provided by Mr H. Yee of Hitchin, whose letter I received in January 1993. Mr Yee wrote with some points about my rating system. This has been the subject of a considerable volume of correspondence over the years and as I view this system as one of the facets which sets *Superplonk* apart from other columns and guides, it was encouraging to see that it attracted so much comment (the great majority of it approving). Mr Yee's analysis of my system was particularly detailed.

I have been reading your articles in the *Guardian* for several years, and I have always enjoyed them and the wines recommended enormously. In common with most readers, however, I could not drum up the energy to write until I had a complaint.

I have always envied your ability to place wines to the

exact point on a scale of 1 to 20. For the first 18 months or so, I relied on my memory to pick up a recommended wine. Then I resorted to writing down some wines on a scrap of paper when I went shopping. Finally, I started to enter each week's wines into my computer database. In the course of doing this, I have found that you do not rate wines consistently from one article to another!

These inconsistencies only appear, of course, when a wine is mentioned in more than one article. I do have your 1992 paperback, and in some cases, I have compared a single article with the rating given in the book.

I am curious as to how this happened. Surely you do not rely on memory? I thought all journalists used computers these days, so how did the rating get changed?

Included in Mr Yee's letter were several examples of inconsistencies and a print-out from his database. Given that the rating system is in many ways the linchpin of my job, I thought this enquiry deserved as full an explanation as I could give. I replied:

You raise an interesting point, several points, and one which exercises me constantly: how can I give a precise rating for a thing which changes over a year, say, or sometimes a shorter period, in bottle?

I find my ratings consistent, considering I'm rating a couple of thousand wines in the book and drinking several thousand more over a year in preparing the book. I am not surprised to find slight variations, because wines can improve in bottle whilst on shelf and sometimes they do the opposite. I am, in fact, tasting a new bottle for each article and often I find the wine different enough to award an extra point to it, or deduct one.

I would really only get distressed when a wine I rated highly deteriorates from a 16-pointer to a 10-pointer within the book's lifetime. This has yet to happen but it could. Equally, the opposite could happen, and certainly when I taste some wines – not many but a few – twelve months apart, I'm often struck how much better they have become.

You're right about my memory. It comes courtesy of AppleMac. What would I do without it? Indeed, if I find myself short-handed in preparing the next edition I know where to look for help.

Arguably, the most flattering compliment a writer – any writer, not just the wine-bottle variety – can be paid is to have an association, wine circle or club formed and named in his or her honour. This may strike some readers as vaguely cultish, but to the author it is genuinely a source of satisfaction (though as a life-long abhorrer of clubs this satisfaction is not entirely unequivocal, nor does it deprive me of the good sense – I hope – not to let such things make me smug). One such Gluck Association has been formed in Swindon by Mr Chris Walton and friends, more details of which can be found in the introduction to the section on the Co-op later in this book.

Julian Saunders and Sheila Maister from south-east London wrote to me in 1993 with details of a *Superplonk* evening they were planning.

We've been following your column in the *Guardian* for a while and we've found your suggestions very helpful in choosing supermarket wines. Our wedding reception this summer was greatly enriched by the Louis Massing Champagne from Tesco's you recommended – a great 16-pointer.

We are planning to hold a *Superplonk* Party on Saturday 19th March 1994 and we would be very pleased if you and your partner would be our guests of honour. We plan to sample some of the wines under £4.00 you've recommended over the last few months and to have a

15

competition to find the cheapest drinking wine on sale in south London. Guests will be invited to bring low-price wines and we would be delighted if you could judge them on their quaffability.

We plan to invite about 30 people at the maximum to the event. We would understand if you're not able to make it to the party but we would be delighted if you could come.

Unfortunately I was unable to attend the party because I was abroad at the time. I remember I recommended that they should include Gateway's Navarra Tinto, then retailing for £1.79, in the tasting. This charming couple later wrote to say that the evening had been an unqualified success (inspiring the heretical idea that had I been able to attend it might not have been so).

Another *Superplonk* tasting was hosted by Bill Deakin, of North Humberside, at one of his wine circle meetings. He wrote to me in December 1991:

As a regular *Guardian* reader and wine consumer I enjoy your *Superplonk* column and often follow your recommendations. Yesterday evening, at a meeting of our local wine circle (a rather grandiose name for what is essentially a good excuse to indulge ourselves), I used your article of 9/10th November on *Superplonk* wines as the basis for a tasting.

I was able to obtain in our local stores a number of the wines you recommended, which proved to be very popular with my fellow members and provided the basis of a very enjoyable evening. The M & S Jeunes Vignes and the Tesco Moscatel de Valencia were particularly appreciated, as was the Sainsbury's Romanian Pinot Noir.

Thank you on behalf of our members, for your contribution to our enjoyment of an ever-growing range of wines.

I do not know whether wine writers generally get letters from readers or whether correspondence is an exception. I suspect that the theme of most letters is always connected with a valuation of an old bottle of wine that the reader has stashed away and has, for some reason, always fought shy of opening. However, for me, such letters form less than 2 per cent of my mailbag. The flavour of this particular container is well represented by the letters in each of the retailer introductions within this book and by the letters reproduced above. If there is a common thread running through them it is that the *Superplonk* idea, arriving as it did (through no foresight of my own but by sheer coincidence) when a vicious recession was forcing tens of thousands of drinkers to rejig their lifestyles for financial reasons, has inspired many people to try wines they might have missed, to have confidence in their own tastes and prejudices, to refuse to pay lip service (an expensive and unnecessary luxury where wine is concerned), and bend the knee to the so-called great wines whose reputations are based on false assumptions and misty perceptions.

I began writing *Superplonk* not as someone with a wine trade background or as an established journalist who wanted to find a way for others to subsidise his thirst. I was invited by the *Guardian* newspaper, a newspaper of which I had been a devotee going back to the days when Manchester featured on its masthead, to contribute a wine column. I was simply a writer with a love of wine; and although that love now and then tempted me into expensive indiscretions – what *amateur* has not so strayed – I was an inveterate tracker-down of bargains from unlikely sources (as supermarkets were in the early days) and I developed a passion for matching wine with food. I would like to believe that my readers recognise these things and relate to them for they can see that my enthusiasm and beliefs spring from the same deep well as theirs.

I don't wish to get maudlin at this point or turn preacher, but I will say this before I finally shut up and let you get on and take this book to your local supermarket and plunder its shelves. Wine and food, of all consumer purchases, are the ones we can possess completely. Everything else we buy is borrowed – borrowed until it breaks down, or is replaced, or we get bored with it, or it becomes dysfunctional or unfashionable, or we get fed up with looking at it or wearing it. The wine we drink and the food we eat becomes part of us – the experience cannot be returned or updated for a newer model. Wine is entertainment, culture, discourse, compassion, education, health, joy and unpretentious pleasure.

I would like to believe I subscribe heavily to those ideals. I do so as a drinker and as a writer. And as long as my readers continue to support me I will soldier on. I may sometimes feel driven to tear out what little hair is still left on my scalp when I get a letter revealing yet another screwup by a supermarket wine department or a failure on my part to have realised that Cornwall does not have any branches of the particular Co-op which stocks some amazing £2.19 bottle of Portuguese red, but these madnesses are occurring less and less frequently. Perhaps the day will come when perfection will be reached and my postman will become a stranger – but I'm most unsure whether I relish the prospect. What will I do with myself on Wednesday afternoons and Friday mornings if I haven't got readers' letters to answer and stamps to stick on?

Indeed, I sometimes wonder what wine would best accompany postage stamp gum. No wine I've yet tasted has been remotely right. But one day the perfect bottle will appear, of that I have no doubt. A reader will write and tell me.

How this Guide Works

Each supermarket in this guide is separately listed alphabetically. Each has its own introduction with the wines logically arranged by country of origin, red and white (including roses). Each wine's name is as printed on its label.

Each wine is rated on points out of 20. In practice, wines

scoring less than 10 points are not included although sometimes, because a particular bottle has really got up my nostrils and scored so lamentably, I feel readers might be amused by its inclusion, I put in a low pointer. In previous books I wrote that over the past few years this miserable vinous underclass had assaulted my palate in steadily decreasing numbers and that the rise in the overall quality of wines was reflected in the rating figures. This year, as in prior years, higher ratings appear more frequently, but not necessarily higher prices. I have been forced, in the interests of fair ratings, to tack on a further half-point, such has been the increase in the quality of fruit without the usual concomitant upping of prices.

I continue to be the only wine writer who genuinely rates wines on a value-for-money basis (the only one, in all likelihood, who even thinks in such terms). I expect expensive wines to be good but I do not always expect good wines to be expensive. Thus, a brilliant £10 bottle may not offer better value than a £3 wine because, although the pricier wine is more impressive it is not, in my eyes, anywhere near three times as impressive. I am increasingly disappointed by wines costing over £10 a bottle and this goes double for those costing over £20.

The full scoring system, from my initial tasting and scoring point of view, works as follows:

20 Is outstanding and faultless in all departments: smell, taste and finish in the throat. Worth the price, even if you have to take out a second mortgage.

19 A superb wine. Almost perfect.

18 An excellent wine of clear complexity but lacking the sublime finesse for the top, yet fabulously good value.

17 An exciting, well-made wine at an affordable price.

16 Very good wine indeed. Good enough for any dinner party. Not expensive.

15 For the money, a great mouthful with real style.

14 The top end of everyday drinking wine. Well made and to be seriously recommended at the price.

13 Good wine, not badly made. Not great, but very drinkable.

12 Everyday drinking wine at a sensible price.

11 Drinkable, but not a wine to dwell on.

10 Average wine (at a low price), yet still a passable mouthful. Also, wines which are expensive and, though drinkable, do not justify their high price.

9 Cheap plonk. Acceptable for parties in dustbin-sized dispensers.

8 Rough stuff. Feeble value.

7 Good for pickling onions.

6 Hardly drinkable except to quench desperate thirsts on an icy night by a raging bonfire.

5 Wine with all its defects and mass-manufacturing methods showing.

4 Not good at any price.

3 A palate polluter and barely drinkable.

2 Rat poison. Not to be recommended to anyone, even winos.

1 Beyond the pale. Awful. Even Lucretia Borgia wouldn't serve it to her worst enemy.

From your viewpoint, the wine buyer's, the rating system can be compressed like this:

10, 11   Nothing nasty but equally nothing worth shouting from the rooftops. Drinkable but not exciting.

12, 13   Above average, interestingly made. A bargain taste.

14,15,16   This is the exceptional stuff, from the very good to the brilliant.

17, 18   Really terrific wine worthy of individual acclaim. The sort of wine you can decant and serve to ignorant snobs who'll think it famous even when it is no such thing. Often a bargain price.

19, 20   Overwhelmingly marvellous. Wine which cannot be faulted, providing an experience never to be forgotten.

Prices

I cannot guarantee the price of any wine in this guide for all the usual trite reasons: inflation, economic conditions overseas, the narrow margins on some supermarket wines making it difficult to maintain consistent prices for very long and, of course, the existence of those freebooters at the Exchequer who are liable to up taxes which the supermarkets cannot help but pass on to the consumer. To get around this problem a price banding code is assigned to each wine:

Price Band

1	2	3	4
A Under £2.50	B £2.50 – £3.50	C £3.50 – £5	D £5 – £7

5	6	7	8
E £7 – £10	F £10 – £13	G £13 – £20	H Over £20

All wines costing under £5 (i.e. A–C) have their price band set against a black background.

STOP PRESS!

Although this is the most thoroughly researched and up-to-date wine guide available, some retailers introduce a few Christmas wines just as this book is going to press. It has always irritated me that these wines, in the past, have escaped my net. But no longer! Thanks to a bend-over-backwards publisher and a printer of unequally untypical flexibility, you will find a Stop Press section at the end of this book. Here are the last-minute bottles – wines I tasted only after the bulk of this book was already printed.

Acknowledgements

Several people are due special thanks for helping me put this book together. Whilst I write it alone, and every wine in it has washed over my palate and my palate alone, I could not enjoy this luxury without Linda Peskin, who organises my workdays and runs the fearful computer system without which I would need the assistance of six secretaries. I could not have written this book either without Ben Cooper's assiduous research back-up and invaluable support. Linda and Ben have been towers of strength. Helen Dore has been her usual immaculate and conscientious copy-editing self and I am in her debt. I would also like to thank Janet Nicholson for her help with the mountain of correspondence, my patient typesetter, Craig Morrison, and all the Hodder folk who seem to me to be unusually bright (thus making it a pleasure to do their bidding): Amanda Ridout, Kerr MacRae, Jamie Hodder-Williams, Karen Geary, and Kate Lyall Grant. And my editor, George Lucas, is a sheer delight to work with.

ASDA

Asda way to confuse 'em

One of the most frequent beefs raised in readers' letters is that they have read splendid reviews of wines, rushed hotfoot to the supermarket, and found either that the wines in question are not there, or the promotional offers have finished. It would be unfair to single out Asda in this regard, though they have had their fair share of such problems over the years.

The most recent episode concerns their Cava which was reviewed in the column at £3.79 a bottle. When readers went to Asda to take advantage of the offer, they found it to be selling at £4.99. Mr and Mrs C. Oulton of Melksham in Wiltshire, preparing for Silver Wedding celebrations and clearly planning to buy in some quantity, were naturally rather miffed when they wrote on 12 November 1995:

> Asda way to confuse 'em.
>
> My wife and I are planning our Silver Wedding Celebration which is to be held on 23rd December. Amongst all the other arrangements, we are enjoying sampling various sparkling white wines in order to choose one to serve to 60 guests. We were therefore very excited that you were recommending the Asda Cava.
>
> When we arrived at the store we were surprised to be told that the price of the wine was £4.99. However, the assistant checked with the manager who agreed that we could have the bottle for £3.79 as shown in your article. We were obviously

pleased that Asda were prepared to honour the price even though it was not apparently their mistake.

If this is the new blend we would like to buy a few cases for our party, but where can we buy it at the price you quote of £3.79?

Mr and Mrs Oulton were not the only readers to be angered by the Cava mix-up, nor were they the only ones to suggest that *Superplonk* could be to blame. From Burcott in Luton, Linda (no surname) wrote:

A great article and very tempting. So I journey to Asda Nottingham to purchase a case of Cava for Christmas. Zut alors! Cava is selling at £4.99 with, according to their wine chappie, no reduction in sight.

Malcolm, don't be a Superplonker. Please inform them before your article so they can stock up, cut down and satisfy your readers!

Linda and Mr and Mrs Oulton were entitled to be confused but the blame for this cock-up lay firmly with Asda, and this needed to be clarified. I replied thus to the Oultons on 3 December:

Quite why this supermarket cannot keep its word I do not know. I have been assured by all manner of individuals at head office that the Cava was reduced from £4.99 to £3.79 and indeed it should have been on a national basis. I'm furious that you were forced to write to me and I shall be sending a copy of your letter, and this reply, to Asda's head office. However, I'm delighted that you're enjoying the wine. I think it's terrific at the price.

The Oultons' predicament reminded me of a letter I received back in 1993 from Mr Gabriel Lancaster of Rochester. Another reader keen to celebrate a long and happy marriage in style, he wrote to *Superplonk* in August 1993:

Some weeks ago you were kind enough to respond to a copy letter I sent to you, the letter being to Asda, concerning certain difficulties experienced in obtaining an Australian sparkling wine (River Run) which you had recommended in your *Guardian* column.

The delay in this reply has been due to the active preparations for the Golden Wedding celebrations of my wife and myself, which occurred recently. The response I had from Asda was a phone call from the Gravesend branch manager, explaining, apologising and offering a case at the offer price mentioned in your column, if I cared to call in and speak with him, during the following three months.

This was followed, just recently, by a letter of apology and explanation from Asda head office, Customer Service.

I took advantage of their offer (obviously!) and I must say that it went down very well, even amongst other prestigious bottles of Mumm's Napa Valley and Lanson, during our celebrations.

I was pleased that Asda head office had done the right thing by the Lancasters. I pass on all such queries to the retailers themselves in the hope that they will correct the mistake. Once a customer has gone away empty-handed, the damage is probably done, but retailers help themselves and their customers – not to mention *Superplonk* – by trying to put things right after the event. In this regard at least, Asda gets it right.

After Mr M. Jones had complained that an Australian Vintage Chardonnay was not available at the Asda in Leamington Spa, he received two letters from said retailer, one from the managing director's office and this one from Asda Customer Relations on 5 November 1990:

Thank you for your recent letter which has been passed from the Managing Director's office.

I was very sorry to hear of the annoyance and inconvenience caused by the unavailability of Australian Vintage

Chardonnay '83 at our Leamington Spa store.

Naturally, we are very pleased by Malcolm Gluck's write-up and are most anxious to respond to the demand it has stimulated. The wine has been available in many of our larger stores for over a year but we are obviously limited by available shelf space in other stores.

Nevertheless, to deter you from returning to Waitrose we have instructed the Leamington Spa store to order the wine as soon as possible. As soon as it arrives Mr Swiatyj, the Food Hall manager, will ring to inform you. If it proves successful the store will stock it permanently.

Once again, thank you for bringing this matter to our attention and I do hope you find the wine to your taste.

Asda seems to be keen on replicating apologies from several different quarters. Whether this is out of utter contrition or a lack of communication is not certain. In any event, Sue Warren of Halifax was doubly, nay trebly grateful, as she wrote on 15 June 1993:

Thank you for your letter about my wine experiences and for contacting Sainsbury's and Asda. Just after I wrote to you I received a letter from the Asda store with apologies and a £3.00 gift voucher. Then I received a letter from their Leeds office with a £5.00 voucher. Philip Clive (Asda) has just replied with a £6.00 voucher. At this rate, maybe I will get to the Caribbean!

In some cases, store staff showed some flexibility on price, as the Oultons had found. Back in 1992, Mr E. Nunn wrote to tell me that he had been allowed to buy a bottle of Valencia Red at the £1.99 quoted in the column. But it would appear that this degree of latitude is far from universal.

One correspondent from North London who must have his reasons for wishing to remain anonymous wrote with this tale of woe in 1991:

Re Your *Superplonk* Column Sat 17.

I dashed the five miles to Asda to buy your recommendations: Valencia Red and Chateau de Cabriac to find that whilst other Valencias were being sold at £1.99, this red was £2.39 (not even the £2.29 you mention). On the latter, the price you gave also seems incorrect. The Manager, clearly not a *Guardian* reader, was not at all sympathetic, but what went wrong? Incidentally, I have found before that the prices you give are sometimes below the actual shelf price.

Moreover, the same correspondent wrote again several months later to say that his complaint had fallen on deaf ears at Asda head office, most unusual for the voucher-happy Philip Clive, who is no longer with the store. However, Catherine Goundry, writing in September 1993, found Asda back to their normal helpful selves.

Many thanks for giving me the phone number of Asda's PR people. I rang them this morning and not only did they tell me which local store stocked Goundrey Langton Chardonnay but also exactly where in the store to find it. So this lunchtime I ventured south of the river (Trent), into our esteemed Chancellor of the Exchequer's constituency, to Asda's West Bridgford shop, and bought a couple of bottles, which I am looking forward to drinking.

Just one thing though – the recommendation on the shelf was by a guy called Oz Clarke writing for a newspaper other than the *Guardian*!

Asda's ex-PR people, Lynne Franks, may have won plaudits from Ms Goundry, but Mr D.J. Alonso of Bristol, writing in May 1993, kindly recognised the part played by *Superplonk* in Asda's PR.

Re : *Weekend Guardian* 1 May 1993 – Asda

Clearly, Lynne Franks PR do not appear very impressive and Asda have been doing well enough for themselves through your column. However I write because I feel that you have gone over the top.

Although I shop regularly in Asda (Bedminster), I am not excited about their wines. My own consumption of Leon '86 doubled last year – I bought a second bottle as I could not believe that you had rated it so highly. Never again.

I bought the first bottle shortly after you recommended the Leon '85, but this was nowhere to be seen, just the '86, with year date in small print. A Chilean Rowanbrook red, suggested by yourself at the same time (14pts), was much better.

Asda has some reasonable wines but the Leon '86 does not deserve 16pts. You deserve something special from Asda for promoting it so well.

Mr Alonso is quite right. The retailers do derive enormous benefit from write-ups their wines receive in wine columns and they pay people like Lynne Franks large sums of money to look after the press. Asda and their ilk are generally very appreciative though any relationship is tested from time to time.

Late in 1995, Nick Dymoke-Marr, senior wine buyer at Asda, wrote to the *Guardian*, dismayed at some 'inaccuracies' in my column of 23 September. Mr Dymoke-Marr accepted that endorsements from wine writers heighten consumer interest in Asda wines, and told us that positive comments from *Superplonk* were used on point-of-sale material. In the light of all these positives that *Superplonk* can offer a retailer, the *Guardian* clearly took exception to his complaint, and wrote:

The error in the version of Malcolm Gluck's copy that appeared in the *Weekend Guardian* on 23 September is regrettable. However I feel strongly disinclined to apologise for it. For a start, the whole tone of your letter is bumptious, presumptuous and impertinent.

As you rightly point out in your letter 'such endorsements heighten the interest in the wine'. Comments of people like Malcolm help you sell a lot of bottles. In effect,

wine writers act as publicity agents for organisations such
as your own. You benefit handsomely from our interest in
you. There is no reciprocal benefit for us.

I am, however, quite prepared to apologise to our readers, for it is they who may have suffered from this inadvert-
ent misinformation. A correction will appear as soon as it
is feasible to print it.

I also differed with Asda in 1995 over the retailer's new way
of laying out its wine department, organising the wines in grades
of sweetness for the whites and degrees of fullness for the reds. I
voiced my reservations over this system and received letters both
for and against from readers.

Chris Cade of Fareham, who wrote in September 1995, shared
my doubts. 'Having visited Asda stores quite recently I agree with
your lack of conviction about that store's changed presentation
policy,' Mr Cade wrote. 'I have found it deeply confusing and far
from helpful!'

On the other hand, Helen Neuenhaus of Birmingham wrote in
praise of the new system, suggesting that I adopt the Asda system
for the *Superplonk* guide.

On the recommendation of a friend, I have just bought a
copy of your book *Superplonk 1996*. On the whole it is a
treasure-house of wine tips, but I have to disagree with your
comments on Asda's new method of displaying wines. I'm
a regular Asda customer and, having read your comments,
felt I had to write to poor Mr Dymoke-Marr to tell him to
ignore you completely!!

Despite books such as *Superplonk*, the majority of the
great unwashed plonk purchasers (myself included) wan-
der along the aisles of supermarkets in abject confusion.

It's all very well to dash off in search of a specific bottle
of wine, recommended by a wine writer such as yourself –
and to find that it is indeed a good buy. But then how do
you progress? Asda, in my humble opinion, have got it spot

on. Having found that I enjoy, for example, a St Chinian, I can try other similar styles from other countries and wine producers.

Armed with your book, I can check what else you recommend in the Asda wine section which I've found I prefer (Reds B–C).

Of course it would be a lot easier if you followed Asda's lead and sectioned your book in the same way, as a lot of us 'plonk drinkers' think the same way. We know we like certain styles of wine (rich, fruity red, or crisp whites) but when faced with an aisle of wines which are sorted according to country we're not sure where to start.

That said, your book is still a great buy. I'm looking forward to *Superplonk 1997* but if Asda take your comments to heart and revert to displaying wines by country again, I shall hold you personally responsible!

In conclusion, my description in 1991 of Asda's wine, Est! Est! Est!, as ludicrously named, clearly touched a nerve. A number of readers were swift to offer explanations. This from Mr W. Pain of Aylesbury:

I am not sure why you describe Asda's wine Est! Est! Est! as 'ludicrously named' in last Saturday's edition of the *Guardian* but if perchance the exclamatory title has meant little till now then I suggest you might pay a visit to a restaurant of the same name in Didsbury, Manchester. This very well ordered restaurant carries at the top of its menu a delightful explanation of the derivation of such a name for a restaurant.

Mr G. Todeschini of Hatfield offered a fuller explanation of the provenance of this unusually, if not ludicrously, named wine. Those engaged in selling wine will frequently tell you that it is easier to sell a wine with a story behind it.

In the *Superplonk* article of Saturday, 23 November you refer to the 'ludicrously named' Est! Est! Est! wine sold by Asda.

Minus exclamation marks, however, in the name there lies a tale: In 12 or 1300 a German bishop was on his lifetime's pilgrimage to Rome with servants and courtiers. Being rather fond of wine, he had one of his servants travel a day's ride ahead, not to arrange for the next night's lodgings, but to taste the wine in each village his master would pass through, and chalk up his comments on the wall of the first house on the road from the north. Depending on the wine, the bishop would then decide where to spend the night.

When the wine taster reached the town of Montefiascone near Lake Bolsena he thought the wine was the best encountered on the trip that far and wrote Est Est Est, meaning *this is it*.

The bishop obviously agreed because he never did reach Rome but is buried in the little church of which there is a sketch on the label of Asda's wine. The above story is carved on his tombstone. The wine from Montefiascone has been called Est! Est! Est! ever since.

Asda Stores Limited
Asda House
Great Wilson Street
Leeds
LS11 5AD

Tel 0113 2435435
Fax 0113 2418146

SEE STOP PRESS SECTION AT END OF BOOK FOR LAST-MINUTE ADDITIONS TO THIS RETAILER'S RANGE.

ARGENTINIAN WINE RED

Argentinian Red, Asda `13.5` `B`

ARGENTINIAN WINE WHITE

Argentinian White 1995, Asda `11` `B`

AUSTRALIAN WINE RED

Chateau Reynella Basket-Pressed Cabernet/Merlot 1993 `16` `E`

Hardys Nottage Hill Cabernet Sauvignon/ Shiraz 1994 `15` `C`

Mount Hurtle Grenache Shiraz, Geoff Merrill 1994 `15` `C`

So richly fruity you can't believe it comes from grapes. It is like an addition to meat as a sauce in itself. It is soft, very ripe, audacious and completely riveting.

Penfolds Bin 389 Cabernet/Shiraz 1993 `15` `E`

Husky fruit which will develop better over the next eighteen months.

Penfolds Rawson's Retreat Bin 35 Cabernet/Shiraz 1995 `14` `C`

Peter Lehmann Vine Vale Shiraz 1994 | 16 | C |

Will awaken the dead. Use it as an invalid's reviver or with any roast or grilled meat meal and the food itself will come alive and go snorting, baaing, mooing and oinking round the table.

Rosemount Estate Shiraz 1994 | 14 | D |

Rosemount Shiraz/Cabernet 1995 | 15 | C |

Such smoothness and velvet-textured fruit. A gentility of fruit which surprises and delights.

South Australian Cabernet Sauvignon 1994 | 13.5 | C |

Positive, fruity, balanced, but a touch too prone to collapse with food.

South Eastern Australia Shiraz/Cabernet 1995 | 14 | B |

Very soft and lengthy. Stretches itself most agreeably around roast chicken.

AUSTRALIAN WINE WHITE

Chateau Reynella Chardonnay 1994 | 16 | D |

Lushness, weight, richness and a silky stylishness.

Cranswick Oak Aged Marsanne 1994 | 14 | C |

Hardys Nottage Hill Chardonnay 1995 | 15.5 | C |

When a wine gets so close to a fiver, it must equally offer fiver fruit. This one succeeds.

Jackdaw Ridge Australian White | 11 | B |

Kingston Estate Chenin/Verdelho 1995   13   C

Penfolds Bin 202 Riesling 1994   14   C

A delicious, dry, off-beat riesling with lots of flavour and soft fruit saved from squashy lushness by lemonic acids. Will age well for a couple of years, but terrific with shellfish now.

Penfolds Rawson's Retreat Bin 21 Semillon/Chardonnay/Colombard 1995   15.5   C

Apples, walnuts, pineapple, melon – quite an impressive medley here. The acidity is pure, crisp Golden Delicious.

Peter Lehmann Semillon, Barossa Valley 1995   15   C

Scrumptious without being overflavoured.

Rosemount Estate Chardonnay 1995   16   D

Beautiful controlled fruit with vivacity and restraint. This paradox is Rosemount's hallmark.

South Australian Chardonnay 1995, Asda   16   C

Fabulous bottle of rich, full, deep, beautifully arranged chardonnay with oodles of flavour and richness. Terrific quaffing wine as well as sufficiently brawny to lift food. Terrific price.

South East Australian Semillon Chardonnay 1995, Asda   14.5   B

Lots of soft, almost lush fruit. Not your blowsy over-the-top Aussie chardonnay but an attractive, flavoursome one.

BULGARIAN WINE   RED

Assenovgrad Mavrud Reserve   `14` `B`

A simple, delicious, cheerful glug with a nice dusky edge of fresh fruit.

Bulgarian Vintage Premium Merlot 1994   `13` `B`

Burgas Barrel Aged Merlot   `15` `B`

Excellent varietal interpretation with a vigorous bite of acidity and fruit. A bookish wine to dwell over with a cheese omelette and grilled leeks.

Domaine Boyar Suhindol Cabernet Sauvignon/Merlot 1992   `15` `B`

Terrific tannins, great fruit, fine structure, this wine has character and real class. Smashing food wine – great with cheese dishes.

Liubimetz Merlot Premiere 1994   `16` `B`

Stunning value. Lovely ripe fruit, soft as crumpled satin, with good tannins and acidity. Has depth, style and flavour – and an astounding price.

CHILEAN WINE   RED

Alto Plano Chilean Red   `15` `B`

Has a touch of dry seriousness to its otherwise big smile of fruity welcome but this only makes it the better with food. Terrific stuff.

Cono Sur Cabernet Sauvignon 1994 | 15 | C

Depth, richness, insistency of flavour and a striking finish. Excellent value.

Cono Sur Pinot Noir Reserve 1995 | 14.5 | D

I like it as a wine more than I like it as a pinot noir. Rich and most gripping.

Rowanbrook Cabernet Sauvignon Reserve 1994 | 14 | C

Rowanbrook Cabernet Sauvignon/Malbec 1995 | 15.5 | B

Softness, deftness, fruit and great length. Wonderful fruity value.

Rowanbrook Chilean Zinfandel 1995 | 14.5 | C

Not the full-blooded, scary Californian beast, but gently intimidating.

Terre Noble Chilean Merlot 1994 | 15.5 | C

Terra Noble Chilean Merlot 1995 | 16.5 | C

A stunning concentration of flavour and rich, youthful fruit. It testifies to great grapes and skilled wine-making. It is a wonderfully delicious wine of style, class and great depth.

CHILEAN WINE   WHITE

Alto Plano Chilean White | 12 | B

Chilean Sauvignon Blanc 1995, Asda | 14 | B

Softly rich but not overdone or too full of itself. Not a classic, lean sauvignon but a flavoursome one and good with food.

Cono Sur Chilean Chardonnay 1995   14   C

Oiliness slicked over the fruit like pomade.

Rowanbrook Chardonnay Reserve 1995   16   C

Deliciousness personified. Come home from work, stretch our your legs, kick off your shoes and relax.

Rowanbrook Sauvignon Blanc Reserve 1995   14.5   C

An odd sauvignon but an interesting contender to set against rich fish dishes, poultry, complex salads and soups.

ENGLISH WINE   WHITE

Carden Vale 1995   14.5   C

This is crisp, delicious and quietly impressive. From a Cheshire vineyard!

FRENCH WINE   RED

Beaujolais, Asda   12   C

Beaujolais Villages Domaine des Ronzes 1995   13.5   C

Not bad, this beaujolais! Has tannin, my life!

Bourgogne Pinot Noir 1994, Asda   11   C

Cabernet Sauvignon VdP d'Oc, Asda

Terrific value. Brisk, dry, deep, excellently structured, characterful, good with all sorts of food. Demonstrates that the Languedoc can grow superb cabernet grapes.

Cahors, Asda

Good bangers 'n' mash wine. But do fry the sausages well – the wine likes blackened grub.

Chateau la Domeque, Corbieres 1993 15 C

Lovely, soft, gently herby fruit.

Chateau l'Eglise Vieille, Haut Medoc 1994 15.5 C

Proper claret with lots of rich fruit but six months have softened the initial austerity of the wine beautifully, mitigated by sympathetic tannins and supported by acidity. A terrific claret at a terrific price.

Chateau Peybonnehomme Les Tours
Cotes de Blaye 1993 14 D

An approachable bordeaux with a touch of fruit to it.

Chevalier d'Aymon Oak Aged, Graves 1993

Claret, Asda 15.5 B

Terrific-value claret. Soft but dry and well-textured. Won't disappoint claret lovers or others who simply want a sturdy companion for meat dishes.

Cotes du Rhone Villages Domaine de
Belugue 1994 16.5 C

Brilliant, New World sweetness and lushness with big Old World tannins. Lovely wine. Lovely concentration of flavour here.

Domaine de Grangeneuve, Coteaux du Tricastin 1994 `16` `C`

Big, earthy fruit brilliantly scaffolded by acidity and tannins.

Domaine de la Baume Merlot VdP d'Oc 1993 `17` `D`

Quite brilliant balance of fruit and acidity and tannin. A bustling, handsome brute with couth manners and massive richness. For the money, one of France's finest merlots.

Fitou, Asda `14` `B`

Lovely dry tannins here. Great food wine.

Fleurie Domaine Verpoix Clos de la Chapelle de Bois 1994 `14` `D`

What's happening with the world? Another beaujolais with tannin and some decent fruit. Has character, structure, weight and texture. (Phew. I can't believe I wrote that.)

Fortant Cabernet Sauvignon VdP d'Oc 1995 `13` `C`

Fortant Merlot VdP d'Oc 1995 `13` `C`

Seems expensive compared to, say, Chilean wines at the same price and Bulgarian at 50p less. Basic fruit, dry cherry to finish. Drinkable, pleasant, uncomplicated.

James Herrick 'Cuvee Simone' VdP 1994 `17.5` `C`

A wine to love for its rocky, sun-drenched fruit and compacted herbiness. Very tannic and rich, it'll improve for a few years.

Mas Segala Cotes du Roussillon Villages 1995 `16` `C`

Has more rigid tannins and acidity than previous vintages. Will soften brilliantly over the next two years.

Merlot, Vin de Pays d'Oc, Asda · 15 · B

Lovely, fruity touch on the dry, brisk yet soft fruit gives this charming wine bite, vigour, style and flavour. Terrific food wine.

Montange Moire Syrah/Merlot 1995 · 14.5 · B

Has interacting dark cherry and blackcurrant flavours.

Morgon, Michel Jambon 1994 · 12 · D

Moulin A Vents 'Les Hospices' 1994 · 13.5 · E

My God! A stylish, rich beaujolais! Sadly, it's hugely overpriced.

Spring Vale Rouge VdP de l'Aude 1995 · 15 · B

Warm, soft, full of flavour. Excellent value. Has charm and style without a hint of coarseness.

St Chinian, Asda · 14 · B

The earthiness is tightly held by the fruitiness and so the result is a simple, great-value bangers 'n' mash wine.

St Emilion, Asda · 13 · C

Stylish, dry, good weight of fruit.

Vacqueyras 'Les Cailles' 1994 · 13.5 · C

Good teeth-clinging fruit.

FRENCH WINE · WHITE

Blanc de Blancs, Asda · 11 · A

Chablis 1994, Asda · 12.5 · D

Chablis Premier Cru Les Fourchaumes, 1994   `13.5` `F`

Quietly impressive; edgily rich, not especially acidically over-blown. A £10-plus wine? Well, it's certainly stylish and well-intentioned but it's lousy value except to the chablis freak – who is of course beyond the help of this writer.

Chardonnay, Vin de Pays d'Oc, Asda   `14.5` `C`

Lovely nutty undertone to young, ripe fruit. Good food wine.

Chateau la Blanquerie Entre Deux Mers 1995   `14` `C`

Gripping stuff. Real flavour. An organic beauty.

Cotes du Roussillon Vignerons Catalans   `10` `B`

Cuckoo Hill Viognier VdP d'Oc 1995   `15.5` `C`

Classic viognier with clean apricot fruit and fresh finish. Delicious tippling here.

Cuvee Frimont Entre Deux Mers 1995   `13` `C`

Curious subdued fruit salad of a wine.

Domaine Baud Chardonnay, VdP du Jardin de la France 1995   `15` `B`

Hints at richness but never goes over the top and assaults the palate brutally. Rather it steals over the tastebuds with melony fruit and lemony acidity. Good value.

Domaine de Trignon Cotes du Rhone 1995   `15` `D`

Terrific with trout and other freshwater fish. Made for the job. A lovely, soft-textured, gently earthy wine.

Domaine des Deux Roches St Veran 1995   `14.5` `D`

Rather classy. Has real fruit but doesn't abandon altogether its

41

Old World credentials in its vegetal, earthy edge. Great with all sorts of fish, poultry, salads, etc.

Domaine St Francois Sauvignon Blanc 1995

`13.5` **B**

Fortant Blanc Sec Sauvignon Blanc VdP d'Oc 1995

`13` **C**

Hardly sec. Finishes full and fruity and far from dry (but never sweet).

Fortant Cabernet Rose, VdP d'Oc 1995

`13.5` **C**

Delicate and tasty.

Fortant Chardonnay VdP d'Oc 1995

`12.5` **C**

Fortant Sauvignon Blanc Vin de Pays d'Oc 1995

`15` **C**

Brilliant New World, Old World French sauvignon with loads of attractive fruit. Not a classic perhaps and won't improve with age (as classics do) but it's clean, limpid and thoroughly drinkable.

James Herrick Chardonnay 1995

`15` **C**

Elegant, restrained, classic, delightfully fruity and stylish.

Montagne Noire Chardonnay, VdP d'Oc 1995

`15.5` **C**

Delicious. Hints at a New World richness and bluster then reins itself in elegantly with balancing acidity.

Muscadet de Sevre et Maine Sur Lie, Domaine Gautron 1994

`13` **C**

Lacks the bite a £4.50 bottle should have but it wouldn't be nice with oysters (unlike the Walrus, for example, who was downright beastly and underhand with them).

Pouilly Fume, Domaine Coulbois 1994 `12` `E`

Sancerre La Vigne des Rocs 1995 `11` `E`

Sauvignon de Bordeaux, Asda `14.5` `B`

Terrific nutty fish wine. Fresh flavour and pert acidity in polished liaison.

Southern Cross Grenache/Chardonnay 1995 `15` `B`

Rich-edged fruit with flavour and style.

Southern Cross Viognier/Chardonnay 1995 `15` `C`

Lovely balance of crisp acidity and a nutty fruitiness.

Spring Vale Blanc VdP 1995 `13.5` `B`

Excellent clean shellfish wine. Like a steely muscadet of way back.

Vin de Pays des Cotes de Gascogne, Asda `15` `B`

Light, delicious, fun drinking combining citric fruit and acidity in refreshing harmony. A delightful wine at a delightful price.

GERMAN WINE   WHITE

Devil's Rock Riesling, St Ursula, Pfalz 1994 `15.5` `C`

Delicate true-riesling aroma, delicate acidity and good fruit, and fresh, mineral-edged finish. Excellent smoked fish wine. Developing very subtle petrolly undertones. Will improve for eighteen months or more.

Hochheimer Holle Riesling Kabinett
Geheimrat Aschrott'sche Erben, Rheingau
1995   `10` `D`

10 now. 15/16 in AD 2000.

Jordan & Jordan Wiltinger Braunfels
Riesling Kabinett 1995   `10` `D`

Niersteiner Spiegelberg Kabinett 1995,
Asda   `14` `B`

Excellent warm-summer-evening aperitif. Will age well for a
couple of years, too.

Northern Star German White 1995   `11` `B`

Ruppertsberger Hofstuck Riesling
Kabinett 1993   `15` `B`

Delicious demonstration of whistle-clean fruit without a touch
of sweetness or rawness of acidity. Brilliant aperitif. Great with
smoked fish.

Ruppertsberger Nussbein Riesling Auslese
1993 (50cl)   `13.5` `C`

Dessert wine.

St Ursula Deidesheimer Hofstuck Kabinett
1994   `13.5` `B`

Lemony wine for Thai food.

Wild Boar Vineyards Riesling 1995   `12.5` `C`

Wiltinger Scharzberg Riesling Kabinett
1995   `11` `B`

HUNGARIAN WINE RED

Hungarian Cabernet Sauvignon 1995, Asda `12` `B`

Dry and austere. Has tannin and juice. Odd. Needs pasta.

Hungarian Merlot 1995, Asda `11` `B`

Kekfrankos 1995, Asda `10` `B`

HUNGARIAN WINE WHITE

Badger Hill Dry White Wine 1995 `15.5` `B`

A brilliant little aperitif. Aromatic, clean, gently florally fruity.
Superb value.

Hill Top Winery Dry White Wine 1995 `12` `C`

Hungarian Chardonnay 1995, Asda `13` `B`

Lemony. Great with fish and chips.

Hungarian Chardonnay Private Reserve
1995 `15.5` `B`

Full, rich, rolling edge – gently voluptuous, never blowsy.
Fresh finish.

Hungarian Muscat 1995, Asda `12` `B`

Hungarian Pinot Blanc 1995, Asda `13` `B`

Excellent aperitif. Good value.

45

Hungarian Sauvignon Blanc Private Reserve 1995   13   B

Stark, grassy and wide-awake, but yawns and gets sleepy as it finishes.

ITALIAN WINE   RED

Barbera d'Asti Cascini Garona 1994   13   C

Barolo, Veglio Angelo 1990   14   E

Expensive, but with a rugged charm of subdued rich fruit, and with a great length of flavour. Terrific with food. Coming along nicely in bottle.

Chianti 1994, Asda   13.5   B

Brilliant-value party wine. Smashing.

Chianti Classico 1994, Asda   15   C

A cracker of a chianti for the money. Has a lovely backbone of tannin holding the rich fruit and firm acidity and the result is a perfectly shaped specimen.

Chianti Colli Senesi Salvanza 1994   13   C

Coltiva Il Rosso 1995   11   B

Sweetish, young, very babyish.

Lambrusco Rosso, Asda   12   A

Apples and cherries, sweet and bubbly. Great for beginners.

Merlot del Veneto   13   A

Sunny to the point of tanning the tongue. Warms the cockles most engagingly, this wine.

Merlot del Veneto Gabbia d'Oro 12 A

A large party wine for uncritical palates.

**Montepulciano d'Abruzzo, Cantina
Tollo 1995** 10 B

Fruit juice.

Rozzano Villa Pigna 1994 14 C

Sangiovese di Romagna Riva 1995 13 B

Cheap, but not the exciting Riva of previous vintages.

Santa Barbara Rosso di Salento 1993 13 C

Lots of sweet fruit.

Sicilian Rosso, Asda 16.5 B

New blend of an old favourite, which hit a low sweet note last
year, but it's back to form with oodles of soft, rich fruit, a
tannic touch on the finish and a very good grip. Terrific value.
Fun slurping.

Squinzano Santa Barbara 1993 13.5 C

Valpolicella NV, Asda 11 B

Cheap. And a cheerful soul.

ITALIAN WINE WHITE

Coltiva Il Bianco 1995 14 B

Brilliant value for a crowd of pasta eaters and no mean performer
for the solo diner in front of the TV with a tuna salad.

Frascati 'Colli di Catone' Superiore 1995 `10` `C`

Frascati Superiore 1995, Asda `11` `B`

La Vis Trentino Chardonnay 1995 `14.5` `C`

Good value for such crisp, clean fruit. Hardly a classic
chardonnay but an amusing one.

Lambrusco Bianco, Asda `12.5` `A`

Fun aperitif for young minds.

Lambrusco Rosato, Asda `12` `A`

Apple skin and sweet cherries. Good for beginners.

Lambrusco Secco, Asda `11` `A`

Recioto di Soave Castelcerino 1993
(half bottle) `13.5` `C`

Expensive and perhaps needs cellaring for several years to reach
its high point of honeyed sweetness.

Sicilian Bianco, Asda `13.5` `B`

Dry, nutty, much better value than frascati or soave.

Soave, Asda `12.5` `B`

Soave Classico Superiore Sanroseda 1995 `13.5` `C`

MORAVIAN WINE WHITE

Moravian Vineyard Gewurztraminer 1994 `12` `B`

Cheap gewurz for light Thai food.

Moravian Vineyard Sauvignon Pinot Blanc 1995 `13.5` `B`

Should be under £3. Rather too full and floral on the finish. Has some nectarine and peach fruitiness which is not as spritely balanced by the acidity as it might be.

MOROCCAN WINE   RED

Domaine Mellil Moroccan Red Wine `15` `B`

Brilliant as ever. Plump, ripe, not coarse or rasping, this is a bundle of lovely fruit.

NEW ZEALAND WINE   WHITE

St Clair New Zealand Chardonnay 1995 `12.5` `D`

St Clair New Zealand Sauvignon Blanc 1995 `13` `D`

Attractive herbaceousness. Crushed grass gently pressed.

PORTUGUESE WINE   RED

Bela Fonte Tinto Vinho de Mes `13.5` `B`

Rich (almost piercingly rich tone on the finish).

Bright Brothers Estremadura 1994 `13.5` `C`

Dao 1992, Asda `13` `B`

Tiring a bit.

Fiuza Oak Aged Cabernet Sauvignon 1994 `14.5` `C`

Richness and liveliness.

PORTUGUESE WINE WHITE

Bela Fonte Branco Vinho de Mesa 1995 `11` `B`

Bright Brothers Sercial-Arinto 1995 `10` `C`

Fiuza Barrel Fermented Chardonnay 1995 `16` `C`

Woody undertone gives this wine purpose and style. Good fruit well coated in flavoursomeness which finishes very elegantly.

Vinho Verde, Asda `11` `B`

ROMANIAN WINE WHITE

River Route Sauvignon/Muscat 1994 `12.5` `B`

SOUTH AFRICAN WINE RED

Bouwland Bush Vine Pinotage 1995 `16.5` `C`

Has cherries, plums and blackberries in its complexity of flavours, very fruity but never sweet, and a concentrated finish of black cherry.

Cape Red, Asda `15` `B`

Smashing flavour here. It screams with fruit yet it's not at all rancorous or ugly. Soft, rich, deep, gluggable. You would pour it for Bacchus himself.

Kanonkop Bouwland Red 1994 `14` `C`

The Kanonkop estate is in love with fruit and this example is full of its obsession. This wine is a soft, deep, loving mouthful of deliciousness.

Kumala Shiraz/Cabernet Sauvignon 1995 `15` `B`

Faintly exotic, rich, handsome, good value, and understanding and sympathetic to good cooking, this wine writes its own lonely hearts ad.

Stellenzicht Block Zinfandel 1995 `16.5` `C`

Lovely depraved stuff!!! Rich and rounded, vigorous and purposeful, this is a terrifically fulfilling wine. It oozes fruit, style and depth. Has a brazen, bawdy edge.

SOUTH AFRICAN WINE WHITE

Cape White, Asda `13.5` `B`

Bargain food wine – especially spaghetti with clams and lots of hungry friends.

Fairview Estate Dry Rose 1995 `15` `B`

One of the better roses I've tasted. Great flavour and serious depth. Has a taunting dryness and fruitiness – great with rich fish dishes.

Kumala Chenin/Chardonnay 1995 `13` `B`

Stellenzicht Noble Late Harvest 1995 (half bottle) `14` `D`

Dessert wine.

Van Loveren Sauvignon Blanc 1995

With the '96 about to hit the shops at time of writing, the '95 is feeling a mite tuckered out and at a loose end.

SPANISH WINE RED

Baron de Ley Rioja Reserva 1991

Rates half a point more than at Thresher, where it costs over seven quid at time of writing.

Bodegas Campillo, Rioja Crianza 1991

An elegant, deeply flavoured, vanilla-tinged wine. Stylish and good value.

Don Darias

Brilliant with curry, just brilliant.

El Meson Rioja CVC

Good vanilla softness, quiet and not overdone. Should be £3.50 though.

Leon 1992, Asda

Curious edge to the aroma, like the inside of a wellie, but the fruit on the palate is simply brilliant: rich, biting, dry, deep and wonderful with robust food.

Remonte Navarra Tinto 1995

Good rich earthy stuff. No nonsense. No rubbish.

Ribera del Duero Senorio de Nava 1991

What savoury depth here! It's a sauce in itself! Rich, exciting, wild, raunchy, packed with flavour and personality, it's an astonishing combination of finesse and muscle.

Terra Alta Bush Vine Garnacha 1995   `13.5` `C`

More honest and exciting than 90 per cent of beaujolais.

Terra Alta Cabernet Sauvignon/Garnacha 1995   `15` `B`

Bags of personality and flavour.

Torres Coronas 1992   `13` `C`

Rather dry and humourless for such exuberant Catalan provenance. Hard to believe Gaudi is related to such wine. The fruit is there but it seems reluctant to smile.

Valencia Red, Asda   `14` `B`

If you're looking for a dirt-cheap, decently fruity, food-friendly wine for a thirsty crowd of chili con carne eaters, this is your wine.

Vina Albali, Valdepenas Reserva 1989   `15` `B`

Great vintage of an old favourite. Riper than previous vintages, it has richness and real style. Yes, it's a swashbuckler but it's no lightweight and it meets food head on.

SPANISH WINE   WHITE

La Mancha, Asda   `12` `A`

Rather falls flat as it hits the finishing line.

Moscatel de Valencia, Asda   `14` `B`

Soft edition of the breed, only faintly marmaladey. Great with soft fruit desserts.

Raimat Chardonnay 1995 `14` `D`

Elegant, clean and nicely organised.

Remonte Navarra Blanco 1995 `11` `B`

Terra Alta Garnacha Blanco 1995 `13` `B`

Valencia Dry, Asda `12` `B`

Valencia Medium Dry, Asda `11` `B`

Good for those on their way up from lambrusco.

USA WINE   RED

Arius Neu Californian Red Wine 1993 `12.5` `D`

Californian Red, Asda `14` `B`

The label says it's medium-bodied and spicy which no more conveys the whole story than if you read those words on a card stuck in a telephone box. It smells of carbolic, armpit and burnt fruit. It is a lovely fruity glug, deliciously soft and bright.

E. & J. Gallo Turning Leaf Cabernet Sauvignon 1994 `13.5` `D`

Warm and possessing some depth but uncompetitively priced compared with Chile or South Africa. But you're getting better, Gallo, so stick at it! You might just make a terrific wine at a dirt-cheap price one day.

E. & J. Gallo Turning Leaf Zinfandel 1994 `12` `D`

Not bad, but very overpriced at nigh on six quid. Anodyne and characterless, it lacks the oomph of real red zin. It fails to finish with £6 worth of vivacity. If it was £3.29 it would be a good buy. A partially turned new leaf.

Gallo Sonoma County Cabernet Sauvignon 1992 `14` `E`

Delicious cab sauv. A touch pricey but good.

Grant Canyon Select Red (California) `14` `C`

A Cal wine for under four quid! A miracle. So is the fruit – for the money.

Quivira Cabernet Cuvee 1992 `17` `D`

Magnificent hairiness of fruit: virile, deep, concentrated, bushy and tickles as it goes down.

Sebastiani Zinfandel 1995 `14` `C`

The easiest-drinking red zin you can find.

USA WINE WHITE

Californian White, Asda `13` `B`

Almost sweet on the finish.

E. & J. Gallo Turning Leaf Chardonnay 1994 `14` `D`

Classy and rich. Not especially elegant or finely balanced as great Californian chardonnays are but it's good with chicken.

Grant Canyon Californian White `10.5` `C`

I like that half point.

Sebastiani Semillon/Chardonnay 1994 `14.5` `C`

Delicious blend of grapes. The best Sebastiani white on sale.

Sebastiani White Zinfandel 1995 `10` `C`

Sweet but almost nothing.

FORTIFIED WINE

Fine Ruby Port, Asda   13.5 D

Good with a nutty fruit cake (if you're married to one, lucky for you).

LBV Port, Asda   13 C

Sweet but fails to carry through its fruity sweetness to the finish.

Stanton & Killeen, Liqueur Muscat, Rutherglen (half bottle)   14 D

A sweet, wonderful thing to drink with Christmas cake.

Tawny Port, Asda   14 D

Sweet but not aggressively so. Good with ice cream.

Vintage Character Port, Asda   14 D

Has the fine acidity under the fruit to suit all manner of cheeses.

SPARKLING WINE/CHAMPAGNE

Asda Cava   17 C

A brilliant, elegant, classic bubbly of gentle fruit, no hint of yesteryear's earthiness, and fresh, whistle-clean finish. Superb for the money for which it gives the finest champagne a run.

Asti Spumante, Asda   12 C

Very sweet.

Barramundi Australian Brut   `15.5`   `D`

Terrific bubbly. Has personality and style.

Blue Ridge Australian Brut   `13`   `C`

Champagne Brut , Asda   `13`   `F`

Champagne Rose, Asda   `12.5`   `F`

Cordoniu Chardonnay Brut (Spain)   `16`   `D`

Delicious, classy, lively aperitif or to be drunk with smoked fish.

Cordoniu Premier Cuvee Brut (Spain)   `14`   `D`

Cranswick Pinot/Chardonnay Brut (Australia)   `13.5`   `D`

Fruity.

Nicholas Feuillate Blanc de Blancs   `13.5`   `G`

A very stylish champers. It is pricey but it is not half bad.

Scharffenberger Brut (USA)   `14`   `E`

Very elegant, very classic, but with a touch of Californian warmth.

Varichon et Clerc Sparkling Chardonnay   `14`   `C`

Soft and peachy, this makes an excellent aperitif. But champagne it ain't.

BUDGENS

What is a Budgen?

It is a shame that I do not receive more correspondence about Budgens. The letters I receive from readers and customers about the foibles of this or that retailer not only provide me with the most useful feedback on how well I am doing my job and how well the retailers are doing theirs, but can from time to time give me the most penetrating of insights into how a particular retailer is perceived, what its typical customers are like and what they expect. It is a source of considerable frustration that I receive the most correspondence concerning the retailers which I know best, and the least about fellows like Budgens who have always been something of a mystery to me.

Never mind; I can at least deduce one thing about Budgens customers from my correspondence: they don't appear to be great letter writers. I can also say that everything I have ever received about Budgens has been complimentary and there have been no complaints whatsoever with regard to wines not being available or at prices other than those quoted in my column.

Mr Harry Browne of Cambridge even marked his first ever visit to a Budgens store by writing to me to report on one of my recommendations back in May 1989. It would appear that Alsatian wines are one of this retailer's specialties.

Another Saturday *Guardian* without your wine column . . . . I do hope this doesn't mean you've been posted to other realms.

You have in me a dedicated follower (together with some friends and relatives who have sampled your recommendations).

We've enjoyed the 1981 Musar (what a find this is), the Gisselbrecht Gewurztraminer (my first-time ever visit to Budgens for wine) and the two excellent Tesco wines: Chateau des Condats and Chateau Les Gravieres. Perhaps I should mention that the Budgen visit led also to a bottle of the Gisselbrecht Pinot at £2.99 which was very drinkable.

Please do return to the supermarkets and to your word processor, and give us more of your sturdy judgements written with such enjoyable verve.

I heard from Mr Browne again in 1995, but sadly there was no mention of Budgens in his later letter. Whether he had lost his taste for Alsatian wines or been seduced by one of the larger, out-of-town supermarkets that Budgens has to compete with, I am not sure. However, I cannot believe that his first visit to a Budgens store would have been his last. For one thing, the retailer isn't often beaten on price. Despite the fact that its stores are smaller and in more expensive locations than many edge-of-town giants and the fact that there are less of them, Budgens' prices are some of the most competitive I have found.

Budgens has been trading since 1872, making it older than Sainsbury's and many other illustrious retailing names. And it has endured even when, particularly in the 1980s, 'analysts' suggested that the medium-sized high street supermarket was a thing of the past. The recent resurgence of the high street and the arrival of concepts such as Tesco Metro, not to mention all the discount stores which operate successfully in locations very similar to Budgens', has left those analysts with egg on their face and Budgens in pretty good shape.

Given that there have been so few letters about Budgens, I feel particularly guilty that one of the most amusing discourses on said retailer has in fact ended up in another section of this book, namely the introduction to the Morrisons shelves. As I have mentioned elsewhere, there is something of a north–south divide among *Superplonk* readers. Readers from the north write quizzically about southern-based Waitrose, as if to ask 'Why do you write about such an irrelevance?', while southerners write, 'Morrisons? Never heard of them!' Budgens stores can be found primarily in London and the south of England. Hence, Greg Long's postscript to his letter concerning Morrisons: 'What on earth is a Budgen?'. I replied to Mr Long that 'A Budgen is a supermarket chain, rare and lesser-spotted in your neck of the woods I daresay, but the old folk down south appreciate its city centre locations' (see page 161).

Budgens Stores Limited
PO Box 9
Stonefield Way
Ruislip
Middlesex
HA4 0JR

Tel 0181 422 9511
Fax 0181 422 1596

AUSTRALIAN WINE   RED

Jacob's Creek Dry Red

**Orlando Jacob's Creek Shiraz/Cabernet
1994**

Not worth over the fiver it is unless you're stuck and it's the
only bottle on the shelf. A £3.49 bottle of decent, dry fruit –
nothing more.

AUTRALIAN WINE   WHITE

Brown Brothers Dry Muscat Blanc 1993
An intriguing aperitif. Or you could try splashing it behind
your ears.

Rosemount Estate Chardonnay 1995
Beautiful controlled fruit with vivacity and restraint. This
paradox is Rosemount's hallmark.

Rosemount Semillon Chardonnay 1995
Softly melonic and gently lemonic. A tasty bottle.

AUSTRIAN WINE — WHITE

Gruner Veltliner Kremstal 1994   16 C

A deliciously soft yet nuttily alive wine of length and flavour. Uniquely fruity, fresh, deep and stylish.

BULGARIAN WINE — RED

Star Zagora Cabernet Sauvignon/Merlot 1993   15 B

Delicious combo of blackcurranty, plummy fruit and incisive tannins. Good value.

BULGARIAN WINE — WHITE

Preslav Chardonnay/Sauvignon Blanc 1995   14 B

An excellently balanced, firmly fruity fish wine. Good depth of flavour.

CHILEAN WINE — RED

Casablanca Miraflores Cabernet Sauvignon 1991   14 C

Very mature. At the peak of its fitness with food. Dry, full fruit of some depth and flavour.

CHILEAN RED

Vina Tarapaca Cabernet Sauvignon 1994 `14` `C`
Brisk, lots of flavour, savoury and gently rustic. Good food bottle.

CHILEAN WINE   WHITE

Vina Casablanca Sauvignon Blanc 1994 `14` `C`
Soft, gently oily, positively fruity and nicely balanced. Good with fish and gentle chicken dishes.

Vina Tarapaca Chardonnay 1995 `12` `C`
Possibly the least exciting Chilean chardonnay I've tasted.

ENGLISH WINE   WHITE

Lamberhurst High Ridge Fume 1994 `7` `C`
Absurdly pretentious in label, price and dull fruit.

Lamberhurst High Ridge Medium Dry 1994 `8` `B`
Silly price for a sweetish, gawky wine of nil personality.

Lamberhurst High Ridge Pink 1994 `9` `C`

FRENCH WINE   RED

Abbaye Saint Hilaire, Coteaux Varois 1994 `13` `B`

Chateau Bassenel, Minervois 1993 `12` `C`

Chateau de Malijay, Cotes du Rhone 1994
`12` `C`

Soft and soupy. Good with game dishes.

Claret
`10` `B`

Costieres de Nimes Fontanilles 1994
`13.5` `C`

Tasty, dry, handsomely rustic. Great casserole wine.

Cotes du Rhone Villages Cuvee Reserve 1994
`13` `C`

Has a gold label on its neck telling us the wine was bottled in the region of production. Does it give you a warm feeling to know that? The fruit is earthy and soft.

Crozes Hermitage 1993
`12` `C`

Domaine St Roch VdP de l'Aude
`11` `B`

Faugeres, Jean Jean 1994
`14` `B`

Soft yet characterful, brisk, dry and fruity with a good savoury edge.

Le Croix Teyssier St-Emilion 1993
`12` `D`

Le Haut Colombier, Vin de Pays de la Drome 1994
`11` `B`

Touch flat and a mite dull.

Vin de Pays d'Agenais Rouge 1994
`10` `B`

Rather limping and short on style.

Vin de Pays de l'Aude
`10` `B`

Party wine for parties held in rough houses.

**Vin de Pays des Coteaux de l'Ardeche,
1991** `12` `B`

Nice dry cherry fruit.

FRENCH WINE WHITE

Blanc de Blancs Cuvee Speciale `11` `B`

Bordeaux Blanc Sec 1995 `15` `B`

Brilliant value here for such decisively fruity and well-balanced
wine.

Corbieres, Blanc de Blancs, 1992 `12` `B`

Basic rather than brilliant.

Cotes de Provence Rose `10` `C`

**'D' Chardonnay VdP de la Ile de Beaute
1995** `12.5` `B`

Great price, great appellation (in the romance of the name) but
try as hard as I might I can't find more points for the fruit in
the bottle.

**Domaine de Villeroy-Castellas Sauvignon
Blanc 1995** `14.5` `C`

An individual almond-edged wine of depth and evident class.

**Domaine l'Argentier Terret, VdP Cotes de
Thau 1994** `13.5` `C`

Nearly very good. Needs a complex salad to set its fruit off.

Domaine Pascaly VdP de l'Aude `12` `B`

Basic but not completely broken.

Les Chasseignes, Sancerre 1993 `10` `E`

Listel, Domaine de Bosquet-Canet `11` `C`

Macon-Ige 1994 `14` `C`
Hints of vegetality in the old-style Burgundian way but this only enhances the typicity of the fruit.

Vin de Pays des Coteaux de l'Ardeche 1993 `13` `B`
Agreeably fruity and firm.

GERMAN WINE   RED

Dornfelder 1993 `13.5` `C`
Try its soft, unGermanic fruitiness.

GERMAN WINE   WHITE

Bereich Bernkastel 1993 `11` `B`

Bereich Bernkastel Mosel Saar Ruwer 1995 `11` `C`

Flonheimer Adelberg Auslese 1993 `12` `C`

Rudesheimer Rosengarten Gustav Adolf Schmitt, Nahe 1995 `10` `C`
Expensive for what it is: sweet and simple.

Schmitt vom Schmitt Niersteiner Spatlese, Late Harvest 1994 `11` `C`

Drink it in a few years – say about the time America lands a manned spacecraft on Mars and brings back a Little Green Man.

HUNGARIAN WINE RED

Cabernet Franc Szekszard 1992 `13` `B`

'Fill your glass and feel like a Royalty' (sic). I filled my glass – and lo! I felt like a king! Wacky bottle of wine from label to throat!

Hungarian Cabernet Sauvignon 1994 `12` `B`

HUNGARIAN WINE WHITE

Hungarian Chardonnay 1993 `10` `B`

Sauvignon Blanc `10` `B`

ITALIAN WINE RED

Merlot del Veneto, Pergola di Vento `12` `B`

Merlot del Veneto Zonin `12` `B`

ITALIAN WINE WHITE

Frascati 'Casale de Grillo' 1994 `13.5` `C`

Expensive for the breed but a very solidly fruity, well-made frascati with more than a touch of good breeding.

Tocai del Veneto Zonin `11` `B`

MACEDONIAN WINE WHITE

Country White `11` `B`

NEW ZEALAND WINE RED

Montana Cabernet Sauvignon 1993 `13` `C`

Waimanu Red `11` `C`

Without doubt the weediest New Zealand red I've ever tasted.

NEW ZEALAND WINE WHITE

Waimanu Premium Dry `10` `C`

Possibly the least adventurously fruity Kiwi white I've ever tasted.

PORTUGUESE WINE RED

Alta Mesa Tinto 1994 `14` `B`

Simple, soft, ripe, very fruity, delicious chilled and poured over parched tongues.

Dao Reserva Dom Ferraz 1990 `13` `C`

Overpriced, really. A dry, brisk, vegetal, maturely fruity £3.29 bottle.

PORTUGUESE WINE WHITE

Alta Mesa Medium Dry White 1994 `12` `B`

Alta Mesa White 1994 `14` `B`

Good value fish and chip wine. Has some flavour and crispness.

SOUTH AFRICAN WINE RED

Clear Mountain Pinotage `14.5` `C`

Smoky, tobacco-edged fruit of some personality.

Table Mountain 1994 `13` `B`

Some flavour and fruit here.

SOUTH AFRICAN WINE   WHITE

Clear Mountain Chenin Blanc   `13.5` `B`
Some cleanly tasty fruit here. Bit muddy on the finish.

SPANISH WINE   RED

Diego de Almagro Valdepenas 1991   `14` `B`
Tasty, mature, ripe, smooth, dry yet well finished off with a
coating of sweet fruit. Perfect for pasta parties.

Lagunilla Rioja Crianza 1991   `14` `C`
Soft, subtly vanilla-like, dry, good with a herb-stuffed roast
fowl.

Vina Albali Reserva 1989   `14.5` `C`
Great vintage of an old favourite. Riper than previous vintages,
it has richness and real style. Yes, it's a swashbuckler but it's no
lightweight and it meets food head on. Rates half a point lower
than at Asda where, at time of writing, it costs under £3.50.

USA WINE   RED

**E. & J. Gallo Turning Leaf Cabernet
Sauvignon 1994**   `13.5` `D`
Warm and possessing some depth but uncompetitively priced
compared with Chile or South Africa. But you're getting better,
Gallo, so stick at it! You might just make a terrific wine at a dirt-
cheap price one day.

E. & J. Gallo Turning Leaf Zinfandel 1994 `12` `D`

Not bad, but very overpriced at nigh on six quid. Anodyne and characterless, it lacks the oomph of real red zin. It fails to finish with £6 worth of vivacity. If it was £3.29 it would be a good buy. A partially turned new leaf.

Pepperwood Grove Zinfandel 1994 `13` `C`

A most soft and soppy zin.

USA WINE WHITE

E. & J. Gallo Turning Leaf Chardonnay 1994 `14` `D`

Classy and rich. Not especially elegant or finely balanced as great California chardonnays are but it's good with chicken.

SPARKLING WINE/CHAMPAGNE

Brossault Rose Champagne `14` `E`

Espuma Prima Sparkling Muscat (Spain) `12` `B`

Fun for children.

Germain Brut Champagne `8` `G`

The most overpriced and least congenial bubbly from Rheims I've ever tasted.

Seaview Brut `14` `D`

CO-OP

Admiration with a hint of frustration

The Co-operative movement has at its foundation some fine guiding principles based on mutual trust and collectivism. It is therefore not surprising, though heart-warming nonetheless, to find a spirit of goodwill pervading the correspondence received from Co-op customers. In short, they are a friendly bunch, and none more so than Mr John Lewis of Deeping St James near Peterborough.

A devoted Co-op customer, Mr Lewis was glad to see that the store had been given some recognition in my *Guardian* column. As the Co-op is sometimes accused of not being as 'marketing-led' as some of the thrusting retailing giants, I was particularly interested in some examples of point-of-sale material which had recently been introduced at the store and which Mr Lewis kindly enclosed with his letter of January 1991. The tone and content of his letters in many ways express what the Co-operative ideal is really about.

A few weeks ago you had an article extolling the virtues of the Co-op – I was very pleased to see this and thought some recognition was long overdue. I have purchased most of my wine from our local Co-op superstore for some years and have hardly ever been disappointed.

I thought you might like to see some leaflets which they've just produced (at least I've not seen them before last week in our Co-op). From the consumer's point of view I think this represents very good practice; I hope there are also leaflets for their wines from other places.

Should you ever be around Deeping St James – gateway to the Fens! – do come round: the good lady makes an excellent elderflower wine which we drink in large quantities.

Good drinking!

I was pleased to hear from Mr Lewis again in 1995, and to learn that his enthusiasm for the Co-op was undimmed. Having read so many diatribes from shoppers peeved, albeit justly, at not being able to find the wine they are looking for, Mr Lewis's calm acceptance of a wine being out of stock was rather refreshing.

I have just enjoyed a bottle of Romanian Classic Pinot Noir 1990 from my local Co-op store, as recommended in your column last Saturday – very good. I'm bound to say that in general I've avoided Romanian wines because of one or two disappointments in the past. I shall stock up now with several bottles. Unfortunately the other Romanian wine you recommended was out of stock.

I'm glad you recognise the Co-op from time to time. I am a Co-operator of many years' standing and our local society, the Greater Anglia Regional Co-op, is one of the very successful and efficient ones. I buy virtually all my wine from our local Rainbow store, amounting to 12 to 15 bottles per month.

I think, in view of your remarks about the Co-op in last Saturday's column, you should explain to readers that unlike other stores which have unified ownership, the Co-op is made up of different retail societies and thus there is no central policy on purchasing wine. I am aware that amongst the wine-drinking classes in the south-east (where there are some very good Co-op outlets), it is somewhat unfashionable to shop at the Co-op, whereas to shop at Sainsbury's is a sine qua non of the quality of life. However, I do have a number of friends who read the *Guardian*, buy wine and shop at the Co-op!

Keep on writing an interesting column but let's hear more of the Co-op from time to time.

This letter had been partly in response to comments in my column in March 1995 regarding the inconsistency of range in Co-op stores which results from the fragmented nature of the organisation. As I have written previously and at some length, there are many regional retail societies, in addition to Co-operative Retail Services and the Co-operative Wholesale Society which operates like a central buying group, but is by no means responsible for the entire product range which varies significantly from store to store. I am sure like many before me, I found that it is one thing to be passionate about the Co-operative ethic, but quite another to understand or muster the slightest enthusiasm for how the organisation actually works.

On a practical note, however, the fragmented nature of the organisation does mean that when a Co-op wine is recommended by a wine writer, readers stand a strong chance of being disappointed when they go out in search of their quarry. The Mr Lewises of this world may be able to co-operate their way around such problems, but others, such as Peter Booth of Southwark, who wrote to me in December 1995, have a different solution:

I read your column every week and purchase all your recommendations at under £5.

You have, in the past, referred to the difficulties readers have encountered in tracing some of your recommendations, especially those at the Co-op. Personally, I don't even bother with the Co-op anymore; I've never found a wine I was looking for in one of their shops.

Also exasperated by the lack of consistency in the Co-op wine range was Jill Glanden of London. Responding to the same article in March 1995, she asserted that it was the responsibility of the journalist to identify and specify which Co-op stores carry the wine, and she phrased herself thus:

> There are, I'm told, more than 50 societies (or companies). Unless the writer specifies from which store or society he has received the wine he is tasting, the reader will not know where to buy it. It is (I believe) the responsibility of the journalist to suss out this kind of essential information, and accuracy here is no less necessary than the details about the wine itself.
>
> I have spent much frustrating effort trying to track down Co-operative wines, and never once succeeding. Most vexing.

A letter written in March 1995 from Mr R.J. Delamare of Cranleigh in Surrey to the Customer Relations Manager at the Co-operative Wholesale Society illustrates the two defining yet contrasting reactions which the Co-op seemingly evokes in so many of its customers: admiration and frustration.

> For a couple of years now since receiving a copy as a gift, I have been a regular user of Mr Malcolm Gluck's excellent wine guide *Superplonk*. Faced with the average supermarket wine display, yards of bottles on five or six shelves, in the past I was totally stumped.
>
> Nowadays, armed with Mr Gluck's invaluable advice, I look for anything that he has given a grade 14 or better and preferably on an A or B price level. For the past couple of years we have not had a disappointing bottle. My family and I have drunk some very pleasant wines at modest prices, and have bought a lot of them from your store here in Cranleigh.
>
> Since Christmas, though, I have begun to suspect that we (Mr Gluck and I) are not on the same wavelength as the Co-op. I can find few of his selections on your shelves.

Some of last year's favourites, the Portuguese Santos for example, are there. Also some new favourites, like the Australian Jacaranda Hill, have appeared, but there is an awful lot of other stuff unknown. This is not to imply that the unknown stuff is awful but it might not be quite what I expect.

You, the Co-op, have recently distributed at, I imagine, enormous expense, a glossy catalogue 'Your Choice – Easter 95' in which Arabella Woodrow, Linda Bellingham and others recommend some 62 wines. Checking with Mr Gluck I find that he only mentions, let alone recommends, 18 of these wines in his 1995 edition. This either means he didn't think them worth a mention, lower than a grade 10 in his opinion, or he didn't taste them.

As *Superplonk 1995* was in the best-sellers list for some weeks over Christmas, I suggest there are a lot more confused guys than just me, wandering round your store. I must admit it is a funny sort of place, they don't have eating apples on Fridays, for example, when all the mums are doing the weekly shop. Perhaps they don't care that there is a free bus to Tesco from just over the road, not to mention Budgens and Gateway just down the street.

As I am not a *Guardian* reader I don't know if this conundrum has been mentioned in his weekly column but I'll send Mr Gluck a copy of this letter. You never know, there might be some little gems in those 62 but I am not really keen on buying all 62 bottles to find out.

P.S. One of my earliest memories of the old Co-op in West Norwood is biscuits in big tins sold in brown paper bags and the money whizzed across the shop on those overhead wires. I used to take my mum's order book down for 6d and they delivered in those days, on Friday night, even to council houses. Ah, progress!

One reader who thankfully did find what he was looking for at the Co-op was Chris Walton of Swindon. As I discovered from his wonderful letter, Mr Walton is a founder member of The Old Town Gluck Association of Swindon, a worthy co-operative in its own right. He wrote:

Pissed! Well, a bit. I write to you after two bottles (between the two of us, I hasten to add!) of your 15-pointer Chilean Cabernet Sauvignon from the Co-op. We never used to think it was worth buying fizzy water in the Co-op until you came up with one or two Portuguese ideas – not for fizzy water! – and now we go there on the same pilgrimage as we do elsewhere.

'We' are a group of five couples in the soft-bellied, pine-tabled muesli belt of Swindon who have formed – wait for it – a Gluck Association. It's what my in-laws would have called a thrift club, my friends an excuse for a piss-up. The rules? We each pay eight pounds a month into a building society account. We get together at each others' houses for food and drink, and the hosts, on each occasion, have the awesome responsibility of spending our savings on Gluck-only wine, a range of points, supermarket sources and countries of origin, both for the evening and for the rest of us to take some bottles away.

Thus, we form an appalling stereotype of bourgeois provincial life, so much so that none of us would dare show this letter to our children: *Guardian* readers, low-paid professionals (we number six comprehensive school teachers, two junior, one Open University lecturer and an engineer), vegetarians, soft left, besotted by your weekly column and annual paperback. Need I say more.

Anyway, should you wish in any way to recognise your increasing fame, our next get-together is on Saturday, 4 March, at the above address – you might wish to recommend us something special for the occasion (we'll be noshing Italian on the night). You and yours are of course cordially welcome to join us.

I said Co-op customers were a friendly bunch, and if that letter does not convey what I meant by that then nothing will.

Co-operative Wholesale Society Limited
PO Box 53
New Century House
Manchester
M60 4ES

Tel 0161 834 1212
Fax 0161 834 4507

SEE STOP PRESS SECTION AT END OF BOOK FOR LAST-MINUTE ADDITIONS TO THIS RETAILER'S RANGE.

ARGENTINIAN WINE — RED

Argentine Malbec Sangiovese 1995, Co-op `15` `C`

Masses of flavour and soft, ripe fruit.

Lost Pampas Cabernet Malbec 1996 `14` `C`

Deep rich edge to the fruit, which is lengthy and bold.

Mission Peak Argentine Red NV `15` `B`

Dry yet fruity and with enough personality and depth to partner pasta, risotto and sausages.

Weinert Malbec 1991 `17` `E`

An expensive treat of such mature, tannic richness and lingering muscle-bound fruit that it cries out for food. Great with meat and cheese dishes. The texture is world-class. Puts scores of major bordeaux to shame. At top Co-ops only.

ARGENTINIAN WINE — WHITE

Argentine Sauvignon-Torrontes 1996, Co-op `15` `C`

Delicious complexity and flavour here. Young and fresh, but full of twists and turns.

Balbi Syrah Rose 1996 `14` `C`

One of the richest, yet dry, food-friendliest roses around.

Lost Pampas Oak-aged Chardonnay 1996 `14` `C`

Oily texture but over-embroidered or too fussy.

Mission Peak Argentine White NV `14.5` `B`

Clean but austere. Good with oysters.

AUSTRALIAN WINE RED

Australian Red, Co-op `13.5` `B`

This is a simple, soft, fruity pasta and pizza wine.

Chateau Reynella Cabernet/Merlot 1993 `17` `D`

A point more than at Asda where it costs £1 more at time of writing.

**Hardys Nottage Hill Cabernet Sauvignon/
Shiraz 1993** `16` `C`

Controlled soft spice laid on smooth blackcurrant fruit. Delicious, firm, well-styled. Also available in half bottles.

Jacaranda Hill Grenache 1996, Co-op `14.5` `C`

Biscuity textured fruit, cherries and rich plum, which is smooth and well polished.

**Jacaranda Hill Shiraz/Cabernet 1993,
Co-op** `13` `C`

Ripe plums with a touch of red earth.

**Kasbah Shiraz/Malbec/Mourvedre, Alambie
Wine Co 1993** `14` `C`

Juicy fruity finish on the soft fruits makes this a food wine – chilled with fish, more temperature with meat and vegetables, and cheese dishes.

Kingston Shiraz Mataro `14` `C`

A soft, yielding wine of depth and flavour.

Leasingham Domaine Cabernet Malbec 1993   15   E

Such vivid fruit! It is a real treat of a wine with its aromatic depth and tarry richness. A heady, compelling balsam.

Lindemans Bin 45 Cabernet Sauvignon 1994   14.5   D

Seems more insistently rich than previous vintages. Quite deliciously cheeky. Rates half a point less than at Fullers, where it costs under five quid at time of writing.

Vine Vale Shiraz   14   C

Famous bruising Aussie style.

AUSTRALIAN WINE   WHITE

Australian White, Co-op   10   B

Best's Late Harvest Muscat 1995   14.5   D

Delicious aperitif. Sweet? A touch. But it is gripping and fine.

Butterfly Ridge Sauvignon Blanc   11   C

Curious wine: sticky lollipop edge. Might be acceptable with Thai coconut/chicken soup.

Butterfly Ridge Sauvignon Blanc/Chenin Blanc   15.5   C

Brilliant blend of flavours and marriage of styles. Has structure, texture and balance. Lovely controlled exoticism to the fruit with buttery pineapple undertones. Delicious.

Hardys Nottage Hill Chardonnay 1994   17   C

Best vintage yet. Lovely textured, oily fruit, never overdone or blowsy and a buttery, melony finish of surefooted delivery. Terrific value for such classy drinking.

Jacaranda Hill Chenin Verdelho 1996, Co-op   14 C

Interesting marriage of gentle apricot fruit and subtle pineapple acidity. Pert and positive.

Jacaranda Hill Semillon/Chardonnay 1994, Co-op   13 C

Mite subdued.

Kingston Colombard Chardonnay 1995   14 C

Fruity with a hint of dryness. A touch fruit-salad but very naive and agreeable.

Koala Creek Dry White 1996   14 B

Adolescent in attitude, too, this raw, fresh, keen, whistle-clean wine. Floral aroma, delicious fruit, great price.

Leasingham Domaine Semillon 1993   15 D

Rich and ready but not aggressively so.

Loxton Low Alcohol Chardonnay NV   0 B

Horrible. Drink water from the nearest ditch rather than this abomination.

Murrumbidgee Estate Fruity Australian White NV   12.5 B

Richmond Grove Verdelho, Cowra Vineyard 1993   15.5 D

Delicious complexity. Soft, subtle (yet decidedly peach/apricot edged) – appeals to all the senses.

South Australian Chardonnay 1994, Co-op `15` `C`

Buttered bread, sprinkled with the faintest touch of lemon. Delicious.

AUSTRIAN WINE WHITE

Winzerhaus Gruner Veltliner 1995 `13.5` `C`

Curious, but appealing, muted richness on the finish.

BRAZILIAN WINE RED

Amazon Cabernet Sauvignon `13.5` `C`

Fresh, cherry-cheeked, good chilled with salads.

BRAZILIAN WINE WHITE

Amazon Chardonnay `11` `C`

Rather a confected wine. Might work under the arms as a deodorant or as a gnat deterrent.

BULGARIAN WINE RED

**Bulgarian Vintners' Reserve Cabernet
Sauvignon, Rousse 1990** `14.5` `C`

Hits you at two levels: rich, gently savoury fruit and a dry, slightly serious finish.

Cabernet Sauvignon, Co-op `11` `B`

**Rousse Cabernet Sauvignon/Cinsault
Country Wine** `15` `B`

Soft yet fresh fruit which combines maturity and youth. Terrific
with food.

Suhindol Merlot/Gamza, Co-op `12` `B`

CHILEAN WINE RED

Chilean Cabernet Sauvignon, Co-op `15` `B`

Coffee and chocolate fruit.

Four Rivers Cabernet Sauvignon 1995 `14.5` `C`

Warmth and complexity, good humour and depth. A wine to
wed.

Long Slim Red Cabernet Merlot 1994 `14` `B`

Rollicking fruity finish with a serious edge to it.

Santa Carolina Merlot 1993 `14` `C`

A classy mouthful of smooth, polished, gently tannic fruit. Great
with cheese dishes.

Santa Carolina Merlot 1994 `15` `C`

Soft, gently warm and leathery, subtly dry and dusty, this is a
young fogey of a wine masquerading as a literature don.

Tierra del Rey Chilean Red NV `14` `B`

Soft, dry, very food-friendly.

CHILEAN WINE   WHITE

Caliterra Casablanca Chardonnay 1994   `16.5`   `C`

Superb rich edge to the final thrust of the elegant fruit. Impressive wine with gusto, flavour and real style.

Casablanca Sauvignon Blanc, Lontue 1995   `14.5`   `C`

Stylish, striking, calm, very classy.

Long Slim White Chardonnay/Semillon 1995   `15.5`   `B`

Terrific food wine with its soft fruit shell containing a fresh acidic centre. Wonderful price.

CHINESE WINE   RED

Dragon Seal Cabernet Sauvignon 1993   `14`   `C`

Bordeaux in feel and taste with an uplift of exotic warmth on the final finish.

CHINESE WINE   WHITE

Dragon Seal Chardonnay 1993   `14`   `C`

Fat and full yet not overexotic acidically and so this turns in a very credible performance.

ENGLISH WINE · WHITE

English Table Wine 1994, Co-op · 15 · B

A terrific English wine at a perfect weight of fruit, acid and alcohol (10%), at a terrific price. It does Blighty proud. It beats muscadet (and many sancerres) hollow.

Denbies English Table Wine 1992 · 10 · C

FRENCH WINE · RED

Bad Tempered Cyril NV · 15.5 · C

Great texture and polish.

Barton & Guestier Margaux Tradition 1992 · 13 · E

Classy, without a doubt. But is it worth nine quid? Hum . . .

Bergerac Rouge, Co-op · 13 · B

Cahors NV, Co-op · 13 · C

Fruity and soft. Juicy.

Chateau Babeau St Chinian 1994 · 13 · C

Light cherry finish to the wine. Good chilled with salmon.

Chateau Cissac 1986 · 11 · F

Dry, but at this price I want more excitement and far more enrichment.

Chateau Les Hauts de Pontet, Pauillac 1991 · 13.5 · E

Bold, subtly chocolatey, rather expensive.

Chateau Pierrousselle Bordeaux 1995   `13.5` `C`

Most drinkable and grilled food-friendly.

Claret, Co-op   `12` `B`

Also available in half bottles now.

Corbieres, Co-op   `11` `B`

Cotes du Luberon, Co-op   `13` `B`

Attractive, gentle charcoal/rubber bouquet, plus a good dollop of cheering fruit. Good value.

Cotes du Rhone, Co-op   `11` `B`

Cotes du Roussillon, Co-op   `15` `B`

Dry, earthy-edged (rich tannins) and wonderfully purposeful and fruity. A really good food wine. Has bite and character and rustic charm.

Cotes du Ventoux NV, Co-op   `14` `B`

Rich, dry, oily, gently earthy and not so mountainous that it can't be ascended by anyone.

Crozes Hermitage Louis Mousset 1994   `13.5` `C`

A friendly example of an often fierce tribe.

Domaine de Conquet Merlot, J. & F. Lurton 1994   `13.5` `C`

Domaine Serjac Grenache VdP d'Oc 1994   `14` `C`

Good earthy grenache character. Great with grilled bangers.

Fitou, Co-op   `13` `C`

Expensive for such sweetness of disposition.

Fleurie, Mommessin 1995 `12.5` `D`

Soft as an old carpet slipper.

Laperouse Val d'Orbieu & Penfolds, VdP d'Oc 1994 `13.5` `C`

The fruit has a somewhat namby pamby attitude to the tannins. Needs time to develop in bottle (six months or more).

Mediterre Rouge, VdP d'Oc `14` `B`

Soft, simple, fruity red without a hint of rustic coarseness.

Medoc Vieilles Vignes 1993 `12` `C`

Too dry for me.

Merlot/Cabernet Sauvignon NV, Co-op `14` `B`

Great value bangers 'n' mash bottle.

Morgon, Les Charmes 1994 `13.5` `D`

Goodness! I might get to like beaujolais again if the wines were more like this (though not at £6.99).

Oak-Aged Claret NV, Co-op `13.5` `C`

Good claret style at a reasonable price.

Oak-Aged Cotes du Rhone 1995, Co-op `13.5` `C`

A soft specimen. Gives in the middle.

St Emilion, Bernard Taillan (half bottle) `13` `C`

Vin de Pays de l'Aude, Co-op `10` `B`

Vin de Pays de l'Herault Rouge, Co-op `12` `B`

Vin de Table Red, Co-op (1 litre) `11` `B`

Winter Hill Red 1995   `15` `B`

Brilliant-value rich, dry red which will make even claret fans
purse their lips and pat their purses.

FRENCH WINE   WHITE

Alsace Gewurztraminer, Co-op   `14` `C`

Lychee and grapefruit to the nose, mulled fruit, richly edged
for the mouth, spicy tickle in the throat. An interesting aperitif,
or to drink solo with a book, or for mild Chinese food.

Bergerac Blanc, Co-op   `11` `B`

Blanc de Blancs, Co-op   `11` `B`

Bordeaux Blanc Medium Dry, Co-op   `12` `B`

Chateau Pierrousselle Entre-deux-Mers
1995   `13.5` `C`

Hint of depth to the fruit here.

Domaine de Haut Rauly Monbazillac 1994
(half bottle)   `14.5` `C`

A waxy, honeyed wine for blue cheese.

Fair Martina Vermentino NV   `14.5` `C`

Hermitage Blanc, Les Nobles Rives 1992   `13` `F`

True Rhone dry white earthiness and class but what a price!

Les Pavois d'Or, Sauternes (half bottle)   `13` `D`

Sweetie for puds – or just fruit.

Mediterre Blanc, VdP d'Oc | 13 | B

Some attractive fruit here.

Montagny Premier Cru 1995 | 11 | D

Philippe de Baudin Chardonnay 1994 | 15 | C

A richly edged wine of some class with a lot of flavour. It is perfect with lemon chicken for the ripe melon fruit and acid meld with the dish perfectly.

Premieres Cotes de Bordeaux, Co-op | 13 | C

Too sweet for the average tooth, but not richly textured enough for desserts. Perhaps best with blue cheese and a bunch of grapes.

Rose d'Anjou, Co-op | 12 | B

A pleasant little rose.

Sauvignon Blanc Bordeaux, Co-op | 13 | B

Some flavour. Touch grudging.

VdP d'Oc Chardonnay, Co-op | 12 | C

VdP de l'Herault Blush, Co-op | 11 | C

Vin de Pays des Cotes de Gascogne, Co-op | 12 | B

Vin de Pays des Cotes des Pyrenees Orientales NV, Co-op | 12 | B

Solid, unexciting, but very, very far from undrinkable. Also available in 3-litre boxes.

Vin de Pays Sauvignon Blanc 1995, Co-op | 13.5 | C

Well-made, fresh, clean.

Viognier VdP d'Oc 1994 `13` `C`

Winter Hill White 1995 `13.5` `B`

Cheap and cheerful – with shellfish.

GERMAN WINE RED

Dornfelder, Co-op `13` `C`

Drink it chilled with grilled salmon or mackerel.

GERMAN WINE WHITE

**Bad Bergzaberner Kloster Liebfrauenberg
Auslese 1994** `15` `C`

Honey-edged, but far from simply sweet. The lemon acid knits
the fruit together brilliantly and stylishly.

Hock Deutscher Tafelwein, Co-op `11` `A`

Huesgen Graacher Himmelreich Spatlese `8` `C`

Sweet – little else. Disgracefully feeble brew.

**Kirchheimer Schwarzerde Beerenauslese,
Zimmerman Graeff 1993 (half bottle)** `14` `C`

I'd lay this down for five years (AD 2000) to reach 17.5
points.

Liebfraumilch, Co-op `10`

Morio Muskat, Co-op `12.5` `B`

Pleasant aperitif.

Mosel Deutscher Tafelwein, Co-op `11` `B`

Muller Thurgau, Co-op `12` `B`

Oppenheimer Krotenbrunnen 1994, Co-op `12` `B`

Rudesheimer Rosengarten 1994, Co-op `13` `B`

Chilled as an aperitif? Or a TV soap opera glug? Possibly. Possibly.

GREEK WINE RED

Kourtaki Vin de Crete Rouge 1995 `13` `B`

Pleasant brew which might work with pickled boar's snout.

HUNGARIAN WINE RED

Chapel Hill Cabernet Sauvignon, Balaton 1994 `14` `B`

Good-value pasta plonking. A dry, fruity wine with some personality, it's earthy, rich and energetic.

Frontier Island Ripe Fruity Red 1995 `9` `B`

Hungarian Red Country Wine, Balaton Region, Co-Op `12` `B`

Hungaroo Merlot 1994　　14.5　B

Invigorating, distinctive, fruity, dry(ish), subtly quirky, great with food.

HUNGARIAN WINE　　WHITE

Chapel Hill Irsai Oliver 1995　　15　B

Brilliant muscat-scented aperitif.

Frontier Island White 1995　　11　A

Talcum-powder fruit – rather stumbling.

Gyongyos Estate Chardonnay 1995　　13.5　B

**Hungarian White Country Wine, Nagyrede,
Co-op**　　14　B

Delicious fruit for the money. Gooseberry/melon/musky peach. Good with food or solo.

Hungaroo Pinot Gris 1995　　15　B

Delicious aperitif wine with a soft apricot subtlety and a gently nutty finish.

ITALIAN WINE　　RED

Chianti, Co-op　　10　B

Country Collection Puglian Red　　15.5　B

Cherry/plum fruit and considerable verve and style. Dry, fruity, very flavourful and frisky.

Le Volte Ornellaia 1993 `12` `E`

Overpriced novelty.

Merlot del Veneto, Co-op `12.5` `C`

Rather more fruit than flab – so it's good with mildly sauced pastas.

Monferrato Rosso 1995 `12` `B`

Montepulciano d'Abruzzo 1994, Co-op `13.5` `B`

Great fun drinking. Soft and mellow.

Principato Rosso, Co-op `12` `B`

Sangiovese di Toscana, Fiordaliso 1994 `15` `C`

Wonderful sweet fruit finish in this deliciously dry red gives it a superb versatility with food (anything from red meats to rice dishes).

Sicilian Red, Co-op `15` `B`

Big, rich, smooth, dark cherry fruit, raisiny yet soft and soupy. This is a terrific savoury pasta plonk.

Valpolicella, Co-op `12` `A`

Villa Mantinera, Montepulciano de Molise NV   `14` `C`

Fun, sloppy, jammy but with an underlying dryness. Great with all sorts of Italian meat and pasta dishes.

Vino da Tavola Rosso NV, Co-op `13` `B`

Beginners' Red. A soft, fresh bowl of cherries.

ITALIAN WINE WHITE

Alasia Chardonnay del Piemonte 1995 `14` `C`

Rather classy in a demure sort of way. Delicious texture and muted richness.

Bianco di Custoza Vignagrande 1995 `12` `C`

Chardonnay Atesino, Co-op `10` `B`

Chardonnay del Salento, 'Le Trulle' 1994 `15.5` `C`

Butters the tongue with highly civilised fruit at a very reasonable price.

Frascati 1995, Co-op `11` `C`

Frascati Superiore, Co-op `11` `B`

Frascati Villa Catone 1994 `11` `C`

Monferrato White 1995 `13` `B`

Nutty in the Italian way, but agrees with you in the end. Good price.

Orvieto Secco, Co-op `12` `C`

Pinot Grigio del Veneto, Co-op `10` `B`

Sicilian White, Co-op `13` `B`

Good value. Solid fruit, lacking a little acidic punch.

Soave, Co-op `10` `B`

Vino da Tavola Bianco NV, Co-op `13.5` `B`

Good value here – as a tuna salad accompaniment.

LEBANESE WINE — RED

Chateau Musar 1977 `13` `G`
£20? An eight-quid wine at best. It has a refined muscularity, immensely dry, perfectly mature, and it's wonderfully aromatic with its cigar-box scents and fruit. Strictly for the nut who loves old books with musty leather covers. Top stores only. The 1988 is in wider distribution (qv).

Chateau Musar 1988 `13` `G`
Not the great wine it once was. Getting too juicy and one-dimensional (and expensive).

MEXICAN WINE — WHITE

L. A. Cetto Petite Syrah 1993 `15.5` `C`
Wonderful texture and weighted richness of fruit.

MOLDOVAN WINE — RED

Kirkwood Cabernet Merlot 1994 `14.5` `B`
Brilliant softness and freshness.

MOLDOVAN WINE — WHITE

Kirkwood Chardonnay 1995 `14` `B`
Fresh hint of pineapple, clean – not as varietally impactful as it might be but very attractive.

MOROCCAN WINE   RED

Moroccan Cabernet Syrah 1995

A cracking wine! Full of flavour and depth but it also has a hint of warmth and herbiness.

NEW ZEALAND WINE   RED

New Zealand Cabernet Merlot 1994, Co-op
Very soft and light.

NEW ZEALAND WINE   WHITE

Explorers Vineyard Sauvignon Blanc

A delightful fish wine which is not typical NZ sauvignon blanc but is delicate and delicious.

Forest Flower Fruity Dry White 1995

Just fails by a whisker to garner more points. Sound texture and fruit – the finish pales.

Millton Vineyard Semillon/Chardonnay 1995   12 D

Somewhat disappointing at this price. Rather uncertain fruit – showing a nervous disposition.

**New Zealand Semillon Sauvignon Blanc
1995, Co-op**   14.5 C

Has its grassy Kiwi grip handsomely muted by the solid fruit
coating. Bespoke fruit at a pret-a-porter price.

Nobilo White Cloud 1995   13 C

Fish 'n' chips wine.

PORTUGUESE WINE   RED

**Campos dos Frades Cabernet Sauvignon
1994**   15.5 C

A most approachable and soft-finishing cabernet with a dark
side to its fruit and a freshness to the acidity – so it's balanced
and bonny.

**Quinta da Pancas Cabernet Sauvignon
1994**   15 C

Great value under a fiver. Has serious fruit of great style.

PORTUGUESE WINE   WHITE

Campos dos Frades Chardonnay 1995   14 C

Depth of flavour surprising in a Portuguese wine. Great with
chicken dishes.

Fiuza Sauvignon Blanc 1995   16 C

A brilliantly conceived wine of striking, balanced fruit. Richness
and style in abundance.

Joao Pires Muscat Branco 1995 `15.5` `C`

Cheering aperitif and great with oriental fish and wonderful
with scallops with a minted pea puree.

Portuguese Rose, Co-op `10` `B`

Vinho Verde, Co-op `11` `B`

ROMANIAN WINE RED

Classic Pinot Noir 1991 `16` `B`

Mature yet lithe, soft, fruity, complex and, incredibly, a proper
gamy pinot. Great value.

Romanian Priarie Merlot 1995, Co-op `13` `B`

ROMANIAN WINE WHITE

Romanian Prairie Sauvignon Blanc
1995, Co-op `15` `B`

Great value here. The fruit is delicately rich, nicely textured and
finely stitched to the acidity.

SOUTH AFRICAN WINE RED

Cape Afrika Pinotage 1992 `16` `C`

Wonderful fruit. Deeply sensual, rich, dry, balanced and truly
flavoursome. Lovely wine.

Cape Red, Co-op   15 B

Distinctive fruit, rich and rolling without being overripe or blowsy, and there is an attractive dry edge of real class. Drink chilled like beaujolais (or rather, like beaujolais used to be). Brilliant soft fresh aromatic fruit. Bargain.

Kumala Cinsault/Pinotage   16 B

Burnt rubber fruit of great charm. Distinctive, soft, deliciously well formed and stylish! Exceptional depth of flavour and lingering-finish fruitiness.

Long Mountain Shiraz 1993   15 C

An exotic shiraz with a depth of flavour and warmth which wins you over by its sheer texture of fruit.

Oak Village Cabernet Sauvignon 1992   13.5 C

Juicy style of cabernet. Touch expensive when compared with the more expensive Bulgars and Chileans.

Oak Village Pinotage 1994   15 C

Not even the most rampant stick-in-the-mud, including the direst stick-in-the-primordial-slime dinosaur, could fail to find this rich, meaty, aromatic, fruity wine charming.

Robertson Cabernet Sauvignon 1994   14.5 C

Soft, friendly, plummy. Quietly mannered, demurely fruity.

SOUTH AFRICAN WINE   WHITE

Cape Afrika Rhine Riesling 1995   14 C

Rich yet dry and oily-textured. Lovely bottle for rich fish dishes – like crab cakes.

Cape White, Co-op

Bargain. Most attractive dry peach fruit with subtle acidic backcloth providing modernity and freshness. Really terrifically tasty for the money.

Kumala Chenin/Chardonnay 1995

Oak Village Chardonnay 1995

Deliciously rich yet calm and refreshing, vigorous and stylish – good value.

Welmoed Sauvignon Blanc 1995

Interesting grassy opening leading on to rich fruit of some texture and weight. Good with roast chicken.

SPANISH WINE   RED

Campo Rojo, Carinena

Thundering bargain. An edge of earthy tannins to the mature plum fruit makes this a solid food wine (cheese dishes and stews).

Enate Tempranillo Cabernet 1992

Aromatic, smooth, classy, well-mannered. It's perhaps almost TOO smooth and classy for its rustic background. It has the politeness perhaps to be expected from a wine made by a man who worked at Chateau Margaux and Torres.

Marques de la Sierra Garnacha 1994

Brilliant value and simply terrific with casseroles and roasts. Has a good shroud of dry, rich tannin and an undercoat of soft berry fruit. Lovely texture, solid fruit with a hint of spice. It has a concentration of flavour and complexity which is stunning for the money.

Marquis de Monistrol Merlot 1992 · 15 · C

Delightfully textured dry wine with depth, flavour and real class.

Palacio de la Vega Cabernet Sauvignon 1992 · 16 · D

Texture, warmth, richness, style, humour and personality. Dry yet full of fruit.

Rioja Crianza, Co-op · 12 · C

Rioja Tinto NV, Co-op · 13 · C

A very soft rioja of the new school of easy entry.

Tempranillo Oak-Aged, Co-op · 13.5 · B

Astonishing power and astonishing vanilla-tinged fruit. Almost medicinal on the finish.

Torres Gran Sangredetoro 1989 · 14 · D

Rich and stylish.

Valencia Red, Co-op · 12 · A

Now available in 3 litres as well.

Vina Pomal Rioja Crianza 1990 · 13.5 · C

Ripe and very ready for a chorizo sausage.

SPANISH WINE · WHITE

Castillo de Monjardin Unoaked Chardonnay 1994 · 14.5 · C

Superb lemony fruit with poise, purpose and subtly rich intentions.

Gandia Hoya Valley Grenache Rose 1995 `14` `B`

A delicious, well-priced rose. Great fragrant drinking.

Moscatel de Valencia, Co-op `16` `B`

Marmalade and toffee caramel – rich and exciting. Fabulous value for the Christmas pud.

Torres Sangredetoro 1992 `12` `C`

Not as rich or thrilling as previous vintages.

Valencia White, Co-op `14` `A`

Good level of fruit – balanced. Now available in 3 litres as well.

Valle de Monterrey Dry White Wine, Co-op `13` `B`

Good price and a solid wine for a party of bouillabaisse diners. Good rich overture not sustained climactically.

USA WINE   RED

Barefoot Cellars Gamay/Zinfandel 1994 `11` `C`

Beringer Zinfandel 1992 `14` `D`

California Red, Co-op `B`

Like burnt blackcurrant jam. How a wine can even LEAVE California let alone sell on a Co-op shelf at this price is beyond belief. The corners cut to achieve such risibly meagre pricing don't bear thinking about.

Gallo Sonoma County Cabernet Sauvignon 1992 `14` `E`

Delicious cab sauv. A touch pricey but good.

Glen Ellen Merlot 1994 `15` `C`

Deeply soft, like a well-plumped pillow. Great to quaff with the TV on.

USA WINE   WHITE

Barefoot Colombard/Chardonnay 1994 `13.5` `C`

Pleasant, balanced, fruity.

California Colombard, Co-op `11` `B`

Gallo Sonoma Chardonnay 1993 `17` `E`

This is an extremely classy chardonnay. Good oak/fruit/acid. Very delicate, very fine.

Sebastiani's White Zinfandel 1995 `10` `C`

**Stowells of Chelsea California Blush
(3-litre box)** `12.5` `F`

SPARKLING WINE/CHAMPAGNE

Barramundi Sparkling (Australia) `15.5` `D`

I love its cheeky label. I love its irreverent fruitiness and citric acidity. It offers finesse with a big smile.

Cava, Co-op `14` `C`

Bargain – whistle-clean and fault-free.

De Clairveaux Champagne NV   13.5   F

Attractive fruit here, really attractive. Pity about the price. (If it was under a tenner we'd really be in business.)

Marino Cava del Mediterraneo   16.5   C

An absolute block-buster of a bottle: delicate, lemony, classically fresh, clean and elegant and just so ridiculously well-priced it makes you think twice and drink time and time again (and at £3.99 a bottle you can afford it).

Sparkling Saumur, Co-op   13   D

Clean and classic.

Veuve Honorian Champagne Brut NV   12   E

KWIK SAVE

Don Cortez rides again

Kwik Save, Britain's most successful indigenous discount retailer, was not featured in the early editions of *Superplonk*. It made its debut in the 1994 guide, and readers were swift to welcome its arrival. Indeed, the tenor of the correspondence about Kwik Save suggests that leaving it out in the first place was something of an omission.

Having noticed a mention for Kwik Save in my *Guardian* column, Robert Watkins wrote in July 1993, paying tribute to the retailer's value-for-money philosophy:

> I was pleased to see Kwik Save surface in your columns. Not before time, this store should be encouraged. For a while I have been saving 50p or so on Bulgarian Merlot, compared to Tesco's price for the same bottle, but because my local Kwik Save had only a limited range I didn't realise that they had more than one or two lines – thank you.
>
> Kwik Save has had a raw deal from food writers – and I agree you can't live on baked beans, but a Heinz baked bean from Kwik Save has the same properties as one from Tesco – or even Sainsbury's. This is especially useful knowledge when one has a 10-year-old son who will happily sit down and eat two cans of the same at one sitting.
>
> To return to the point, this letter was prompted by your endorsement of Romanian Cellars Feteasca Neagra

and Cab Sauv – Littlewoods £2.89. The same bottle is available from Kwik Save at £2.29 – it was £1.99 a month ago – and we enjoyed several bottles. At that price even 60p out of £2.89 is more than 20% saving. i.e. £7.20 a case. Kwik Save should be given some credit for this.

No. I'm not a paid supporter of Kwik Save – I just don't want to pay over the odds.

Another good bottle from the same store is Crooked Creek Red – an Aussie with some of the qualities that you would expect in an over-£3.00 bottle.

Keep up the good work, we enjoyed particularly Lezeria – and Contesse de Lorancay – as cheap drinkable whites are less abundant.

Equally warm was the welcome from Brian Jackson of Preston in July 1993 who was particularly pleased to be reunited with an old friend on the Kwik Save shelves.

Like many people I always enjoy reading your *Superplonk* column. Perhaps this is because of your obvious enjoyment of the wines and the fact that I have never progressed much beyond the cheap and cheerful stuff I was introduced to as a student and long-distance hitch-hiker in the late 1960s.

I was interested to note that you have recently discovered the ubiquitous (except in the south) Kwik Save. Last September I was also pleased to be able to browse the Kwik Save wine shelves. It was the occasion of the Preston Guild and I was devising a little wine-tasting competition for a group of friends I had invited to this once every 20 years celebration.

I wanted to throw in a bottle of good old plonk from our days at college some 20 or more years ago. What better, I thought, than that old student party stand-by Don Cortez? The problem was that I had not seen it for several years and despaired of finding it. I then hit on Kwik Save. They had plenty of it at a mere £2.37 a bottle.

The old Don Cortez really fooled the competitors. It didn't seem anything like as they had remembered it 20 years before. What has happened to it? It now seems quite palatable and even has DO status. What will it taste like at the next Preston Guild in 2012?

Mr Jackson is not the only person who remembers Don Cortez from his student days, when I recall it cost 2s 6d. It was, I believe, first introduced by Gough Brothers and was one of the best-selling wines in the country for a while.

Incidentally, Mr Jackson's comment on Kwik Save's northern bias is not really fair. True, once upon a time, a Kwik Save was a rare sight south of the Watford Gap, but since the early '90s, the chain has been steadily expanding southwards, and now has a fair representation down in the south-east.

Given his enthusiasm for Kwik Save, I was happy to be able to tell Mr Jackson that it was to be included in *Superplonk 1994*.

The improvements in the Kwik Save wine department have been closely monitored by Mr Nelson Wallace of Cleveland, a *Superplonk* fan but interestingly not a *Guardian* reader. Mr Wallace had written as early as August 1993 asking for Kwik Save to be included in the guide.

I have two objects in writing this letter. First is to thank you for the pleasure my wife and I have had from this last year's *Superplonk*. We normally like to have a bottle of wine with dinner and it is a great help to have informed guidance rather than the blurb or description on the label.

The second object is to suggest that you consider the inclusion of Kwik Save in the next edition. I read some time ago that Kwik Save had appointed a lady MW as their wine buyer. We are well served here with every firm in *Superplonk* except Waitrose so we hardly ever buy in Kwik

Save even though we have had a store nearby for about two years. In that time we have noticed a difference in the appearance and sources of the wines on the shelves and have been happy with the odd 'cheapie' we have tried.

Yesterday I saw they were quoting from your *Guardian* recommendation of Domaine Reschause (Merlot) as delicious. Having bought one and sampled it in the evening, we agree completely with the description. At £2.85 the bottle is a bargain, so we've bought a few more in case stocks run out. Other prices seem equally modest.

Of course our experience of Kwik Save's wines is very slight and it may be that you will dismiss the idea of including them in *Superplonk* as unjustified on the basis of your knowledge of them. However, I thought it a suggestion worth making.

Two years later, Mr Wallace wrote again, concluding his letter with an update on his local Kwik Save which underlines how the retailer's wine offer has developed over the years. His one gripe is that the wines come and go rather too quickly:

... As regards Kwik Save, whose branch nearby was opened two or three years ago to serve a constantly growing neighbourhood of new executive houses, we have noticed a change and improvement in the off licence part. Originally the shelves were biased in favour of beers and lagers, but the balance has swung towards the wines, partly we think due to the improving quality of wines and partly because the clientele will have turned out to be more sophisticated than the management had anticipated.

The snag about Kwik Save is that new names appear on the shelves but don't last long there presumably because Kwik Save can't buy the larger parcels that the 'big boys' normally take.

It has been interesting, though, to find some bottle with labels saying (for the first time I think) 'produced and bottled for Kwik Save'. These are the Vins de Pays d'Oc near Beziers given the most un-French title of 'Skylark Hill'. We hope you will endorse our liking for 'Vermentino' white and 'Very Special Red', that we find very acceptable for everyday drinking at £2.89 to £2.99.

In fact, in my mailbag, Kwik Save was the subject of just one complaint concerning quality, from Kenneth Bryan of Powys regarding the Bulgarian wine, Oriachovitza 1990. But the retailer's prompt and honest response does them credit. In raising the issue, Kenneth Bryan asked for hints on detecting a duff wine prior to opening.

Can anything be done to intercept really dud, if not downright contaminated, wines getting through to the customer?

I have had a marvellous run of good Oriachovitza 1990 from Kwik Save and blessed the name of Angela Muir, but now the stuff is a minefield.

This has been going on for about six months until I have had to stop buying and as we are addicts, we are suffering from withdrawal symptoms.

Staff at Kwik Save Welshpool and Oswestry could not be more amiable, if slightly puzzled, when you take it back but it is an effort to do it, particularly if it is just drinkable. Now the really good Oriachovitza seems to be rare. It is mostly adequate, poor or absolutely undrinkable.

Can they get back the happy red-nosed communists who used to enjoy quality control in Bulgaria? Or is it an intentional confidence trick played by someone sending over stuff which is not of marketable quality, hoping that the Kwik Save customers will just take the medicine without making sufficient fuss to cause a stir at buying level?

I have raised this with counter staff at Kwik Save and I am writing to you because if you cared to take it up you would be most likely to have other drinker feedback and to be able to get at someone at their HQ who is able to take a look at the problem, which cannot be doing Kwik Save any good, and may require action that is painful.

Thank you for your book which my family all buy. It is sad about the 16 rating on the Oriachovitza which should now be about 1 to 8.

As Oriachovitza had been such a superb wine, I was as dismayed as Mr Bryan to hear of its decline. I wrote to Angela Muir, Kwik Save's aforementioned wine consultant, for enlightenment, and replied to Mr Bryan thus.

I was appalled to get your letter of February 3rd concerning the Oriachovitza 1990 at Kwik Save. I will contact the Kwik Save people immediately with a copy of your letter and of this reply, and ask them what is going on with this wine. Please keep me in touch with future developments.

I'm especially disappointed to hear this about this wine because, as you say, it's a solid 16–pointer, or rather was, and now I shall have to revise this view – maybe even write an article about the problems of retailers and quality control of certain East European wines.

On 16 May 1995, Kwik Save's Trading Controller, Richard Graves, had sad news for Mr Bryan, *Superplonk* and Oriachovitza fans everywhere.

Further to my letter of 17 February, I am now able to confirm that we have decided to de-list Oriachovitza. The reason for the delay in making this decision is that we asked our consultant to visit Bulgaria on our behalf, to review quality-control procedures at our existing supplier's wineries and to find new sources for possible replacement wines. We have now received her report and as a result, will soon be replacing Oriachovitza with a Cabernet Sauvignon Reserve from the Vinenka winery.

May I thank you for drawing this matter to our attention which was in fact the first occasion when quality problems came to our notice. Meanwhile, please accept the enclosed £5.00 voucher which I hope you will use to acquire a bottle of wine from your nearest Kwik Save Store.

Kwik Save Stores Limited
Warren Drive
Prestatyn
Clwyd
LL19 7HU

Tel 01745 887111
Fax 01745 882504

ARGENTINIAN WINE

RED

Balbi Vineyard Malbec Syrah 1995

Has a somewhat dull, mass-produced feel as if someone said, 'Let's turn out an agreeably priced, warmly fruity wine which won't upset anyone.' It won't.

Mendoza Red, J. & F. Lurton

Dirt-cheap party plonking. Takes to chilling, this red, too.

AUSTRALIAN WINE

RED

Butterfly Ridge Cabernet Sauvignon/Shiraz

Very soft and nearly jammy.

Pelican Bay Shiraz Cabernet 1996

Has a zip to it. Is it enough? Well, it's enough if you've a plate of pasta in front of you. By itself, it may not tease you for very long.

AUSTRALIAN WINE

WHITE

Angove's Classic Reserve Chardonnay 1995

A rounded, rich-to-finish chardonnay with a gentle oiliness and firm, fruity structure. Great grilled-fish wine.

Pelican Bay Chardonnay 1996

Delicious rich-edged, opulently fruity tipple. Great to quaff, terrific with fish and chicken.

BULGARIAN WINE — RED

Burgas Cabernet Sauvignon 1993

Just about at its peak. Dry, rich, fulsome, serious. A bargain until the fruit gives out by spring 1997.

Cabernet Sauvignon Reserve, Elhovo 1992

Soft but with enough briskness of blackcurrant fruit on the finish to make an admirable mouthful.

**Domaine Boyar Cabernet Sauvignon,
Straldja 1993**

Beautifully soft, rich, calm, deep, subtle, ripe cabernet of great style and class. Brilliant value for money.

**Domaine Boyar Lovico Suhindol Cabernet
Sauvignon/Merlot Country Wine** 13 B

A somewhat dry, wrinkled wine.

**Domaine Boyar Merlot/Cabernet
Sauvignon 1995** 15.5 B

Superb value. Lots of swirling, serious-intentioned blackcurrant fruit. Terrific with food.

**Domaine Sakar Reserve Merlot, Liubimetz
1992**

A soft, very ready merlot with perfectly integrated fruit, acid and tannin.

BULGARIAN WINE — WHITE

Khan Krum Riesling-Dimiat   14

If you want a cheap, fresh, perfectly satisfying aperitif, you have it here.

Preslav Barrel Fermented Chardonnay 1995   13

Preslav Vintage Blend Chardonnay/ Sauvignon 1995   14

Perfectly balanced, excellently priced, terrific with complex salads.

FRENCH WINE — RED

Cabernet Sauvignon VdP d'Oc 1995   16

Soft cherries and juicy blackcurrant fruit immediately strike but then the tannins' beautiful return stroke as a back taste gives the wine depth, character, style and brilliant value for money.

Claret Cuvee VE 1995   12

Tastes clarety enough. Rich food might give it the brush-off, though.

Cotes du Rhone Francois Dubessy 1995   12

Soft, utterly yielding. Goes with saliva but not a lot else.

Domaine Trianon, St Chinian 1995   15

Soft, cherry-edged, terrific texture and a good price. Rather delicious fruit here.

Domaine de Bruyeres, Cotes de Malepere
1994   `16` B

Great value to be had here. Also style, dry classy fruit, great
balance and a structure which commands respect. Will serve as
a posh dinner-party red.

Rouge de France, Selection Cuvee VE   `12` B

Skylark Hill Cabernet Sauvignon/Shiraz
VdP d'Oc   `14` B

Rich, invigoratingly dry wine with plenty of fruit and enough
weight to handle lots of richly flavoured dishes.

Skylark Hill Merlot, VdP d'Oc   `15.5` B

Excellent, simply excellent for the money. The leather is there
but the flavour is rich.

Skylark Hill Very Special Red VdP d'Oc   `14` B

A high note of ripe cherry and plum on the finish is a
counterpoint to the very dry start.

Vin de Pays de l'Herault Domaine Virginie   `11` B

FRENCH WINE   WHITE

Blanc de France Vin de Table Selection
Cuvee   `13` B

Excellent price for such freshly turned-out fruit.

Bordeaux Sauvignon 1995   `14.5` B

A subtly rich, clean, fresh, perfectly weighted bordeaux blanc
– has style and a very welcoming price tag.

Rose de France Selection Cuvee VE

Will do, at this price. But it does need a hot day in the back garden.

Skylark Hill Chardonnay VdP d'Oc

Not a very fat chardonnay but it is authentic – and how many wines can you say that of under four quid (well under)?

Skylark Hill Very Special White, VdP d'Oc

Softly nutty, gently melony – with a surge of freshness on the finish. Quality quaffing for not a lot of dosh.

Stowells of Chelsea Vin de Pays du Tarn (3-litre box)

Sound but dullish – not a lot of fruit.

Vin de Pays de l'Herault, Domaine Virginie

'Two pounds sixty nine pence.' It should be in a display case in a museum – or will be, soon.

GERMAN WINE WHITE

Deutscher Tafelwein, Rhein, K. Linden 1995

Piesporter Michelsberg, K. Linden 1995

Valley Home Riesling 1995   `11` `B`

Dull, but not to Liebfraumilch drinkers.

HUNGARIAN WINE   WHITE

Hungarian Chardonnay, Mor Region
1995   `13` `B`

A fresh style of chardonnay.

Hungarian Country White 1995   `11` `A`

Talcum-powder fruit – rather stumbling.

Hungarian Country Wine Pinot Gris/
Riesling, Kiskoros Region   `12` `B`

Starts well, finishes limply.

Hungarian Pinot Gris, Neszmely 1995   `14` `B`

Pleasant, varietally faithful aperitif: delicious pre-prandial potion.

ITALIAN WINE   RED

Il Paesano   `13` `B`

Light and juicy. Fun.

Montepulciano d'Abruzzo 1995   `14.5` `B`

Soft with a hug from a gently squeezing earthiness of fruit. Good pizza plonk.

Valpolicella Venier   `11` `B`

ITALIAN WINE WHITE

Frascati Superiore, Villa Pani 1995 `12` `B`

Gabbia d'Oro `10` `A`

Soave Venier `11` `B`
Rather an austere example.

MACEDONIAN WINE RED

Cabernet Sauvignon 1993 `13` `B`
Juicy – very, very juicy.

Macedonian Country Red 1995 `10` `A`

PORTUGUESE WINE RED

Alta Mesa Estremadura 1994 `14` `B`
Soft cherry fruit, pleasantly priced.

PORTUGUESE WINE WHITE

Rosado Vinho de Mesa `10` `B`

ROMANIAN WINE RED

Danube Meadow Young Vatted Merlot
1995

Lovely cheekpuckering tannins on the leathery, blackcurranty fruit. Delightful wine.

Prokova Valley Young Vatted Pinot
Noir 1995

Not especially appealing to die-hard pinot freaks but appealing to anyone who likes simply fruity, dry red wine.

SOUTH AFRICAN WINE RED

Clearsprings Cape Red, Simonsvlei

Some good, clean, well-polished fruit.

SOUTH AFRICAN WINE WHITE

Clearsprings Cape Medium White,
Simonsvlei

Residual sugar gives it the fruit.

SPANISH WINE RED

Berberana Tempranillo Rioja 1994

Solid rioja at a decent price. Has typical tempranillo fruit with that edge of candied cherry and vanilla on the finish.

Flamenco Spanish Full Red `10` `B`

Roughish, not very couth.

Jun Carillo Fruity Red Wine 1995 `13` `B`

Marino, El Tinto del Mediterraneo `14` `B`

A prune-edged food wine. Has a handsome tannic touch.

Promesa Tinto `14` `B`

Cheap and cheering. Great bangers 'n' mash bottle (fruity yet with a grilled earthy edge).

SPANISH WINE WHITE

Castillo de Liria Moscatel, Valencia `15.5` `B`

Brilliant pudding wine for the money. Also, well chilled, an effective aperitif.

Gandia Hoya Valley Chardonnay 1994 `14.5` `B`

Only a slight softening of the finish fails to get this otherwise crisp fish wine a higher rating.

Jun Carillo Fruity White 1995 `13` `B`

Perfect for fish parties.

Marino El Vino Blanco de Mediterraneo `12` `B`

Promesa Blanco `11` `B`

Cheap, not altogether cheerful. But acceptable with a horde of fish stew guzzlers.

USA WINE — RED

California Cellars Red 11 B

USA WINE — WHITE

California Cellars White 13 B

California under three quid? Yes. But this is California on a cloudy day.

SPARKLING WINE/CHAMPAGNE

Bonnet Brut Heritage Champagne 12 F

Cava Brunet Brut Reserve (Spain) 15 C

Old-style fruity cava but there is no doubting its deliciousness – and the price is perfect.

Champagne Brut, Louis Raymond 13.5 E

LITTLEWOODS

*'You should know, Malcolm, that Littlewoods are
pulling out of wine and spirit retailing entirely at the
end of 1996 and I think you should be the first to know
. . . I hope our paths cross again in the future . . .'*
Ian Duffy, Littlewoods wine buyer,
on the telephone, summer 1996

In contrast with some of the other larger supermarket chains,
I have received very few letters concerning Littlewoods' wines
and it is now exceedingly unlikely that I ever will. As the above
extract of a conversation reveals, Littlewoods will no longer flog
the stuff after 31 December and I only include this introduction
to the store and its list of wines to give readers an opportunity
to plunder the shelves and, who knows, maybe unearth some
unrepeatable bargains amongst stock which must be cleared to
make way for underwear and fluffy toys.

Littlewoods as a wine retailer and deserving of appearing in
the cast of *Superplonk* will, then, be history as 1997 dawns. It
has become, I guess, a victim of the supermarket's remorseless
march to wine-retailing hegemony and if a tear does not drop
from my eye as I contemplate a Littlewoodsless book in the
future, I do feel a little sad that Mr Duffy will be out of a
job and I will no longer be able to make jokes about wine
retailers who run football pools and stock knitting patterns.
Linguistically, perhaps, the association of Littlewoods and wine
was so dissonant that drinkers could not take the union seriously
and developed little regard for it as a wine retailer.

In the glorious past that was Littlewoods – epistolary history as far as I am concerned – little indeed can be said. The letters that have come my way have only included any reference to the retailer in passing. What could be the explanation for this? There are probably a number.

First, Littlewoods has fewer stores than the big supermarket chains, and not all of them carry wine, though this was something which the retailer claimed it had ambitions to change when it avowed an intention to have wine departments in all of its stores. In the second place, Littlewoods is not strictly a supermarket. It is a department store, and as such wine was just one element of an extensive retailing repertoire. Moreover, unlike in a supermarket, the wine department was tucked away to one side or even on a different floor where it did not necessarily attract passers-by.

Supermarkets on the other hand are designed so that customers 'flow through' from one section to the next in what the retailer perceives as the most logical and practical manner. The supermarket orders its aisles in a way that it believes is in tune with what its customers expect. This is why they have reached the conclusion, doubtless born out of exhaustive consumer research, that we shoppers will always think of fruit and vegetables when we first enter a supermarket because it is fresh produce, unlike wine which is bottled and pulled out of the ground well before yesterday and can therefore be at the 'stale' end of the store. Having the wines at the end of the shop as the final port-of-call for the shopper makes sense, particularly for the customer shopping for one meal, a party or a dinner party. It is only after the food has been selected that a considered choice of wine can be made (though I must say I always do it the other way round when in a restaurant and decide what I want to drink before I crack the problem of what to eat with it, but I can't say I follow this pattern when shopping for wine for a dinner party or even for a special supper for two because in these circumstances the decision about the food has always already been taken). Another factor may be that people pause longer and browse more studiously in the wine sections which, if they were at the beginning or in the middle of the store, could cause an almighty trolley jam. At least, with the wine department being at one end of the store any compromising of the retailer's 'flow-through' strategy is kept to a minimum. Of course, some supermarkets separate their wine departments altogether from the rest of the shop, which is effectively the system Littlewoods operated in its stores.

All this is something of a digression from my original question regarding the paucity of correspondence concerning Littlewoods. Did customers never have any grievances? Were they entirely satisfied with the recommendations I made and the retailer's ability to supply the wines? There is also the possibility that since Littlewoods' wines did not enjoy quite the same exposure through my *Guardian* column as those of some of the big supermarkets and off-licence chains, few readers ventured inside the stores.

However, the most likely explanation for the absence of letters about Littlewoods does, I believe, relate to the make-up of the Littlewoods wine customer – in so far as a high proportion of them wear it (make-up, that is). Littlewoods' wine customers were, and perhaps will continue to the end of the year so to be, predominantly female. I deduce this from the company's list of its six top-selling wines supplied last year which are all whites ranging from Liebfraumilch at the top through lambrusco and hock to Buck's Fizz. But the last one isn't a white wine, I hear you protest; it is nevertheless a product targeted at the female drinker. It is not uncommon for a retailer to have a high proportion of women among its wine customers (though Safeway, for some reason I cannot fathom, has a higher percentage of male customers than its rivals), but at Littlewoods the fairer sex appears to dominate to a considerable degree.

This has probably had a direct bearing on my volume of correspondence, as I have noticed over the years that I receive more letters from men than from women. I would say that letters from men account for around 65 to 70 per cent of the letters I receive. There could be many reasons for this, but by far the most likely rationalisation is that men have more time than women – who have very probably made their wine purchases having finished the rest of the weekly shop, done the housework, the family accounts, cooked the kids' dinner and all that probably after a day at work to boot. True, more and more men, I am happy to say, are sharing in these tasks and in some households devoting themselves to them exclusively, but not amongst the general run of Littlewoods customers. All things considered, therefore, I feel that neither I nor Littlewoods should be too disconsolate about the seeming lack of interest shown in its wines. Mr Duffy should not be downcast. He will, I hope, quickly find another job with another wine retailer or, should he so decide, go off to the Balearics and write a sensational history of his time with the company which will be serialised in the *Daily Mail* and turned into a major motion picture (wonderful phrase that! – *motion picture*) starring Marlon Brando, Jack Palance, Katherine Hepburn and Vanessa Redgrave as various members of the Littlewoods dynasty.

None of this should imply that we will be hearing no more from Littlewoods in the coming few years, even if they have joined, as far as wine is concerned, those other shops and myriad merchants whose memorial tablets have so swelled the cemetery of ex-wine retailers over the past decade. It was reported in the *Financial Times* in June that Littlewoods intends to spend some £500 million expanding its retail chain, opening 40 new stores, bringing the total in the chain to 170. The new stores will all be around 25,000 sq ft in size and the expansion will create 3,000 new jobs in the next four years.

I am sorry that Mr Duffy's will be amongst the old jobs lost. I look forward to our paths crossing at the premiere of his movie – to which I trust I will be invited.

Littlewoods Stores Support Centre
Atlantic Pavilion
Albert Dock
Liverpool
L70 1AD

Tel 0151 242 6000
Fax 0151 242 6390

AUSTRALIAN WINE — RED

Andrew Garrett Black Shiraz, McWilliams Vale 1993 — `13` `D`

Angove's Misty Moorings Australian Red — `13` `B`

Hardy's Nottage Hill Cabernet Sauvignon/Shiraz 1993 — `16` `C`

Hardy's Shiraz/Cabernet Sauvignon 1994 — `15.5` `B`

Jacobs Creek — `13` `C`

Orlando Jacobs Creek Shiraz/Cabernet 1993 — `13` `C`

Orlando RF Cabernet Sauvignon 1991 — `14` `C`

Wolf Blass Yellow Label Cabernet Sauvignon 1993 — `13.5` `D`

AUSTRALIAN WINE — WHITE

Andrew Garrett Fume Blanc 1993 — `15` `D`

Angove's Misty Moorings Australian White — `13.5` `B`

Hardys Nottage Hill Chardonnay 1994 — `17` `C`

Hardys Padthaway Chardonnay 1993 — `16` `D`

Hardys RR Medium White 1993 ⬜11 ⬛B

Hardys Semillon/Chardonnay ⬜13 ⬛B

Hardys Stamp Semillon/Chardonnay 1993 ⬜13 ⬜C

Orlando RF Chardonnay 1993 ⬜14.5 ⬜D

Wolf Blass South Australian Chardonnay
1994 ⬜14 ⬜D

BULGARIAN WINE   RED

Bulgarian Classic Cabernet Sauvignon
1991 ⬜14 ⬛B

CHILEAN WINE   RED

Chilean Cabernet Sauvignon 1993 ⬜14 ⬛B

CHILEAN WINE   WHITE

Chilean Sauvignon Blanc 1994 ⬜13.5 ⬛B

FRENCH WINE   RED

Beaujolais, Littlewoods ⬜8 ⬛B

Chateau d'Aigueville Cotes du Rhone 1993	13	C
Chateau Grand-Jean, Bordeaux 1989	13	C
Claret, Littlewoods	12.5	B
Corbieres NV, Littlewoods	12	B
Cotes du Rhone, Littlewoods	13	B
Cotes du Roussillon Villages 1993, Littlewoods	13.5	B
French Red Table Wine	11	B
Vin de Pays de l'Aude Red	10	B
Vin de Pays Pyrenees Orientales Red	12.5	B

FRENCH WINE WHITE

Bordeaux Blanc, Littlewoods	10	B
French Dry White Table Wine, Littlewoods	8	B
French Medium White Table Wine, Littlewoods	2	B
Muscadet de Sevre et Maine 1993, Littlewoods	10	B
Premieres Cotes de Bordeaux, Littlewoods	12	C
Rose d'Anjou, Littlewoods	12	B

Vin de Pays Pyrenees Orientales White	10	B
Vin de Table Dry White	10	B
Vin de Table Medium, Littlewoods	10	B

GERMAN WINE WHITE

Bereich Niersteiner Rheinhessen 1990, Littlewoods	12	C
Hock, Littlewoods	7	B
Liebfraumilch Rheinhessen 1990, Littlewoods	8	C
Piesporter Michelsberg 1993, Littlewoods	11	C
St Johanner Abtei Auslese Rheinhessen 1993	13.5	C

HUNGARIAN WINE RED

Cabernet Sauvignon, Szekszard 1993	8	C
Hungarian Merlot, Eger 1990	10	B

HUNGARIAN WINE WHITE

Gewurztraminer	10	B

**Hungarian Chardonnay, Badacsony
Region 1993** `5` **C**

Hungarian Sauvignon Blanc, Zemplen 1993 `9` **B**

ITALIAN WINE RED

Chianti Il Borgo `10` **B**

Valpolicella Il Borgo `11` **B**

ITALIAN WINE WHITE

Frascati, Il Borgo `8` **C**

Lambrusco White, Il Borgo `8` **B**

Soave Il Borgo `11` **B**

PORTUGUESE WINE RED

Bairrada `13` **B**

Borges Bairrada Reserva 1989 `10` **C**

ROMANIAN WINE RED

Romanian Cabernet Sauvignon 1985 `15` **B**

Romanian Classic Merlot 1990	12	B

Romanian Classic Pinot Noir 1990	13.5	B

ROMANIAN WINE · WHITE

Transylvania Pinot Gris 1992	14	B

SOUTH AFRICAN WINE · RED

Great Trek Pinotage	15.5	B

SOUTH AFRICAN WINE · WHITE

Great Trek Chenin Blanc	14	B

SPANISH WINE · RED

Carreras Cabernet Sauvignon	10	B
Marques de Caceres Rioja 1991	14	C
Rioja Romancero Crianza 1990	14.5	C

135

SPANISH WINE WHITE

Carreras Chardonnay	10	B
Carreras Sauvignon Blanc	9	B

USA WINE RED

Eagle Ridge Cabernet Sauvignon, California 1992	15	B
Eagle Ridge California Red NV	14	B

USA WINE WHITE

Eagle Ridge California Chardonnay 1993	12	C

SPARKLING WINE/CHAMPAGNE

Asti Spumante, Martini	10	D
Cavalino Sparkling Moscato (Italy)	6	A
Champagne Brut Francois Daumale	13.5	F
Marques de Monistrol 1991	13	D
Monsigny Champagne, Littlewoods	11	F

MARKS & SPENCER

Oh, what a lovely job!

In common with other retailers, Marks & Spencer use wine writers' recommendations on shelf-stickers in their stores to promote their wines. However, Mrs Peggy Wibberley of Ashford wondered whether M & S is rather more selective than other retailers in this regard, as she explained in her letter of 16 June 1991:

> I buy food at Marks & Spencer at least once a week, so I went in search of the two wines you recommended. You may be interested to hear of my experiences. At Ashford there was no sign of either wine, though other wines recommended by the *Independent* and by another newspaper the name of which I cannot now remember were prominently displayed.
>
> I happened to visit the Canterbury store shortly afterwards. Here again were large notices at waist level proclaiming 'Recommended by the *Independent*', 'Recommended by the *Sunday Times*' and another lot recommended by, I think, the *Daily Mail*. No mention of the *Guardian*. Having grovelled about at floor level and hit my head on my own trolley, I eventually managed to spot and drag out from the back of the shelf the two wines you mentioned. Is M & S afraid of inadvertently advertising the *Guardian* or does it think no one round here could possibly be reading it?

Also having difficulty in finding recommended wines in M & S stores was George Hipperson of Bath. His letter about the availability of M & S wine boxes particularly caught my attention:

> Re. Boxing Clever – M & S Australian Shiraz/Cabernet.
>
> On the strength of receiving a copy of your '93 *Superplonk* guide for Christmas, I purchased last week's Saturday *Guardian* and read your column; following your favourable comment on the above boxed number I visited Marks in Bath that same day. The white was there in gaudy boxes as described but no sign of the red. Likewise today I visited again; can you shed any light on this?
>
> Perhaps you can discover which M & S stores do have it, and let me know. Thank you.

I passed on a similar query from Peter Meadows in November 1994 to Marks & Spencer and, thoroughly placated, Mr Meadows sent me a copy of M & S's reply.

> I was informed by Malcolm Gluck of the *Guardian* that you have had difficulty in finding his recommendations in our Manchester store.
>
> Manchester is one of our biggest and best stores and does very well on wine – they carry most of the catalogue – we are therefore surprised to learn of your problem. Could you please let me know which particular lines and I will be delighted to help. In the meantime please accept a bottle of our Gran Calesa with our compliments.

No wonder Mr Meadows was satisfied. The M & S Gran Calesa is that sort of wine. However, owing to an unfortunate error in the 1996 edition of *Superplonk*, some readers may have been denied the opportunity to experience its calming and salubrious qualities.

It is therefore *Superplonk* and not M & S which must answer for the frustrations suffered by Mr W. Clegg of Bolton and Norman Cartmell of Wilmslow, whom I thank for writing to point out the error. They had both gone to M & S stores in search of a Spanish red, Costers del Segre, awarded 18.5 points in the 1996 guide. Unfortunately, I had tasted this wine before it had been labelled, and it was only subsequently named Gran Calesa. It was therefore simply listed by its denomination of origin, Costers del Segre. Wine names and labelling can be a minefield at the best of times without such additional crossed wires. With much beating of the chest, I informed both readers of the correct name and, as Gran Calesa is widely distributed in the M & S chain, trust that they were eventually able to partake of this cracking wine.

It is not only the elusive qualities of certain recommendations which spurred readers to write to me, but also inconsistencies between shelf prices and those quoted in *Superplonk*. Indeed, it was an enquiry about the price of a Marks & Spencer wine which elicited the most succinct item of correspondence to fall on the *Superplonk* door-mat, from the not entirely inappropriately named Margaret Penny of Harrogate. Quite rightly, Ms Penny was upset at having to pay 30 pennies more for a bottle of wine than had been stated in the column that week. She wrote in September 1991:

What was that you said in last Saturday's *Guardian* about M & S Cotes de Saint Mont being £2.99?

Attached to the letter was a receipt for the wine which had cost £3.29. Also on this receipt were the words 'Discover the difference of Marks & Spencer', the difference in this case being 30p. One would hardly imagine that M & S would need reminding of the old adage: Look after the Pennys and the pounds will look after themselves.

Interestingly, a letter from Mr J.R. Ewans of Truro in 1989 suggested that M & S was more profligate with the pounds than one would expect from one of our nation's longest-living bastions of commerce. Having read my endorsement of an M & S champagne at £9.99, he had gone to the Truro store to purchase the said bottle, only to find that it was in fact £10.99. While Mr Ewans was incensed, I was glad to inform him that he had actually got himself a bargain, as I replied on 13 March 1990:

> After receiving your letter of 29 Feb, I can only say congratulations! You did not pay one pound more for your bottle of champagne, but one pound less.
> Between my writing of the article you refer to and its publication, M & S has raised the price of the Blanc de Noirs from £9.99 to £11.99.

Writing at greater length to point out an inaccuracy in the column relating to M & S was Pamela Frankel of Lewes whose letter regarding the origination of the idea of 'Flying Wine-makers' I received in July 1994. I had rather zealously given M & S the credit for this successful innovation in the wine market, an assertion Ms Frankel wished to challenge.

> I read your article in this Saturday's *Guardian* with interest. However, I am somewhat puzzled by your claim that Marks & Spencer initiated the Flying Wine-makers as if my memory serves me correctly, it was Tony Laithwaite of Bordeaux Direct who gathered together his crew of Australians to visit vineyards which could do with some modern techniques – and what a change they made!
> This is not a plug for Mr Laithwaite but I have had wines from Bordeaux Direct for many years and always felt I had good value for money and good wines.
> I appreciate that his business is not in the same category as the supermarket but I feel that honour should be given to Mr Laithwaite for his part in innovating the flying wine-makers – his title – with the logo and name on

every bottle. So perhaps we shall see him as Lord Clariere of Bordeaux (his own vineyard) in the next honours list!

P.S. You have a lovely job!

In my reply to Ms Frankel, I found myself agreeing on both counts. Yes, Mr Laithwaite should be given credit for being in the vanguard of the flying wine-maker revolution, and yes, I do have a job I love.

You're absolutely right about Tony Laithwaite, I believe he was one of the first to get Australians to make French wines and it may well be that the term 'flying wine-maker' is of his origination. Thank you for pointing this out, it was remiss of me not to touch on Mr Laithwaite's role in my article in the *Guardian*. You're quite right. I do have a lovely job. I just wish I could do it without making errors like the above.

Nevertheless, while I may have underestimated Tony Laithwaite's part in the arrival of Flying Wine-makers, I wonder whether an endorsement on every bottle is perhaps overdoing the attribution. Furthermore, to my knowledge, we are still awaiting his own elevation, as advocated by Ms Frankel.

Marks & Spencer
Michael House
57 Baker Street
London
W1A 1DN

Tel 0171 935 4422
Fax 0171 487 2679

ARGENTINIAN WINE   RED

Trapiche Malbec Oak Cask Reserve 1992   `15` `C`

Delicious layered, fruity complexity. Flavourful, deep, good with food.

ARGENTINIAN WINE   WHITE

Chenin Blanc Mendoza 1995   `15` `B`

Pleasurable fruit of striking freshness and gently exotic shading. Hints of richness with a nutty finish. Delicious.

AUSTRALIAN WINE   RED

Honey Tree Shiraz Cabernet 1995   `13` `C`

It's so bloody sweet! Honey tree indeed!

James Halliday Coonawarra Cabernet Sauvignon 1992   `12` `F`

Difficult to rate this £12 wine higher. Fine Wine Stores only.

Langhorne Creek Cabernet Sauvignon 1994   `13.5` `D`

Doesn't quite reach the fair shores of a 14-point rating. The finish, at this price, is not firm or rich enough.

Lindemans Australian Shiraz 1993   `15` `C`

Flavour, flavour, flavour.

Pheasant Gully Riverina Shiraz   `13` `C`

A sweet shiraz of little character but some flavour.

Rosemount Estate Shiraz 1994   `14` `D`

Rosemount McLaren Vale Shiraz 1993   `14` `E`

Impressive weight of fruit and price tag.

Shiraz Cabernet Bin 505, 1994   `13` `C`

AUSTRALIAN WINE   WHITE

Australian Medium Dry   `12` `C`

Honey Tree Semillon Chardonnay 1995   `13` `C`

Curious fruit.

Lindemans Bin 65 Australian Chardonnay, 1995   `15.5` `C`

Rich, satisfying, brooding, gently oily – this is a textbook Aussie chardonnay of elegance and style. Superb with grilled veggies.

Orange Vineyard Chardonnay 1994   `14` `E`

Impressively fruity and it introduces itself with real style. Perhaps a tenner is a lot to swallow, though.

Pheasant Gully Colombard   `12.5` `C`

Rosemount Estate Chardonnay, Hunter Valley 1995   `16` `D`

Flourish of woody fruit on the finish of a balanced, delicate wine provides delicious compensation for seven quid.

Rosemount Estate Fume Blanc 1994 `13.5` `D`

Expensive – a touch. Sauvignon blancish – a touch.

Rosemount Orange Vineyard Chardonnay 1994 `16.5` `D`

A quite stunning wine of elegance and fruity finesse. Gently woody, ripely melony and citric acidity.

South East Australian Semillon/ Chardonnay `14.5` `C`

Crisp and vaguely gooseberryish with a distant richness on the finish (which is mostly lemonic). Tasty brew here.

BULGARIAN WINE RED

Bulgarian Cabernet Sauvignon, Svischtov Region 1991 `12` `B`

CHILEAN WINE RED

Casa Leona Cabernet Merlot 1994 `15` `C`

Chocolate and subtle cassis. Good firm wine for Christmas; will improve over a couple of years.

Central Valley Cabernet Sauvignon, Carmen Vineyards 1994 `14` `C`

Maipo Cabernet Sauvignon Reserve 1994 `15` `D`

Has unusual bite and earthiness for a Chilean. Gives the classy, supple fruit some balance and character.

CHILEAN WINE WHITE

Carmen Chardonnay/Semillon 1995 15.5 C

Chewiness to the well-flavoured fruit gives this wine class and weight. Good with light chicken dishes.

Casa Leona Chardonnay 1995 16.5 C

Lovely oily opulence which teases the tongue with its delicious texture and firm fruitiness. A dream of a wine at a good price.

Casablanca Valley Sauvignon Reserve, Carmen 1995 16 C

Class sauvignon with a hint of South American loucheness. Terrific force yet great gentility. Stylish, elegant, superb shellfish wine and aperitif tipple.

Chardonnay Lontue 1994 15.5 C

Restrained yet impressive. Not a big wine nor one to go with robust food, but pleasantly beguiling experience for the undemanding palate fresh home from work.

Sauvignon Blanc Lontue 1995 10 C

Extraordinary fruit here. Has a sort of soft celery undertone and flabby finish. I suppose it might taste wonderful with raw oysters but I can't eat 'em.

FRENCH WINE RED

Beaujolais, Cellier des Samsons 1995 13 C

Beaune Premier Cru, Les Theurons 1989 `11` `H`

**Bordeaux Matured in Oak, AC Bordeaux
1993** `12` `D`

**Cabernet Sauvignon 'Domaine de
Mandeville' 1995** `15` `C`

Has a pleasing richness with hints of dry, charcoal savouriness.
Good with roast chicken.

**Chateauneuf du Pape AC, Les Couversets
1993** `12.5` `E`

Classic Claret Chateau Cazeau 1995 `13.5` `C`

Solid, respectable stuff.

Corbieres Chateau de Serame 1994 `15.5` `C`

Meaty, savoury, subtly rich, very agile (leaps over casseroles and
stew with ease) and has character without coarseness. And being
sealed with a synthetic cork, no more dud fruit! So it gets an
extra half point for this.

**Domaine de Belle Feuille Cotes du
Rhone 1995** `11` `C`

**Domaine de Mandeville Merlot, VdP
d'Oc 1995** `13` `C`

Rounded, unctuous, highly polished.

**Domaine de Mandeville Syrah, VdP
d'Oc 1995** `14.5` `C`

Muscular yet lithe. Rustic yet classy.

Domaine St Germain Minervois 1994 `14` `C`

Good earthy shroud to the fruit.

Domaine St Pierre, VdP de l'Herault 1995 `13.5` `B`
Synthetic cork.

Domaine Virginie Merlot VdP d'Oc, 1995 `13` `C`

Fitou, Caves de Mont Tauch 1994 `13` `C`
Not typical. Rather a sweet young thing.

Fleurie AC, Cellier des Samsons 1995 `12` `E`

**French Country Red Vignerons des
Catalans, VdP des Pyrenees Orientales** `13` `A`

**Full Red, Cotes du Roussillon Villages
(1 litre)** `13` `C`

**Gold Label Cabernet Sauvignon, Domaine
Virginie VdP d'Oc 1994** `15` `C`
Vigorous, dry, classy, varietally impactful, rich and balanced.

**Gold Label Pinot Noir, Domaine Virginie
VdP d'Oc 1994** `12` `C`

**Gold Medal Cabernet Sauvignon, VdP
d'Oc 1994** `14` `C`
Flavour and depth.

House Red Wine `13` `B`
Not bad. But is it a £2.99 wine? Not compared with Bulgarian
blockbusters.

Margaux 1993 `12.5` `E`

Merlot Moueix 1993 `13` `D`

Moueix St Emilion 1993 `13` `E`

Portan, VdP d'Oc 1995 `13` `C`

FRENCH WINE WHITE

Chardonnay 'Domaine de Mandeville', VdP d'Oc 1995 `14` `C`

Quiet, classic, demure.

Chardonnay VdP du Jardin de la France, Cellier des Samsons 1995 `12.5` `C`

Cotes de Gascogne Blanc Plaimont 1995 `13.5` `B`

Real fruit salad freshness and zip. Good basic shellfish wine for beginners. Synthetic cork.

Domaine Virginie Roussanne VdP d'Oc, 1995 `14` `C`

Gentle touch of creamy fruit on the freshness. Classy country wine.

Domaine Virginie Vermentino VdP d'Oc, 1995 `13.5` `C`

French Country White `12` `B`

Gold Label Chardonnay VdP d'Oc 1995 `14` `C`

Nice gentle sort of chardonnay. Has rhythm and bite but is quite pricey.

House White Wine `12.5` `B`

Has some freshness but not a lot of fruit. Hint of elegance. I like the plastic cork.

Jeunes Vignes, La Chablisienne 1994 | 12 | D

Malvasia del Salento 1995 | 13 | C

Meursault Louis Jadot 1992 | 12 | H
Fine Wine Stores only.

Montagny Premier Cru, Cave de Buxy 1993 | 13.5 | D
Very proper and purposeful. Lots of flavour and style.

Petit Chablis, La Chablisienne 1995 | 12 | D

Pouilly Fume Domaine Mathilde de Favray 1995 | 10 | E

Pudding Wine Muscat de Rivesaltes (50cl) | 13.5 | C
Rather expensive for a half bottle.

Puligny Montrachet, Domaine Maroslavac-Leger 1991 | 11 | G

Rose de Syrah, Domaines Virginie 1995 | 11 | C

Sancerre Les Ruettes 1995 | 12 | D

Vin de Pays du Gers White, Plaimont 1995 | 13.5 | B

Viognier 'Domaine de Mandeville', VdP d'Oc 1995 | 15 | C
Delicious example of the big hearty viognier grape. Real zip and fruit, style and flavour.

Vouvray AC, Domaine Pouvraie 1995 | 11 | C

White Burgundy AC, Caves de Lugny 1995 | 11 | C

ITALIAN WINE   RED

Barbera del Piemonte, Giordano 1995   `14.5` `C`

Rustic, earthy edge which never vulgarises the cherry/plum fruit.
Good price for a good food wine.

Cardillo Rosso di Sicilia 1995   `14` `B`

Simple fruity stuff. Not a whiff nor a trace of any Sicilian
herbiness or sun.

Chianti Classico, Basilica Cafaggio 1994   `13.5` `D`

Very fruity and almost sweet to finish. Has little of the
character, earthiness and generally piratical cut and thrust of
previous vintages.

Il Caberno Giordano 1992   `14` `C`

Subtle licorice edges to the fig and blackberry fruit. Delightful
tannins underneath.

Italian Red Table Wine (1 litre)   `14` `C`

What a charming party wine! (Even if the party is merely a
thirsty individual.)

Merlot del Veneto, Casa Girelli NV   `12` `B`

Montepulciano d'Abruzzo 1995   `13` `B`

A soft pasta plonk.

Primitivo di Manduria 1993   `16` `D`

Meaty stuff: warm, spicy, earthy, inviting, all-embracing. Has
rough charm – great with meat dishes.

Rosso di Puglia, Casa Girelli 1994   `13` `C`

Sangiovese Cabernet Sauvignon della Toscana 1994 `14.5` `C`

Bristles with characterful fruit; soft but effective.

ITALIAN WINE WHITE

Bellaura Bianco di Sicilia 1995 `14.5` `C`

Lovely aperitif. Gorgeous touch of fruit on the initial perfumed crispness.

Bianco di Puglia 1995 `14` `C`

Only just 14. I thought £3.79 a touch steep for this clean, simple, barely fruity wine.

Bianco Veronese `13` `B`

Canellino 1995 (4%) `10` `B`

For teenagers as an introduction to wine.

Chardonnay delle Tre Venezie `12` `C`

Curiously austere chardonnay. I've tasted fruitier trebbianos.

Frascati Superiore DOC, Estate Bottled 1994 Girelli `12` `C`

Frascati Superiore Pallavicini 1995 `12` `C`

Italian White Table Wine (1 litre) `13.5` `C`

Great-value fruity party wine. Good with barbecue food too.

La Rime Pinot Grigio della Toscana 1995 `13` `C`

Orvieto Classico 1995 `13` `B`

Not bad as orvietos go.

Pinot Grigio della Toscana, Le Rime 1995 `12.5` `C`
Pleasant, crisp, light – but overpriced. You can buy stunning, complex Chilean wines at this price.

Pinot Grigio delle Tre Venezie `13.5` `C`
Gently saline clean wine for shellfish.

NEW ZEALAND WÍNE RED

Kaituna Hills Cabernet Merlot, Marlborough 1994 `12` `C`

Kaituna Hills Chardonnay, Gisborne 1995 `12.5` `C`

Kaituna Hills Chardonnay Semillon, Gisborne 1995 `13` `C`

Kaituna Hills Sauvignon Blanc, Marlborough 1995 `13` `C`
Edgily sweet with a grassy undertone.

Saints Gisborne Chardonnay 1995 `14` `D`
M&S's best New Zealand wine. Has flesh and flavour and will go well with mild Thai fish dishes.

Saints Hawkes Bay Cabernet Merlot 1994 `13.5` `D`

SOUTH AFRICAN WINE RED

South African Merlot 1995 `16` `C`
Delicious breezy fruit. Has style and aplomb with oodles of warm fruit.

SOUTH AFRICAN WINE WHITE

Johannesburg Riesling 1995 `10` `C`

Madeba Reserve Chardonnay 1994 `13.5` `D`

McGregor Chenin Blanc 1995 `12.5` `C`

Zell Castle Riesling Spatlese 1995 `12` `C`

SPANISH WINE RED

Gran Calesa Costers del Segre 1992 `17` `D`

Savoury, rich, vibrant, dry yet softly voluptuous and fruity on the finish, this is lovely textured wine of great charm and flavoured, aromatic warmth.

Marques del Romeral, Gran Reserva Rioja 1987 `12` `D`

Penascal Vino de Mesa Tinto, Castilla y Leon NV `13.5` `C`

Rioja type, sweet and vanilla-like.

Raimat Carretela 1991 `15.5` `C`

Ripe, soft and very rich without being annoyingly ostentatious.

Rioja Bodegas AGE `13` `C`

Roseral Rioja Crianza 1993 `13` `C`

Valencia Bodegas Schenk 1993 `15.5` `B`

Brilliant vibrancy of fruit, depth of flavour, polish and bite. Absolutely smashing wine.

SPANISH WINE WHITE

Conca de Barbera 1995 `14` `B`

Clean, fresh, delicate. Good blue mood lifter.

Moscatel de Valencia `14` `C`

Possesses only a distant echo of the usual marmalade-edged fruit of this genre – but a honeyed specimen nonetheless.

Rose de Valencia 1995 `12` `B`

Pleasant drinking at £2.29 but not £3.29.

URUGUAYAN WINE RED

Juanico Merlot Tannat 1995 `12` `C`

USA WINE RED

Canyon Road Cabernet Sauvignon 1994 `16` `D`

A most coolly classy wine. Has a superb balance of fruit, acid and wood. These three strike energetically and authentically in harmony.

Canyon Road Merlot 1995   `13.5` `D`
Sweet interpretation.

USA WINE   WHITE

Canyon Road Chardonnay 1995   `14` `D`
Has an exuberance of warm fruit which is deliciously melded
to the acidity. A balanced wine of flavour and purpose. Rates
a point more at Thresher, where it costs under £4 at time
of writing.

Canyon Road Sauvignon Blanc 1995   `14` `D`
Good upfront fruit. Rather pricey.

FORTIFIED WINE

20 Year Old Port   `15` `G`
Something delicious to go with the nuts and dried fruits at
Christmas.

Cream Sherry   `14` `C`
Good value for the Christmas cake.

Fino Sherry   `16` `C`
Delicate yet slyly fruity. A fino to bring wine lovers back
to sherry?

Medium Amontillado Sherry   `13` `C`

Rich Cream Sherry   `15.5` `C`
Brilliant ice-cream wine.

SPARKLING WINE/CHAMPAGNE

Asti Spumante Consorzio $\boxed{13}$ $\boxed{D}$

One sweet, peachy glass is enough as an aperitif. But dry bubblers will loathe it.

Australian Chardonnay, Blanc de Blancs Bottle Fermented Brut 1992 $\boxed{14}$ $\boxed{E}$

Bluff Hill Sparkling Wine (New Zealand) $\boxed{13.5}$ $\boxed{D}$

Light and delicate.

Brut Sparkling Vin Mousseux (France) $\boxed{13}$ $\boxed{C}$

Cava (Spain) $\boxed{14}$ $\boxed{C}$

Champagne Chevalier de Melline, Premier Cru Blanc de Blancs $\boxed{12}$ $\boxed{G}$

Champagne Orpale 1985 $\boxed{10}$ $\boxed{H}$

Cremant de Bourgogne $\boxed{15}$ $\boxed{D}$

Elegant, seriously classical-style fruit with a touch of crusty bread on the edge. A terrific bubbly which only the naff label undermines.

Oudinot Brut Champagne $\boxed{16}$ $\boxed{F}$

This is one of the softest, most deliciously fruity champagnes at any supermarket anywhere under £12. It has a delicate citric finish to complete its charms.

Oudinot Rose Champagne $\boxed{17}$ $\boxed{F}$

Delightful rose – it justifies its soppy colour and steep price by being aromatically enticing, fruity in a most gentle way, with a finish of finesse.

Prosecco Brut (Italy) `12` `D`

Touch too sweet for me.

Rosato Spumante (Italy) `12` `C`

Rose Sparkling Vin Mousseux `14` `C`

An excellent-value rose with a lilting touch of soft fruit to the well-formed fresh structure of the whole.

Veuve de la Lalande Brut `10` `C`

Suitable only as a base for a spritzer.

Veuve de la Lalande Rose `12` `C`

Veuve de Medts, Premier Cru Brut (France) `14.5` `G`

Expensive but exceptional.

Vintage Champagne, St Gall, Premier Cru Brut 1990 `13` `G`

Vintage Oudinot Grand Cru 1989 `13.5` `G`

MORRISONS

. . . of Portuguese lorry-drivers and Methodist ministers

As early as 1991, readers were enquiring about the exclusion of Morrisons from *Superplonk*. It was a matter I remedied in *Superplonk 1993*, but not before Greg Long of Rotherham had written on 5 January 1992:

> Congratulations on the second edition of your *Superplonk* paperback which was a most welcome gift in my stocking this Christmas. However, may I ask you why there is no coverage of the wines of the Morrison supermarket chain? I realise that they are essentially a north of England organisation but you have never struck me as the sort of journalist who is afraid of travel. After all, you have been to France and the fare there is almost as expensive as a British Rail Away-Day to Sheffield Midland Station.
>
> I bring Morrisons to your attention, not only because they have three fine stores within a short distance of here but also because they make shopping a real pleasure. My wife and I never fall out in Morrisons, unlike a trip to Asda, which is often the prelude for an attack of marital sulks. The wine departments are also stacked full of interesting wines at what appear to be excellent prices and fill me with the thrill of anticipating a new

discovery. For instance, it is worth making the trip just to buy 'La Vieille Ferme' Cotes du Ventoux.

My fear is that the Morrisons wine buyer, totally unappreciated by the influential writers like yourself, will jack it all in and go and do something with greater kudos in the eyes of the press, like write the IQ section in the *Mail on Sunday*. One mention in your Saturday column would be appreciated. A section in the next edition of *Superplonk*? Is it too much to hope for?

PS What on earth is a 'Budgen'?

It was not only Mr Long. Derick Stewart had written in 1991, observing that I included Littlewoods 'who carry a fairly limited range, but omit Wm Morrison Supermarkets, now no longer a regional chain, and who have for many years put a great deal of resource and thought into their wine buying'.

Mr Stewart recalled that 'even Berkmann and Hall listed them in the seventies; since then their operation has spread southward and must now outrank Littlewoods in terms of volume sales, even if not in total number of outlets'.

Addressing the matter of Wm Morrison was clearly becoming pressing. The reason for the omission of Wm Morrison was not down to any southern elitism on the part of *Superplonk* or reluctance to travel. I explained all to Mr Long on 21 January 1992:

Your letter of the 5th of Jan was most amusing and I hope the chief wine buyer at Morrisons appreciated it because I sent him a copy and repeated my request, originally submitted three years ago when my *Superplonk* column began, for a copy of the store's wine list and details of its coverage. I did not receive a reply then but I have now and I hope, all being well, that I can cover the store both in the column and in the book.

P.S. A Budgen is a supermarket chain, rare and lesser-spotted in your neck of the woods I daresay, but the old folk down south appreciate its city centre locations.

Mr Long's ignorance of the Budgen, and the general conclusion among correspondents that the lack of coverage of Morrisons had something to do with its northern location suggests a north–south divide in supermarket retailing, with Budgens and Waitrose cast as the southern archetypes (see page 61).

Morrison's status as a 'northern outpost' was also observed by Dudley Courtman, curiously writing from his home in – Chelmsford? All became clear in his letter of June 1992:

The name Morrison's appeared in your column today. It brought to my mind the last time you extolled the virtues of this northern vintnerial out-post. I was then naif enough, being like you separated from the gold nectar by two hundred miles of roadworks and drivers who deserved them, to draw to the attention of my northern relations the presence of prize purchases awaiting them on Morrison's shelves.

Sad to say I have lost all my southern 'bon viveur' credibility, as the Soveral – a 16-pointer – tasted of Portuguese lorry drivers' seven-day-old socks. This point was proved conclusively to me by the fact that I was presented with the rejected bottles for my own consumption when I last ventured up the A1.

Somebody, somewhere, slipped up. Or is it just my naivete reasserting itself?

Equally brazen about my intimate knowledge of Portuguese lorry drivers, I replied on 17 June 1992:

I loved your description of Soveral – it is exactly like Portuguese lorry drivers' seven-day-old socks. This is the essence of its appeal.

Seriously, I think you should welcome all those free bottles of Soveral. The wine is very ripe and perhaps your northern friends are not frequent enough drinkers to appreciate that, first, the wine should be left to breathe for say two hours, and , second, it is best with food. I can quite understand why many tender-tongued folk would find it ugly. I think it is well worth 16 points at £1.99 the bottle, as long as it's had plenty of air, and the food has got some real gutsy flavours to it.

Morrisons elicits a fairly healthy-sized postbag, and one outlet in particular, Eccles, which I am told is one of the smaller stores in the chain, seems to receive a disproportionate amount of attention. Whatever its size, the Eccles outlet appears to be a wonderful advertisement for the Morrisons operation, if Elizabeth Farrell's praise is anything to go by. She wrote in August 1992:

We bought your book at the beginning of the year and find it essential when choosing which supermarket to patronise on our weekly shopping trips.

I recently started a new job in Eccles, a part of the area that I had not previously frequented. Finding the town had a Morrisons I thought to see what you said about the wines they sell.

I know you cannot possibly cover every supermarket chain in existence but I hope this letter may go some way to helping you decide to add this to the others in your next edition of *Superplonk*. It will help to keep the book balanced – to balance out Budgens and Waitrose that don't exist in the north.

We will definitely be buying the next edition to see whether or not it is in (we would have anyway).

I apologise if you had already discussed Morrisons in your column, but we don't always get round to buying the paper at the weekend.

Hope you will consider including Morrisons. I haven't got any ulterior motives other than I think the food is reasonable and the choice of wine and bottled beers are excellent and I'm glad I got a job which based me in Eccles.

I am pleased to say I had good news for Ms Farrell and for all Morrisons' fans when I replied to her thus on 8 September 1992:

Sorry to take so long to reply to your letter but August is a wicked month for me.

Yes, Morrisons is definitely in the new edition of *Superplonk* (out in November), they feature in my new video (out in November) and they frequently star in the *Superplonk* column (out every Saturday morning).

Good luck with the Eccles job. Isn't Eccles a cake with a lot of currants in it? If so, Morrisons have a wine from Cyprus, Keo red, which is utterly disgusting ordinarily but possibly rather good with a cake overstuffed with currants . . .

I was indebted to another Morrisons customer, Mr T. Whitham of Sheffield, for recommending another interesting pairing. That of Morrisons' Gabbia d'Oro with Dickens. Assuming that he was referring to Charles rather than Monica, I resolved to combine a bottle of Gabbia d'Oro with my favourite Dickens book, *Pickwick Papers*.

The problem of not being able to find recommended wines in the stores after they have been featured in the column has surfaced with almost every retailer, and Morrisons is sadly no exception.

When John Vallans wrote with his concerns in November 1992, I mused once more on the mystical link between *Superplonk* and the Eccles Morrisons.

I write as a grateful *Superplonk* enthusiast who owes you many thanks for bargains bought over several years. Just lately, however, I have had some frustrations when trying to lay my hands on a recommended bottle, and I hope a description of the circumstances may be helpful to you.

This past weekend, I had to go to Manchester and Oldham. Morrisons at Eccles (a small store) had none of the 'Vin Primeur' you had recommended. We went to the giant Morrisons Hypermarket at Oldham. They thought they had something called 'Vin Primeur' three weeks ago. They stocked copies of the *Superplonk* paperback. They had no knowledge of whether they might have any 'Vin Primeur' again. When I told them (on Monday) that it had been advertised in the previous Saturday's *Guardian* they said: 'Oh, that chap's always three weeks out of date.'

I can imagine that, with your set of supermarket recommendations, it's hard, if not impossible, to match the date of publication of your article with availability in the shops but I hope you'll agree that I'm entitled to feel a bit disappointed (I shan't be in Oldham for at least a year). I think you'll understand that when I look for the *Superplonk* column nowadays, I'm bound to be making the inward reservation, 'Don't get too excited . . . even if you trawl from Tesco, Gateway, Safeway stores, and drive 250 miles to Oldham, the chances are you won't get a bottle!'

By the way, the Californian Red was a great success, and Caviade Estates white (I got the last five bottles from the Eccles Morrisons on the Monday after publication) much appreciated.

Perhaps (may I suggest?) there needs to be a warning, or an overall indication that certain wines may just possibly be available if one is very lucky or maybe (if this is possible) an indication of whether a particular wine is a one-off purchase of only a few bottles here and there, or something of which substantial stocks may be expected in a good many stores over a considerable period.

I'm sorry to be a nuisance, but can say I write as a devotee of your column.

Brian Rippin of Sheffield would probably count himself as a less devoted reader. Or at least his devotion was directed in a different, rather more vertical direction. He wrote in June 1992 regarding some recommended Morrisons wines which were not available in his local store. Once more, tones of north–south antagonism pervade.

I am not exactly a disciple of yours but I do enjoy your enthusiasm and when given the chance, tend to agree with your judgements about wine. But I am getting frustrated. You waxed lyrical about three Morrisons' wines recently and today I went to their huge store at Hillsborough and none were on sale. It's emotionally and economically draining, this rushing about at odd moments to no avail.

Is it just that living in the fourth largest city in England is no substitute for not living in London or the Home Counties, or are these recommendations out of date before you make them? (The assistant in Morrisons this morning hadn't even heard of the Chardonnay, but then the name *Guardian* didn't seem to register either.)

I think I may stop reading you!

Mr Rippin may have regretted that last threat, as his plight was given greater public exposure than he might have liked when I referred to him in my column. Exasperation of a different kind in his next letter of 6 July 1992. Had he been the victim of a savage expose?

What are you doing to me?

For your amusement you should know that I am

a Methodist minister and have responsibility for 300 churches in South Yorkshire, North Nottinghamshire and East Derbyshire. Now that you have told the world about my drinking habits I could be in trouble. On the other hand it may be the means of liberating some anxious drinkers!

Stuart Purdie has been in contact with me and kindly sent a bottle of the famous Chardonnay and I have also received a letter from Angela Mount. Stuart Purdie was most solicitous and suggested I made myself known if I went into Morrisons again. After your article on Saturday, I think not. It could be dangerous.

I may never write to a journalist again. I *will* go on reading you; but cautiously.

Wm Morrison Supermarkets
Wakefield 41 Industrial Estate
Wakefield
W Yorks
WF1 0XF

Tel 01924 870000
Fax 01924 821250

SEE STOP PRESS SECTION AT END OF BOOK FOR LAST-MINUTE ADDITIONS TO THIS RETAILER'S RANGE.

ARGENTINIAN WINE RED

Balbi Vineyard Mendoza Rouge 1995

A food wine – because it's so rich and soupy it can't be agreeably quaffed without a plate of something handy. Bread and cheese is enough.

AUSTRALIAN WINE RED

Coldridge Shiraz/Cabernet 1995 13 B

Winningly friendly and cherry ripe.

Lindemans Bin 45 Cabernet Sauvignon 1994

Seems more insistently rich than previous vintages. Quite deliciously cheeky. Rates half a point less than at Fullers (*Streetplonk*), where it costs under five quid at time of writing.

Lindemans Bin 50 Shiraz 1993 15 C

Rich, very textured, deeply flavoured and great company.

Penfolds Bin 35 Shiraz Cabernet 1994

Wyndham Bin 444 Cabernet Sauvignon 1992

Very deep and rich – like a Ken Tynan anecdote.

AUSTRALIAN WINE WHITE

**Coldridge Chenin Blanc/Colombard/
Chardonnay 1995** `12` `B`

Goundrey Riesling 1991 `13` `C`

Lindemans Bin 65 Chardonnay 1995 `15.5` `C`

Still batting well and positively under a fiver.

**Penfolds Rawson's Retreat Bin 21
Semillon/Chardonnay/Colombard
1995** `15.5` `C`

Apples, walnuts, pineapple, melon – quite an impressive medley here. The acidity is pure, crisp Golden Delicious.

BRAZILIAN WINE RED

Amazon Cabernet Sauvignon `13.5` `C`

Interesting, highly drinkable curiosity.

BRAZILIAN WINE WHITE

Amazon Chardonnay `11` `C`

A touch confectionery-fruited and sweet to finish. Good soft wine for those looking to move up from Liebfraumilch.

BULGARIAN WINE

Bear Ridge Gamza NV

Light, richly flavoured, cheering. Suits pasta and thin cooks.

CHILEAN WINE

Entre Rios Chilean Red

Excellent rich dry brew of character and depth. Wonderful sausage dish but will serve duty with posh dinner-party fare.

Gato Negro Cabernet Sauvignon 1994 *5/5/97*

Even smoother and riper than excellent previous vintages. Lovely touch of concentrated fruit (cassis?) on the finish and this is backed up by tannic savouriness of great softness and appeal.

Stowells of Chelsea Chilean Merlot Cabernet (3-litre box)

This wine is soft yet with an agreeably gentle level of proud tannins. Why don't I rate it higher? I simply find the aroma off-puttingly ripe and rubbery. It really ought to be better put together than this.

CHILEAN WINE

Castillo de Molina Reserva 1995

Brilliant, rolling, oily fruit of great texture and fruitiness. Warm, complex, deep.

Entre Rios Chilean White `15` `B`

Delicious dryness, fruitiness, flavoursomeness and stylishness. Full of fruit (never crisp) yet it teeters over the edge into sloppiness.

Gato Negro Sauvignon Blanc 1994 `15.5` `B`

Delicious sauvignon character – good fresh fruit with undertones of ripe raspberry and melon. A perfect thirst-quencher.

Stowells of Chelsea Chilean Sauvignon Blanc (3-litre box) `15.5` `F`

Brilliantly classy fruit of real sauvignon style: clean, fresh, fruity and gently nutty, this is solid, well-made wine of style and modernity. Yet it is sufficiently classic in personality to please the hardened sauvignon fan – especially at 54p a glass.

ENGLISH WINE WHITE

Three Choirs Estates Premium 1993 `14` `C`

One of our more enterprising bottles of English plonk. Good medium-bodied fruit with gentle crispness on the finish. Highly quaffable.

FRENCH WINE RED

Bourgogne Pinot Noir Vallet Freres 1989 `10` `D`

Cabernet Sauvignon, Chais Cuxac, Vin de Pays d'Oc `14` `C`

Soft, rich, fruity, dry. An excellent food wine.

Cellier la Chouf, Minervois 14 B

Cheap and cheerful.

Chais Cuxac Cabernet Sauvignon 14 C

Deliciously approachable cabernet. Real class yet real drinkability.

Chateau de Lauree Bordeaux Rouge 1995 B

Dry, dusky, vegetal fruit in a sort of off-hand claret-like way, this is a sound bordeaux at a remarkable price. The label looks great on the dinner table.

Comtesse de Lorancy 15 A

Swirling black cherry flavours, rich, savoury. Terrific value.

Corbieres, Les Fenouillets 1994 15 B

Remarkable value. Indeed, it's almost unbelievable – a dry, earthy, fruity red, altogether chubby-cheeked and hale of health in cracking form for under three quid? Delicious!

Cotes du Rhone Villages, 1995 14 C

What one might call an excellent house wine. Good flavour, only gently earthy, with some richness of tone and a solid finish of warm fruitiness.

Cotes du Rhone A. Brillac 1993 10 B

Cotes du Ventoux J. P. Leon, 1994 14 B

Engagingly fruity with a savoury undertone and a hint of rich flourish on the finish. Not mountainous but reasonably hilly.

Domaine du Vieux Lazaret Chateauneuf-du-Pape 1993

Dry, earthy, perfectly fruity and great with robust food. But very expensive.

Ginestet Bordeaux

Some typical bordeaux austerity detectable here.

La Source Cabernet Sauvignon VdP d'Oc 1994

Good rich fruit, rolling and polished, a soft texture, not spiky, peppery or overheated, this is a simple, direct cabernet.

La Source Merlot VdP d'Oc 1994

Soft, fruity, winsome – and lose some. You can't drink this wine with rich food but you can with rich company.

La Source Syrah VdP d'Oc 1993

Rolling fruit of smooth texture and dry intent.

Le Millenaire Cotes du Roussillon Villages 1994

A light dry wine of subdued charms. Suits a baked potato stuffed with cheese.

Le Piat d'Or

No character, little style. Unattractive. Slightly toffee-ish bouquet. Sweet fruit. Dry finish.

Louis Fontaine VdP des Pyrenees Orientales

Margaux 1990

Marquis de l'Estouval, VdP de l'Herault 1995

`13` `A`

'A simple wine of character' it says but I'm not sure the character is very large. Still, this is a good wine with soft, easy-to-swallow pastas and at £1.99 it's not demanding on the pocket overmuch.

Medoc La Taste

`14` `C`

Has some taste, ironically. And the tannins give it backbone and savour.

Montregnac Bergerac 1994

`13` `B`

Touch rough, but very ready. Clodful of earthy fruit and great with spicy sausages.

Regnie, Duboeuf 1994

`12` `D`

Not a lot of thrills for such proximity to six quid but it's respectable. Not a little horror like some.

Renaissance Buzet 1994

`14` `C`

Very dry and rich. Great with roast food.

Stowells of Chelsea Claret Bordeaux Rouge (3-litre box)

`13` `G`

A good simple quaffing claret with an agreeable echo of the dry, tannic heritage of the region.

Tradition Coteaux du Languedoc

`15.5` `B`

A new batch of this stunningly good-value wine has landed and it's in fine form. Not as dazzling as last year's wine, it is nevertheless still full of style and flavour.

Vin de Pays des Bouches du Rhone

`13` `B`

Winter Hill VdP de l'Aude 1995   `15` `B`

Brilliant-value rich, dry red which will make even claret fans
purse their lips and pat their purses.

FRENCH WINE   WHITE

Bergerac Montregnac Sauvignon 1994   `13.5` `B`

Dry with good firm flavour.

Cascade Sauvignon Bordeaux 1994   `10` `B`

Cascade Bordeaux Sauvignon 1994   `12` `B`

Fish head soup wine.

Chais Cuxac Chardonnay 1994   `14` `C`

Good rich style of fruit of some class and style. Quenches a
deep thirst with real fruit.

Chateau de Lauree Bordeaux 1995   `12.5` `B`

Chateau Saint Gallier 1994   `14` `C`

Quietly classy.

Comtesse de Lorancy   `13` `A`

Very fresh and breezy. Good fish wine.

Cotes du Rhone Blanc 1995   `10` `C`

Domaine du Rey Cotes de Gascogne 1994   `14` `C`

Lovely fruit and vibrancy, cool acids. Fresh, flavoursome and
good value.

Entre Deux Mers 1995 `12` `B`

Ginestet Graves Blanc 1994 `13` `C`

A good friend to shellfish but not the solo tippler. Bit mean to
the misanthrope, this bottle.

J. P. Chenet, Cinsault Rose 1995 `12` `B`

Mildly amusing. The fruit is certainly more straightforward than
the 'Chesterfield Church Spire' bottle.

La Source Chardonnay VdP d'Oc 1995 `14.5` `C`

Brilliance at a fair price: richness, sanity, calmness yet fullness,
this is a well-textured wine with style.

La Source Sauvignon Blanc VdP d'Oc 1995 `16` `C`

Good fruit here with many winning qualities: soft yet gently
crisp, flavoursome, energetic. Better value and better fruit than
many a New Zealand at twice the price.

La Source Syrah Rose VdP d'Oc 1995 `13` `B`

A pleasant rose with enough guts to stay the course with
salmon.

Le Millenaire Cotes du Roussillon 1994 `12` `C`

Bit austere on the finish and a touch earthy, without compensa-
tory freshness, at the outset. Still, it would suit oysters.

Le Piat d'Or `9` `C`

Interestingly, hypermarkets in the ferry ports put this under the
foreign wines shelf rather than the French, and quite right. In
spite of the brilliant fantasies of the TV commercials no Frog
would be seen dead drinking this wimpish concoction – made
for the British market. Morrisons is the only supermarket brave
enough to send me a sample of this wine and I'm pleased it did.
This wine has no character and little style.

Le Vigneron Catalan Rose   `13.5` `B`

Softer flavour and fruit here.

Macon Villages Domaine Jean-Pierre
Teissedre 1993   `13.5` `C`

Not bad, not bad. I mean, it has some richness and some vegetal typicity and it's good with rough grub.

Meursault Pierre Matrot 1990   `8` `F`

I wouldn't serve it to a dog.

Muscadet La Pantiere 1994   `10` `B`

Pouilly Fume 1994   `11` `D`

Premieres Cotes de Bordeaux   `13` `C`

Has some style. Good with hard cheese and hard fruit.

Rose d'Anjou Vincent de Valloire 1994   `12` `B`

Toffee edge to the sweet fruit.

Terret Vin de Pays Lurton 1994   `12` `B`

Tradition Gewurztraminer de l'Alsace
Preiss Zimmer 1994   `13.5` `D`

Some typicity of a fascinating breed – the roseate, perfumed, spicy gewurztraminer. An example here which is still blossoming.

Tradition Pinot Blanc d'Alsace Preiss
Zimmer 1994   `13` `C`

Rather strains to be rich and it's not an ambition it reaches unless food like crab cakes is on offer.

Vouvray Jean Michel 1995 `10` `C`

Winter Hill White 1995 `13.5` `B`

Cheap and cheerful – with shellfish.

GERMAN WINE WHITE

**Binger St Rochuskapelle Kabinett,
Johannes Egberts 1992** `11` `B`

Devil's Rock Riesling, St Ursula, Pfalz 1994 `C`

Delicate true-riesling aroma, delicate acidity and good fruit,
and fresh, mineral-edged finish. Excellent smoked fish wine.
Developing very subtle petrolly undertones. Will improve for
eighteen months or more.

**Flonheimer Adelberg Kabinett Johannes
Egberts 1995** `13` `B`

An excellent alternative to Liebfraumilch. Sweet but also acidic
– so it isn't badly balanced. Useful warm weather aperitif.

Franz Reh Auslese 1994 `12` `C`

Franz Reh Kabinett 1994 `11` `B`

Franz Reh Spatlese 1993 `12` `B`

Sweet but not entirely nothing. Grandma will like it.

Seafish Dry, Rheinhessen 1993 `B`

Few wines are so well named that they do the wine hack's job
for him but this is a rare exception. I can only add that it is
also a good refreshing glug.

Stowells of Chelsea Liebfraumilch (3-litre box)

As reasonable a proposition as you get with this beast.

Wiltinger Scharzberg Spatlese 1993

13 B

GREEK WINE RED

Mavrodaphne of Patras

11 C

A wine for fruit cakes.

GREEK WINE WHITE

Kourtaki Vin de Crete 1994

This is firmly fruity, not flabby, and it goes very well with complex vegetable salads.

HUNGARIAN WINE WHITE

Barrel Aged Pinot Noir, Szendehely Koruyeki 1993

14.5 B

Simple, dry, finishes weakly but has some earthy aplomb on the palate. A terrific wine for pizza parties.

Chapel Hill Cabernet Sauvignon, Balaton 1994

14 B

Good-value pasta plonking. A dry, fruity wine with some personality, it's earthy, rich and energetic.

ITALIAN WINE RED

Chianti Classico Uggiano 1992 `14` `B`

Flavourful, lingering, dry, controlled earthy fruit – a subtle edge of candied orange. Distinctive. Good value.

Chianti Riserva Uggiano 1990 `15.5` `D`

Very elegant drinking. Soft, rich (but not overripe) character and real calm style.

Chianti Uggiano 1994 `13.5` `C`

Some soft flesh on 'those old bones'.

Eclisse VdT di Puglia Rosso `14.5` `B`

Full of teeth-gripping, soupy fruit of depth, flavour and richness. A most satisfyingly food-friendly wine.

Feyles Barbera d'Alba 1992 `16` `C`

Licorice, aniseed and plums – brilliant fruit, classy, distinctive and lingering. Dry, bright – quite extraordinarily delicious and individual.

Gabbia d'Oro `8` `A`

Ugh.

Montepulciano d'Abruzzo Vigneti del Sole 1995 `13.5` `B`

The distant thunder of falling apple cores in this juicy bottle. Rather fresh and keen on the finish.

Sangiovese di Romagna `13` `B`

Valpolicella, Morrisons `12` `B`

**Vigneti Casterna Amarone della
Valpolicella Classico 1988** `15` `D`

Cloyingly rich, herby fruit with baked undertones, seems hardly to possess any acids so smooth is it. Great with roast meats with herbs.

ITALIAN WINE WHITE

Eclisse VdT di Puglia Bianco `12` `B`

Est! Est!! Est!!! `10` `B`

Gabbia d'Oro `10` `A`

It has tasted like dilute apple juice without the fruit in the past. But the producer of this miracle of mediocrity is improving this formula. This wine rates 3 points more than previous blends. Things are looking up!

Orvieto Classico Uggiano 1994 `11` `B`

Stowells of Chelsea Chardonnay (3-litre box) `13.5` `G`

Some weight to the fruit, and balance. A pleasant glug.

Stowells of Chelsea Chardonnay Trentino (3-litre box) `13.5` `G`

Simple, dry, good fruit.

MOROCCAN WINE RED

Moroccan Red Wine 16 B
Touches of Colombian coffee for this superbly rich, leather-touched wine which slips down superbly.

PORTUGUESE WINE RED

Borges Bairrada Reserva 1989 10 B
Flat. Gone. Popped its clogs.

Soveral Tinto de Mesa 10 A
Oh! What have they done to it?! Bitter almonds and gasoline. Has individuality, I suppose, but then so did Polyphemus the Cyclops. But it will work well with lots of Portuguese dishes and it is rated on this basis.

Val Longa Country Wine NV 14 B
Dry, fruity, good lingering finish. Straightforward but excellent with food like liver and onions.

PORTUGUESE WINE WHITE

'M' Portuguese Rose 13 B
So much better than Mateus at the price and zippier in the fruit department.

Val Longa Country Wine NV 10 B
Might be OK if you've got a heavy cold.

Vinho Verde 12 B

ROMANIAN WINE — RED

Classic Pinot Noir 1990   `15` `B`

Brilliant cherry fruit, dry, bright and weighty without being overripe.

Pietroasa Vineyards Young Merlot 1994   `14.5` `B`

Good with pies, tripe and even roast ape (if you read such omens into the vineyard's name). It certainly is a versatile young red with vigour and bite and lots of young fruit.

Romanian Cellarmasters Feteasca Negra and Cabernet Sauvignon   `13` `B`

Good value for food-related orgies.

Special Reserve Pinot Noir 1990   `15.5` `B`

One of Romania's ultimate fruity treats. Soft, gamy, dry, fruity – this wine is mature, masterful (i.e. goes with food) and perfectly petty-priced.

ROMANIAN WINE — WHITE

Romanian Cellarmasters Chardonnay and Feteasca Regala   `14` `B`

The perfect quaffer at this price and it even has enough fruity oomph to go with food.

Romanian Late Harvest Chardonnay 1985   `14` `B`

Brilliant with hard cheese and fruit.

SOUTH AFRICAN WINE RED

Bainskloof Pass Cabernet 1994 `12` `B`

Bottelary Winery Pinotage, Stellenbosch 1995 `13.5` `C`

A rich, cherry/plum pinotage of dry, rich-edged fruit of some depth. Not complex but very cheering.

Faircape Cinsault 1992 `13` `B`

Faircape Pinotage 1992 `14` `B`

Better than most beaujolais and less money.

SOUTH AFRICAN WINE WHITE

Cape Country Chardonnay 1995 `13` `C`

Dull edge to the acidity marks the chardonnay down.

Faircape Chenin Blanc 1995 `14` `B`

Lots of soft fruit here with a hint of crispness on the finish.

Faircape Sauvignon Blanc 1995 `13` `B`

Excellent price for such unmoody, well-flavoured sauvignon. Has a bright, rich edge which comes through from start to finish. Good rich fish wine.

Stowells of Chelsea Chenin Blanc (3-litre box) `14` `F`

Comes out bright and clean – here are fruit and zip and real style.

SPANISH WINE   RED

Carreras Dry Red, Valencia 1987   15   A

A thundering great bargain: dry, fruity, balanced and flavoursome. Excellent pasta and pizza wine.

Corba, Campo de Borja 1994   13   B

Juicy fruit fun.

Navajas Rioja 1995   15   C

Delicious new vintage of one of Morrisons' best-value reds.

Navajas Rioja Reserva 1986   14   D

Lots of vanilla-edged fruit. Soft, luxurious, delicious – hints of chocolate and wild strawberry – but this is a light airy assemblage in tone for rich food.

Raimat Abadia 1992   15   C

Deeply serious food wine.

Remonte Navarra Crianza Cabernet
Sauvignon 1992   15.5 C

Has the typical Navarra character (i.e. a firm rustic edge of tannin and subtle, vegetal undertone) which is finely mature and fully ripe.

Stowells of Chelsea Tempranillo (3-litre
box)   14   F

Great glugging flavour and texture.

Torres Sangredetoro 1993   13   C

Not as gripping as once it was. But the '94 vintage is the best ever.

SPANISH WINE WHITE

Navarra Perdido 1995 `12` `B`

Solana Torrontes Treixadera 1993 `10` `C`

Interesting, brave, but hopeless. It has an intriguing lemon sherbet smell but the fruit is poor value and spineless to boot.

Spanish Dry, Morrisons `13` `A`

Great value for large groups.

USA WINE RED

Blossom Hill California `10` `C`

E. & J. Gallo Turning Leaf Cabernet Sauvignon 1994 `13.5` `D`

Warm and possessing some depth but uncompetitively priced compared with Chile or South Africa. But you're getting better, Gallo, so stick at it! You might just make a terrific wine at a dirt-cheap price one day.

E. & J. Gallo Turning Leaf Zinfandel 1994 `12` `D`

Not bad, but very overpriced at nigh on six quid. Anodyne and characterless, it lacks the oomph of real red zin. It fails to finish with £6 worth of vivacity. If it was £3.29 it would be a good buy. A partially turned new leaf.

Gallo Cabernet Sauvignon `10` `C`

Why does this dull, overpriced wine insist on having half its back label in French? The pretension of the witless.

Glen Ellen Merlot 1994

Deeply soft, like a well-plumped pillow. Great to quaff with the TV on.

**Sebastiani Californian Cabernet Franc
1994**

Delicious smooth vanilla-ed fruitiness.

Sutter Home Cabernet Sauvignon 1993

Mature, fruity, balanced . . . but it doesn't quite finish with the oomph I'd look for in a £4.50 wine.

Willamette Oregon Pinot Noir 1993

A powerful argument for living in Oregon but not necessarily living in Britain and paying eight quid for this delicious example of Oregon fruit. £4, maybe, but never eight.

USA WINE WHITE

Blossom Hill, California

E. & J. Gallo Turning Leaf Chardonnay 1994

Classy and rich. Not especially elegant or finely balanced as great Californian chardonnays are but it's good with chicken.

**Glen Ellen Proprietor's Reserve
Chardonnay 1994**

What a way to warmly and fruitily coddle a roast chicken. Great fruit here.

Sebastiani White Zinfandel 1995

Sweet but almost nothing.

Sutter Home Chardonnay 1994   `13.5` `C`

Good rich start but finishes almost sweet.

Willamette Oregon Chardonnay 1992   `14` `D`

Mild but effective – like a quiet but devastating word which breaks up a bar-room brawl.

FORTIFIED WINE

Inocente Extra Dry Fino   `16` `D`

Sherry, yes, but so dry it puckers your cheeks. Fabulously satisfying when it's well chilled and taken with grilled prawns. The mineral, flinty fruit tiptoes on the tongue like a ballet dancer on shoes spun from cobwebs. Remarkable value.

Rozes Ruby   `13` `C`

A rich ruby with lots of flavour. Good with currant cakes.

Rozes Special Reserve   `11` `D`

Nothing special. Too reserved.

Rozes Tawny   `12.5` `C`

Mild version of the breed good for putting in gravies.

SPARKLING WINE/CHAMPAGNE

Asti Spumante Gianni (Italian)   `11` `C`

Sweet and peachy. Pour it over ice cream.

Brut de Channay   `16` `C`

This is an outstanding dry wine for the money. It offers good balanced fruit and acid, neither overblown nor sharp, and drops down the throat as smoothly as many an Australian sparking wine. If it was repackaged and the store ditched the hypnotically horrendous black and gold label, which is the only tarty aspect of the wine, it would go like hot cakes – which, incidentally, the wine will cheerfully accompany. Rock cakes, unsweetened, warm from the oven for afternoon tea may not be as fashionable as they once were but this wine is priced handsomely enough to spark a revival. It rates 16 points.

Cava Cristalino Brut (Spanish)

A touch, only a touch, of cava earthiness and restrained fruit, but the acidity's fine and firmly controlled and the balance is excellent. Certain hairy-chested men will wear the gold round their necks.

Moscato Spumante 11 B

Shaving foam in a glass.

Nicole d'Aurigny Champagne 15 E

Still one of the most stylish, serious champagnes under £9 around.

Omar Khayyam, India 12 D

Paul Herard Blanc de Noirs Brut
Champagne (half bottle) 14 D

Delicious, fruity, bold, rich. A solo hedonist's delight.

Paul Herard Blanc de Noirs Demi Sec
Champagne (half bottle) 12 D

Raimat Sparkling Chardonnay (Spain) 15 D

Brilliant flavour here. Real class at a bargain price.

Seaview Brut

Seppelt Great Western Brut `15` `C`

I've said it all before about this wine. Let its rating say it all now.

SAFEWAY

Supers with no plonk

How many days are there in April? Well, according to Safeway, twenty-six. Or at least that's how long April lasted in 1992 according to the Safeway calendar. Having duly reported in the column on 25 April that a wine promotion at Safeway would run for the whole of the month, I received a barrage of letters from Dumbarton to Abergavenny from readers who had found that the offer had already finished.

Nevertheless it does the retailer some credit that the incorrect pricing of these two wines, a Vin de Pays de Vaucluse and Lionel Derens champagne, elicited the most letters I have ever received on a single item. Among the disgruntled was Mr Desmond Wheway of east London who wrote:

> If you go from the *Guardian* office, along Clerkenwell Road to Old Street and turn right down Whitecross Street you'll reach a Safeway where I purchased a bottle of Lionel Derens champagne today for £8.49, and not £7.99, the April price as suggested in last Saturday's column.
>
> Undoubtedly the amount I paid is a reasonable price, but is it a coincidence between your endorsing the wine on the Saturday at £7.99, and my being charged more a few days later – and less than a mile from your own doorstep? I recall, in the past you've noticed rapid price rises for recommended wines. Is some sort of advantage being taken here?

Geoff Nuttall, a resident of the wonderfully named village of Kirkby Overblow near Harrogate, also saw the retailer as the culprit:

> You may care to know that on the day your article appeared about the price reduction at Safeway of the Vin de Pays de Vaucluse and the champagne, my local store in Harrogate quietly raised the price of these lines by 50p a bottle. So those of us who acted on your advice were disappointed. Sharp practice by the store, do you think?

Roger Hall of Faceby, Middlesbrough, clearly wanting to think the best of *Superplonk*, put the blame fairly and squarely on the *Guardian*, writing to the newspaper on 28 April:

> I refer to Malcolm Gluck's column in the *Weekend Guardian* dated 25–26 April. The article recommends Safeway's special offers of Vin de Pays de Vaucluse at £1.99 a bottle, red and white, and Lionel Derens champagne at £7.99 a bottle. I went to my local Safeway to buy some of both of these yesterday to find that the offer finished on 25 April.
>
> What is the point of publishing this advice when the offer ends rather than when it first becomes available? As a service to your readers it rates zero points! I assume that Malcolm wrote the article at an appropriate time and you held up its publication until its advice became virtually useless. This is an example of unprofessionalism fortunately rare in your paper.

For one regular correspondent from Holloway, who for reasons better known to himself prefers to be known as The North London Tippler, it was too much to bear, coming so soon after the election. Why there was such a sudden demand for cheap champagne after such an occasion defeats me. Our north London consumer was persistent and, as has been seen in other similar cases, eventually got his discount.

The election result, naturally, has made me think once more of drink and, armed with your Saturday piece, I today rolled down the road to Safeway (Holloway). Were the wines you praised so effusively available at the prices to which they were supposed to be discounted? Naturally not; the Vaucluse was £2.49 and the Lionel Derens champagne was £8.49.

They were actually selling your book, so I felt confident that waving my piece of newspaper would do the trick, little realising that they would see me as more like Chamberlain returning from Munich. I'm now so jaundiced at this kind of thing that I pressed on, only to be told that prices were changed on Mondays and that they had just been put back.

April, I reminded Safeway, had not yet become a twenty-six-day month. It was impossible to keep sane if a recommendation on a Saturday meant a price increase on Monday. In the end, I was allowed to take both items at the lower price, but it was clear that it was a concession solely for me, for no one else had complained! My God, this particular store is a glum place, and the Vaucluse (already tasted) shames the shop.

I'm not surprised that you sometimes despair. It cannot be happening on the wine shelves alone and going to some of the supermarkets is like walking on quicksand as far as prices are concerned. I have experienced similar problems at Asda and Tesco. You might be able to make something of these inconsistencies in supermarket wine pricing. It infuriates me, but I am rarely apoplectic.

Not all Safeway stores are as accommodating as Holloway. When he found himself in the same bind, Mr D.G. Moore of Lower Claverham near Bristol could not persuade his local to bend on the price. While his letter may suggest to some that the frustration had driven Mr Moore to ale – more specifically

Adnams – I believe he was referring to Adnams, the established wine merchants, rather than Adnams, the beer.

I always thought that a good journalist checked his facts before writing his piece?

The Safeway Vaucluse that you enthused over in your column on Sat 25 April stated that the price would be held throughout APRIL. I had already enjoyed a bottle, so to pick up a half dozen bottles I set off on 27 April only to be told the offer finished on Sat 25 April. The price was now £2.39 and the shirt-sleeved minion would not budge, telling me to take it up with you (some hope) and I should buy the Bulgarian Cab. Sauv. as an adequate substitute.

The wine merchants must be over the moon with your editorials in the broadsheets but please give a thought for the poor sods who spend time and money on a wild goose chase. I have had quite a number of cases of non-availability over the years!

I'll stick to Adnams in future.

So voluminous was the correspondence regarding these wines that there was only one course of action, a circular letter to all the readers which I wrote on 11 May 1992.

Firstly, I apologise for this not being a personal letter but I do not have the resources to answer personally each and every letter I received on this matter. On behalf of *Weekend Guardian*, I also apologise for the late appearance of the article that I wrote extolling the virtues of these Safeway wines; had the article appeared when it should instead of one week later, then you would have been given a week's more time to acquire the wines in question at their special £1.99 prices. I try extremely conscientiously to run a service for readers and I will do my best to make sure this sort of thing does not happen again. (I urge correspondent Mr Moore, in particular, to reconsider his avowed intention to abandon supermarkets altogether and 'stick to Adnams'.)

However, nothing can excuse Safeway who, like Sainsbury a little while back, arbitrarily decided to chop several days off the end of a month and so an offer I was assured would not finish until the end of the month was terminated on the last Saturday of the month. I will supply Safeway with the name and address of every reader who was embarrassed by failing to acquire the wines at the prices promised and I am sure suitable amends will be made.

On a personal note, I can only say that I am more furious over this business than any reader. Headless I may now be, but I will not repent for long: digging up interesting bargain wines is my job and I will continue to do it whatever the pressures put upon the available space in my newspaper or the pressures put upon profits by the supermarkets I cover.

Other occasions where prices have conflicted with those in the column were reported by Jim Kingston from Dartford, who had problems in 1992 with the price of Australian Shiraz and Minervois, and Stephen Harvey in 1993. The frustration is understandable. Supermarkets set themselves very high standards particularly in terms of value for money, and customers naturally have high expectations. But, as the *Superplonk* books bear witness, these standards are by and large achieved and often surpassed by Safeway and its like, in spite of the odd hiccup. And this is how it should be. For all the convenience of one-stop shopping, baby changing rooms and in-store pharmacies, supermarkets are really about giving consumers unbeatable prices. When customers feel they have come away with a bargain, the retailer can genuinely contemplate a job well done, as the following letter from Michael Pender of Cardiff, received in February 1996, perfectly illustrates:

How's this for a 20–point-plus bargain? Our local Safeway at Llanishen is selling Penfolds Magill Estate 1991 Shiraz at £4.49. The same nectar is available down the road at Oddbins at £12.99. Beat that!

Surely this is worth a venture over the Bristol Channel.

I received a number of letters from readers, who found that recommended wines were not available at their local Safeway stores. Such an experience came as a particular disappointment for Kenneth Mason of Edinburgh.

Malcolm Gluck says 'Imagine ... summoning up the nerve to ask for Gyongyos. Worse ... Xinomavro Naoussis'. But that is what his *Superplonk* column has led me to do. Happy at finding Safeway featured – they dominate Edinburgh – I go to the local branch and look for his recommendations.

No luck, so I *do* ask. The young man took it calmly, said they were not in stock and pointed us to the 1990 La Coume de Peyre – not the '91 which moved Gluck to eloquence.

I can understand a column which points us to rare places for rare wines, but what is the point of *Superplonk* if the Supers don't stock the plonk?

Such anomalies are frustrating, but for a retailer with the size of range which Safeway offers they are sometimes unavoidable. Mr Peter Booth of Southwark wrote to me at the end of 1995 with a similar tale of woe and as always I passed his letter on to the retailer. He received a very courteous and prompt response from Nicki Dallison, a PR executive at Safeway, who wrote: 'I was very sorry to hear of your difficulty in obtaining two of our wines which Malcolm recommended. Sadly we do not have the space available to carry the full range of wines in all our stores, which means that some are stocked in larger Safeway stores only.' Having noted that Mr Booth had been searching for wines in the Wimbledon and Morden stores, Ms Dallison advised him that if he travelled a little further south to Sutton he would find the largest Safeway store in the London area with the fullest selection. For my own part, when I am aware that a wine I am reviewing has a particularly limited distribution within a supermarket chain I endeavour to mention that in my article.

But not all Safeway shoppers wrote to complain. One writer with strong Safeway connections is Mr T. Whitham of Sheffield. With the fifth largest Safeway in the country on his doorstep, and someone 'on the inside', Mr Whitham's new-found taste for wine, inspired, he tells us, by *Superplonk*, is regularly exercised. As one of the main aims of the books has been to demystify the idea of buying wine, and give drinkers more confidence in making selections, it is always heartening to hear of such experiences. However, Mr Whitham had a beef about the rating system, and its lack of indication of sweetness for white wines.

I have just bought a copy of the 1994 edition of *Superplonk*, and find it just as fascinating as before.

I've only been drinking wine for just over a year – since just before buying the '93 edition (or should that be 'vintage') of your book, in fact – as I had an unfortunate experience with a bottle of red Hirondelle as an undergraduate which put me off the stuff for twenty years. Now, however, Gluck in hand, I boldly go where I would once never have dreamed of going. With a wife who works at the main Sheffield branch of Safeway and with the Hillsborough Barracks branch of Morrisons only five minutes' walk away, you can imagine how useful your annual opus is to the Whitham household.

But, however useful your book is, there is but one slight niggle: you never mention the sweetness or otherwise of the whites. A number of times I've chased up one of your recommendations, only to find that it would be far too sweet for me.

Please, Mr Gluck, don't put me in a quandary next year: I want to buy your '95 edition (and, let's hope the '96 '97 '98 ...), but I would certainly find their ratings useful.

What's a fellow to do? Answer: get Mr G to put some numbers on his reviews.

You know it makes sense.

Mr Whitham and I have corresponded on a number of occasions and he has continued to lobby for a sweetness indicator in my reviews. While there is a case for including some reference on sweetness – I will always say if I find a wine particularly sweet or particularly dry – the problem of a scale from 1 to 10 is that it means so many different things to different people. With whites, if no sweetness is specified, readers can assume that it is a dry wine.

One final retort from Mr Whitham on 26 June seems to indicate that he is still a fan. He concludes his letter:

> One final thing; so far I've had three letters from you, each with a totally different signature. Which is the one to frame when you're a media celebrity?

On any sweetness indicator, Mr Whitham would surely score maximum points.

Safeway plc
Safeway House
6 Millington Road
Hayes
UB3 4AY

Tel 0181 848 8744
Fax 0181 573 1865

SEE STOP PRESS SECTION AT END OF BOOK FOR LAST-MINUTE ADDITIONS TO THIS RETAILER'S RANGE.

ARGENTINIAN WINE RED

Andean Vineyards Merlot/Malbec, Mendoza 1996
Depth, flavour, fruit. Very tasty.

Balbi Vineyard Malbec 1996
Wonderful!!!

ARGENTINIAN WINE WHITE

Balbi Syrah Rose 1996
One of the richest, yet dry, food-friendliest roses around.

AUSTRALIAN WINE RED

Australian Dry Red, Safeway
A really excellent little food wine with brisk, clean, plummy fruit.

Australian Red, Safeway
A lovely wine for picnics (scissors needed for the Tetrapak rather than a corkscrew) and the fruit is sound, correct and satisfying.

Breakaway Grenache/Shiraz, McLaren 1995
Warm, soft, very sunny.

Hardys Bankside Shiraz 1994 `16` `D`

Classic Aussie shiraz with a touch of mint to the beautifully textured, deeply held flavours. An immensely likeable wine of open charm and fruity resolution.

Hardys Barossa Valley Cabernet Sauvignon 1992 `15` `D`

Hardys Barossa Valley Shiraz 1993 `15` `D`

Some richness and fruit, character and style.

Hardys Collection Coonawarra Cabernet Sauvignon 1994 `14` `E`

Expensive for such juicy fruit – though there is tannin in evidence.

Hardys Private Bin Cabernet Sauvignon 1995 `14.5` `C`

Sweet fruit and very easy-going.

Hardys Private Bin 58 Shiraz 1995 `13.5` `C`

Perfectly respectable. That's its trouble.

Hardys Stamp Shiraz/Cabernet 1995 `14` `C`

Rich and soft – slightly soupy. A good glug.

Houghton Wildflower Ridge Shiraz 1993 `14` `D`

Flavour and depth.

Jacob's Creek Dry Red 1993 `15` `C`

Fun yet serious fun. Great with the usual meaty things.

Mount Hurtle Shiraz 1994 `14` `E`

Only just rates as high as 14. It is a touch overpriced, though it is highly charged with soft fruit.

Penfolds Koonunga Hill Shiraz Cabernet 1992 `14` `C`

Getting pricey at over a fiver, this wine. Has lush sweet finishing fruit but not a lot of complexity.

Penfolds Rawson's Retreat Bin 35 Cabernet Sauvignon/Ruby Cabernet/Shiraz 1993 `10` `C`

Soft and rather expressionless.

Peter Lehmann Barossa Cabernet Sauvignon 1994 `16` `D`

Gorgeous! The texture is unusually rich, clinging, developed and finely tannic for an Aussie under ten quid, and the fruit is simply rich, deep and very lingering.

Poet's Corner Shiraz/Cabernet Sauvignon/Cabernet Franc 1994 `14.5` `C`

A very soupy, rich, most appealingly soft wine of mellow charm.

Rosemount Shiraz/Cabernet 1995 `15` `C`

Such smoothness and velvet-textured fruit. A gentility of fruit which surprises and delights.

South Eastern Australia Oaked Cabernet Sauvignon 1995, Safeway `15` `C`

A very cheery, easy-to-love cabernet of such soft and controlled lush fruitiness you can't quite believe it was made on earth – or in it.

South Eastern Australia Oaked Shiraz 1996 · 14 · C

Brisk, meaty, very soft. Great glugging Aussie.

South Eastern Australia Shiraz/Ruby Cabernet 1996, Safeway · 15 · C

Starts brisk and firm then turns ripe and rich and faintly cherry-edged. Delicious.

Stowells of Chelsea Shiraz Cabernet (3-litre box) · 14 · G

Rich fruit with earthy undertones. Has a long, meaty finish with a firm, purposeful balance of fruit and acid.

Wildflower Ridge Shiraz 1992, Western Australia · 16 · C

Wolf Blass Yellow Label Cabernet Sauvignon 1993 · 13.5 · D

Is this deeply fruity wine worth seven quid? It's a fiver's worth of flavour here, no more.

AUSTRALIAN WINE · WHITE

Australian Chardonnay 1993, Safeway · 14 · C

Australian Chardonnay 1994, Safeway · 13 · C

Australian Dry White 1994, Safeway · 13 · B

Australian Marsanne 1995, Safeway · 14 · C

An excellent fish wine: flavourful, perky, deeply marinely inclined.

Australian Oaked Colombard 1996 `13` `C`

Breakaway Grenache Rose 1995 `13.5` `C`
Touch expensive but effective rose – especially for robust fish and mild chicken dishes.

Breakaway Sauvignon Blanc/Semillon 1996 `13` `C`

Geoff Merrill Chardonnay 1994 `13.5` `E`
Pleasant, but absurdly overpriced.

H. G. Brown Bin No 60 Oaked Colombard `12` `B`

Hardys Barossa Valley Chardonnay 1993 `15` `D`
Has a lovely coarse fruit edge. Great with chicken dishes.

Hardys Nottage Hill Chardonnay 1996 `16` `C`
Superb soft, rolling texture. Brilliant fruit. Great balance.

**Hardys Private Bin Oaked Chardonnay
1994** `15` `C`
Meaty, rich, textured, classy, polished, excellent with chicken and fish. Excellent price.

Hardys RR Medium White 1993 `11` `C`
Quite why Hardys puts its name to this dull wine is one of life's exceedingly tedious mysteries I have no interest in solving.

Hardys Stamp Grenache/Syrah 1996 `13` `C`
A somewhat overpriced rose.

Jacob's Creek Semillon/Chardonnay 1993 `13` `C`

Jacob's Creek Riesling 1995 `14` `C`
Good with Chinese food.

Lindemans Bin 65 Chardonnay 1993　16　C

Longleat Marsanne 1993　12　C
Odd spritzig quality.

Monty's Hill Chardonnay/Colombard 1995　14　C
Doesn't quite come down as effectively as it goes up, but it'll work well with food.

Orlando RF Chardonnay 1994　15.5　D
The essence of Australian white wine-making: bold yet elegant, fruity yet never overblown, this is turbo-charged fruit cruising at a comfortable speed which easily, in second gear, outpaces Old World equivalents at two and three times this price.

Penfolds Organic Chardonnay/Sauvignon Blanc, Clare Valley 1994　13.5　D
Tasty, fresh, decent. Touch expensive.

Penfolds Rawsons Retreat Bin 21 Semillon/Chardonnay/Colombard 1995　15.5　C
Best yet, this vintage.

Peter Lehmann Semillon Barossa Valley 1995　15　C
Lovely.

Peter Lehmann Semillon/Chardonnay, Barossa 1995　15　D
What a character! Individual, soft, smooth, handsome yet very very cheeky.

Poet's Corner Semillon/Sauvignon/ Chardonnay 1995　14　C
Rich, a pasta wine.

Rosemount Estates Chardonnay, Hunter Valley 1993 `17` `C`

Huge fruit (rounded, ripe, brilliant), great balance, class, style and price. Utterly delicious – a wine to love!!

Rosemount Estates Semillon/Chardonnay 1995 `15` `D`

Elegant.

Semillon Chardonnay SE Australia 1994, Safeway `13.5` `C`

Bright and sunny – with a gently lemon hint.

South East Australia Oaked Chardonnay `16` `C`

Great combination of rich-edged, elegant fruit and fine, incisively balancing acids. Great value here.

AUSTRIAN WINE WHITE

Seewinkler Impressionen Ausbruch 1992 (half bottle) `14` `E`

Restrained marmalade finish to the apricot and honey fruit. Expensive but lovely pud wine.

BULGARIAN WINE RED

Aged in Oak Merlot, Rousse 1995 `14.5` `C`

Bulgarian Country Wine, Pinot/Merlot
Sliven, Safeway

Firm and fruity – sound style.

Cabernet Sauvignon Reserve, Sliven 1990

Has a green vegetable undertone to the soft, jammy fruit. Odd but oddly attractive.

Cabernet Sauvignon, Suhindol, Safeway
(3-litre box)

Cabernet Sauvignon Svischtov 1991,
Safeway

Juicy and full with its affections, this is a forward red of charm.

Gorchivka Estate Selection Cabernet
Sauvignon 1993

Individual, serious, dry, gently soft (yet tannic hints) and good with cheese and rice dishes.

Lovico Suhindol Cabernet Sauvignon
Reserve 1990

Has chewiness and flavour in equal amounts. Decant it an hour beforehand into a wellington boot if you like, and the fruit flows like a torrent of velvet.

Vinenka Merlot/Gamza Reserve, Suhindol
1991

Great with cheese dishes.

Young Vatted Cabernet Sauvignon,
Haskovo 1995, Safeway

Brilliant, biting fruit: deep and velvety.

BULGARIAN WINE WHITE

Bulgarian Chardonnay 1995, Safeway `15.5` `B`

Delicious, great value.

Bulgarian Country Wine, Safeway `11` `B`

Chardonnay Reserva 1993 `15` `C`

Great value. Brilliantly deep fruit.

Chardonnay/Sauvignon Preslav 1994 `13.5` `B`

I am strongly opposed to this marriage – usually. This one works.

Sauvignon Blanc & Rikat, Rousse 1995 `14` `B`

Elegance and complexity: real class and style here.

CHILEAN WINE RED

Anakena Cabernet Sauvignon 1993 `13` `C`

Curious fresh-edged wine which seems to be grasping at, but not quite reaching, something better.

Caliterra Cabernet Sauvignon 1995 `16.5` `C`

What flavour! What softness! What lingering depth of fruit! Chile, I kiss your feet.

Carmen Grande Vidure Cabernet 1994 `14.5` `C`

Smooth, rich, classy – very good price for such accomplished fruit.

Chilean Cabernet Sauvignon, Lontue 1995, Safeway
17.5 **C**

A fabulous wine for the money. Has tannins, fruit, acid in beautiful, textured harmony. A great rich complex wine of immediate charm and concentration. 9/4/97 (rdc6)

Grand Vidure Cabernet Reserve 1994
16 **C**

Dry, tannic, fresh – developing. Needs a two-hour breather.

Tocornal Cabernet/Malbec 1994
14 **C**

Soft and cherry-edged. Good with food and cheering company.

Tocornal Chilean Red 1994
15 **C**

Bright and breezy cherry and plum, and very cheerful. Good with food, good without.

Tocornal Malbec 1993
13.5 **B**

Sweet and dusky.

Villa Montes Gran Reserva Merlot 1992
14 **C**

Curious digestive cream biscuit richness to the fruit. Only a limited volume available.

Villard Cabernet Sauvignon 1992
13 **D**

Edge of mint? Dry, a touch austere.

CHILEAN WINE WHITE

Caliboro Semillon/Chardonnay
14 **C**

Fresh, clean, fruity. Charming.

Caliterra Chardonnay 1996

How does Chile pack so much charm in a bottle for such reasonable money?

Caliterra Chardonnay, Curico 1994

Must be the finest chardonnay under £4 in the world. Superb balance of acid and demure fruit, taste and refreshment.

Casablanca Sauvignon Blanc, Lontue 1994

Delicious smoked fish wine. Nice zing on the finish.

Castillo de Molina Sauvignon Blanc 1996

Chilean Chardonnay 1996, Safeway

Lovely structure and high-quality fruit. An outstandingly beautifully textured wine for the money. Classic chardy charms.

Chilean Dry White 1996, Safeway

Like a civilised edition of vinho verde – delicious prickle to the young fruit.

Chilean Sauvignon Blanc, Lontue 1996, Safeway

Another fresh, nutty, supple young white at Safeway.

Concha y Toro Casillero del Diablo Chardonnay 1994

Brilliant woody fruit: elegant, rich, satisfying, complex, utterly delicious, finely wrought, beautifully textured. Made, it seems to me, from grapes kissed by angels.

Concha y Toro Casillero del Diablo Sauvignon Blanc 1994

Lovely rich rolling fruit of assertiveness and style. Deee-licious.

Tocornal Chardonnay 1995

Very elegant, subtle, big-striding yet gentle-stepping wine.

Torconal Chardonnay, Ed Flaherty 1995

Rather muddy finish spoils the effect.

ENGLISH WINE — WHITE

Estate Selection Dry, Sharpham, 1990

Reasonable delivery of fresh fruit, sane and balanced.

Lymington Medium Dry 1991

Stanlake, Thames Valley Vineyards 1994

For a limey bottle, it ain't bad. Should be £2.25 – but blame the Exchequer for this gross distortion, not the wine-maker.

Three Choirs Seyval/Reichensteiner 1990

Apple-bright fruit, developed and attractive, wrapped in wet wool, i.e. that musty feral aroma given off by a sodden sweater drying in front of the fire.

FRENCH WINE — RED

Beaujolais 1995, Safeway

Jammy and almost sweet. Not sure it's great value at this price. But what price complexity and depth? Taste the same store's Chilean Red . . .

Cabernet Sauvignon VdP d'Oc 1995, Safeway   `15.5` `C`

Beautiful price, beautiful fruit, beautiful invigorating bottle of serious, deep, flavourful fruit. Great stuff, Safeway!!

Chateau de Chorey, Chorey-les-Beaune 1992   `10` `E`

Chateau des Gemeaux, Pauillac 1992   `12.5` `D`

Bit hard to like, but will soften in time.

Chateau du Ragon, Bordeaux 1995   `15` `C`

Genuine vegetal tannic bordeaux!

Chateau la Tour de Beraud, Costieres de Nimes 1994   `14` `C`

Stale cigar-like edge to the brisk fruit gives character and sunniness which goes brilliantly with food.

Claret, Safeway   `12` `B`

Approaches a reasonable depth of dry, tannic fruit.

Cotes du Rhone 1995, Safeway   `13` `B`

Soft, juicy, simple – works with food rather than mood.

Cotes du Rhone Oak Aged 1995   `14` `C`

Solidly fruity, good integrated tannin and acidity, and a lovely savoury finish which clings to the tastebuds.

Cotes du Rhone Villages, Meffre 1994   `13.5` `C`

Domaine du Bois des Dames Cotes du Rhone Villages 1995   `14.5` `C`

Hints of raspberries amongst the assorted dry fruits and the whole assemblage comes nicely packaged for the tongue because of the rich texture.

Domaine Vieux Manoir de Maransan Cuvee Speciale 1995

`14` `C`

Not the rich, clinging earth of old-style Rhone but the ringing bright-toned fruit of modernity. Delicious.

French Organic Vin de Table, Safeway

`13` `B`

Fruity, gently earthy.

French Red Wine, Safeway (1.5 litres)

`13.5`

This is the way to package wine! No corks – just a plastic screwcap. The wine is a good soft rustic red.

Gabriel Corcol St Emilion 1993

`12` `C`

La Baume Syrah/Grenache VdP d'Oc 1995

`15` `C`

Has that initial spiky hairiness of the warm south, then the softness and richness of fruit rolls over and shows us its puppyish, playful side. Delicious.

La Chasse du Pape Cotes du Rhone Reserve 1994

`17` `C`

A quite brilliantly characterful, hugely giving wine for the money. It is more alive than many a Chateauneuf-du-Pape at twice the price. It is rich, dark, gently rugged, deeply fruity, dry yet singing with flavour and it lingers like love. Over three-quarters of an hour it develops a licorice chocolate depth. Not at all stores.

La Cuvee Mythique Vin de Pays d'Oc 1993

`14` `D`

This has improved considerably in bottle. Pricey but the opulence of the fruit, dry and rich with herby undertones, is deeply impressive. Has a restrained wildness of exciting drinkability.

Laperouse Val d'Orbieu & Penfolds, VdP d'Oc 1994 `13.5` `C`

The fruit has a somewhat namby-pamby attitude to the tannins. Needs time to develop in bottle (six months or more).

Margaux, Barton & Guestier 1989 `11` `E`

Minervois, Safeway `14` `B`

This is a juicier edition of the Corbieres, less earthy, more eager.

Moulin a Vent Mommessin 1994 `10` `D`

Moulin de Duhart, Pauillac 1993 `12` `F`

Tasty but vastly overpriced.

Oak-aged Medoc 1993 `13` `C`

Impressive in a quiet way.

Oak-aged Claret NV, Safeway `13.5` `C`

A thoroughly solid, drinkable, respectable claret. Lacks excitement but it's from Bordeaux, remember.

Regnie Duboeuf 1994 `12` `D`

Not a lot of thrills for such proximity to six quid but it's respectable. Not a little horror like some.

Sarget du Chateau Gruaud Larose 1992 `13` `E`

St-Julien 1994 `11` `E`

Stowells of Chelsea Vin de Pays du Gard (3-litre box) `14` `F`

Delightful smooth fruit with flavour and balance. A lovely touch – a distant echo, really – of earth.

Syrah Galet Vineyards 1994

A handsome, rugged beast softened by rich tannins of some gentility and a warm, savoury finish. A delicious soupy wine for all sorts of lamb dishes.

Syrah/Merlot VdP d'Oc 1995

Terrific price for such richly endowed, dry, characterful fruit. It really hits the spot with its lovely textured fruit which is well controlled, never coarse or too rustic and, finally, deeply refreshing and delicious.

Vin de Pays de l'Ardeche 1994, Safeway

Seriously drinkable, light and dry, cherryish and agreeable if chilled and drunk with grilled salmon.

Vin de Pays de Vaucluse, Vallee du Soleil 1995

Vigour and bite with a light dusting of cherry fruit.

Vin Rouge, Vin de Pays Catalan, Safeway

Volnay Domaine Michel Lafarge 1992

FRENCH WINE WHITE

Bergerac Sec 1995 Safeway

Chablis Cuvee Domaine Yvon Pautre 1994, Safeway

Chardonnay VdP d'Oc 1995, Safeway

Chateau du Pradier Entre Deux Mers 1995

Chateau Haut Bonfils, Barrel-fermented Bordeaux Semillon 1994
`15` `C`

This has softened and developed more complexity.

Chenin VdP du Jardin de la France 1995, Safeway
`14` `B`

Great-value simplicity: fresh, fruity, clean and very refreshing.

Domaine du Rey Vegetarian White Wine, VdP des Cotes de Gascogne 1995
`14.5` `C`

Gripping concentration of freshness.

Domaine Latour-Giraud Meursault 1994
`11` `F`

Gewurztraminer d'Alsace, Turckheim 1994
`15` `D`

The unique taste of rose-rich gewurztraminer from Alsace. Powerful, rich finish of compressed rose blossoms. Great with Chinese food.

Hugh Ryman Chardonnay Aged in Oak, VdP d'Oc 1994
`14.5` `C`

Delicious firm style with a serious edge.

La Coume de Peyre Vin de Pays des Cotes de Gascogne 1995
`15` `B`

Lovely, slightly exotic fruit tinged with lemon freshness. Great quaffing bottle.

Laperouse Blanc Val d'Orbieu & Penfolds, VdP d'Oc 1994
`14` `C`

Rich rolling elegance. Very attractive wine for grilled sole.

Mercurey 'Les Mauvarennes', Faiveley 1993
`13.5` `E`

Rather tasty. And you can't say that about many burgundies these days.

Montagny Premier Cru 1994 `12.5` `D`

**Philippe de Baudin Sauvignon, VdP
d'Oc 1995** `15` `C`

Warmth of ripe melons, yet cut by citric acidity giving it
balance and charm. A strikingly sane and 'sippin'-nicely-thank-
you' bottle.

Premieres Cotes de Bordeaux, Safeway `11` `C`

Tough to rate. It's too light for puds, too sweet for pre- and
prandial tippling, and not acidic enough to go with other foods.
Quandary.

Sancerre 'Les Bonnes Bouches' 1994 `10` `E`

Sauvignon de Touraine 1995, Safeway `14` `C`

Fresh, light, and elegant. Soft restrained fruit with some
finesse.

**Sauvignon VdP du Jardin de la France
1995, Safeway** `13.5` `B`

**'Terre Vivante' Chardonnay/Viognier, VdP
d'Oc 1995 (Organic)** `15` `C`

Delicate yet decisive. Deliciously perfumed freshness and richness.

**Vieux Manoir de Maransan, Cotes du
Rhone 1995** `15` `C`

A terrific partner for freshwater fish (like trout – grilled or
smoked). It has flavour, a hint of crispness and real weight.

**Vin Blanc (Domaines Virginie) VdP de
l'Herault, Safeway** `12` `C`

Vin Blanc Safeway (1 litre) `10` `B`

Vin de Pays de Vaucluse 1995, Safeway `14` `B`
Good clean fruit.

Vouvray Demi-Sec, Safeway `10` `C`

GERMAN WINE WHITE

Auslese 1993, Pfalz, Safeway `12` `C`

**Bereich Bernkastel, Mosel-Saar-Ruwer,
Safeway** `12` `B`

Bereich Nierstein 1993, Safeway `12.5` `B`
Has some nutty qualities.

Gewurztraminer Pfalz 1995, Safeway `10` `C`
What a perfectly respectable wine. It is well-meaning but so dull
you want to take it out and shoot it.

**Hugh Ryman Almond Grove Riesling Dry,
Pfalz 1993** `12.5` `C`
Curious style. Tries to be something I'm not sure the ries-
ling can be.

HUNGARIAN WINE RED

**Chapel Hill Barrique-Aged Cabernet
Sauvignon 1994** `14.5` `C`
Juicy, friendly, softly bristling with blackcurrant fruit but

217

stays just this side of seriousness by virtue of its gentle tannic shading.

HUNGARIAN WINE WHITE

Chapel Hill Barrique-fermented Chardonnay, Balaton 1995 | 15 | C

Great robustness of texture yet fineness of fruit.

Hungarian Country White 1995, Safeway | 12 | B

Matra Mountain Chardonnay, Nagyrede 1995 | 15 | B

Great classic feel yet spiked with iconoclastic acids leading to a cheeky finish of immense charm.

Nagyrede Estate Pinot Blanc 1995 | 13.5 | B

Neszmely Estate Barrique-Fermented Sauvignon Blanc 1995 | 15.5 | C

Beats sancerre into a cocked chapeau. Delicious conformist sauvignon.

Pinot Grigio, Nagyrede 1995 | 14 | B

Clean and crisp with an echo of fruit on the edge.

River Duna Irsai Oliver, Neszmely 1995 | 15.5 | B

Brilliant.

River Duna Sauvignon Blanc 1995 | 14.5 | B

A touch of peach and pear to the fresh whip-lash finish.

River Duna Sauvignon Blanc Special Cuvee 1995 `13.5` `C`

Riverview Chardonnay/Pinot Gris 1995 `15` `C`
Superb fruit, quite upliftingly firm and fresh.

Silver Swan Olasz Rizling, Balaton Boglar 1993 `13` `B`
Good initial attack on the nose but less punch on the palate.

ISRAELI WINE RED

Carmel Cabernet Sauvignon `12` `C`
An interesting curiosity; dry and respectably clothed in fruit.

ITALIAN WINE RED

Barrel Aged Cabernet Sauvignon, Cecchi 1994 `17` `D`
Stunning concentration of rich dark fruit. Has opulence, class, elegance, huge depth of flavour and developed tannins scaffolding well-built, complex fruit. A sensual wine. If this wine costs £7 or less it rates 17 points; the price is subject to confirmation at time of going to press . . .

Chianti 1995, Safeway `12` `C`
Sweet edge.

Chianti Classico 1994, Safeway `C`
Dry, earthy, good with pizzas.

Concilio Barrique-Aged Merlot, Trentino Riserva 1994 `13` `D`

Montepulciano d'Abruzzo, Barrique Aged 1994 `15.5` `C`

Real class. Great wood, soft spice, fruit, balance. Delicious. Lovely texture. Great with grilled vegetables and cold meats.

Montepulciano d'Abruzzo Miglianico 1993 `15` `C`

Sicilian Red 1995, Safeway `14.5` `B`

Lovely simple soft fruit and teeth-clinging richness. Touch of earthiness gives it character.

Tedeschi Capitel San Rocco Rosso 1991 `14.5` `E`

Expensive but impressively well-structured, rich and characterful.

Tenuta San Vito Chianti 1994 (Organic) `13` `D`

Good but expensive.

Valpolicella 1995, Safeway `11` `B`

Zagara Nero d'Avola 1995 (Sicily) `14.5` `C`

Soft, simple. Can be drunk chilled.

ITALIAN WINE WHITE

Bianco del Lazio 1995, Safeway `13.5` `B`

Warm and soft.

Casa di Giovanni VdT di Sicilia 1995, Safeway `14` `C`

Chardonnay del Salento, Barrique Aged, K. Milne 1995 `16.5` `D`

A rich, elegant, superbly purposeful and confident wine of impressive class. Superb with scallops.

Chardonnay delle Venezie 1995, Safeway `14` `C`

Modern fruit but the acidity seems old-style.

Frascati 1995, Safeway `14` `C`

Solid fruit, clean, decent.

Lambrusco Rose, Safeway `10` `B`

Lambrusco Rosso Safeway `11` `B`

With the Christmas turkey, the sensorily infirm and the sweet-toothed will find this red most agreeable.

Lambrusco, Safeway `10` `B`

Sweet and peachy for total beginners.

Le Monferrine, Moscato d'Asti 1995 `12` `B`

5% alcohol.

Pinot Grigio delle Venezie 1995, Safeway `13` `C`

Has some textured charm.

Puglian White 1995, Safeway `14` `C`

Delicious, soft yet firm fruit. Nutty and fresh.

Sicilian White 1995, Safeway `13` `B`

Soave 1995, Safeway `15` `B`

Very good value. Not fully modern (for there are echoes of

old-style soave here). Delicious fruit, rounded and firm. Good balancing acidity. Catch it while it's young.

Zagara Grillo 1995 `15` `C`

Delicious rich-edged food wine. Character, class, weight, style and great drinkability.

NEW ZEALAND WINE RED

Kirkwood Cabernet/Merlot 1995 `15.5` `B`

Lovely grip of fruit, acid and gentle tannins on the teeth.

NEW ZEALAND WINE WHITE

Kirkwood Chardonnay 1995 `14` `B`

Real class. Real fruit. Real value.

Domaine Sapt Inour `14` `B`

What a dry, earthy, fruity companion to a well-fried merguez sausage!

Millton Vineyard Barrel-fermented Chardonnay 1995 `14` `E`

Organic, and overpriced, but there is no doubting its benevolence.

Montana Sauvignon Blanc, Marlborough 1995 `13.5` `C`

New vintage. Grassy, blurred.

Stowells of Chelsea New Zealand
Sauvignon Blanc (3-litre box)   13.5 G

Keen, grassy aromas, good fruit, rather a quiet finish.

Taurau Valley 1996   14 C

Solidly fruity. Good with poached chicken.

Timara Dry White 1995   14 C

Has flair and precision. Great with fish poached, grilled or roasted.

PORTUGUESE WINE   RED

Fiuza Merlot, Ribatejo 1994   14 C

Attractive texture and fruit.

Joao Pires Tinto da Anfora, Alentejo 1991   14 D

I used to enthuse mightily over previous incarnations of this wine. It's losing its stuffing and at over a fiver this is a pity but it's still a 14-point wine with food – which it loves.

PORTUGUESE WINE   WHITE

Bright Brothers Fernao Pires/Chardonnay,
Ribatejo 1995   15.5 C

Exciting, aromatic and deeply plush marriage of two unlikely grapes. Terrifically well-wrought, well-textured and deliciously fruity.

Falua Ribatejo 1995   14.5 B

Rich, dry, dark and satisfyingly fruity. Great price.

ROMANIAN WINE RED

**Murfatlar Barrel-fermented Chardonnay
1994**

Big fat fruit of caressing charm bringing deep pleasure to palate
and throat.

SOUTH AFRICAN WINE RED

Cape Red 1996, Safeway

A warm, soft, slightly smoky/rubbery pasta wine.

Kleindal Pinotage 1996, Safeway

Brilliant lingering flavour and rounded softness of tone. Terrific
balance makes this wine both deep and quaffable. Humming
value for money.

**Rosenview Cabernet Sauvignon,
Stellenbosch 1996**

Juicy and overripe but not blowsy or too soppy. Very good
richness on the finish.

Rosenview Cinsault 1996

Has a delightful, though serious, dry depth of fruit but only
evident after its juicy freshness has lashed the tongue.

Rosenview Merlot, Stellenbosch 1996

A very shivery (rather than warm-coated) merlot.

Simonsvlei Pinotage Cabernet Reserve 1994 14 C

New vintage. Dry yet soft and gently tannic.

Simonsvlei Shiraz Reserve, Paarl 1994 15.5 C

Pour into mugs and serve it as Cup-a-Soup. It's all savoury fruit. Marvellous with cheese and herb omelette.

SOUTH AFRICAN WINE WHITE

Boschendal Chardonnay, Franschoek 1994 15.5 D

Very elegant, finely cut, mature yet youthful. A strikingly quiet yet delicious, authoritative wine.

Cape Dry White 1996, Safeway 14 B

Nutty, melony, very ripe, delightfully fresh.

Danie de Wet Chardonnay Sur Lie 1995 15 C

Delicate yet really full of flavour (soft ripe melon). Typical de Wet craftsmanship.

Namaqua Dry (3-litre box) 15 F

Modern style, full of ripe fruit. Terrific freshness, too, so it's good for thirsts as well as being good for fish.

Quagga Colombard/Chardonnay, Western Cape 1996, Safeway 13.5 B

Pear-drops, melon and lemon – enough for any palate to grapple with.

South African Chenin Blanc, Swartland 1996, Safeway 13.5 B

Very rounded and ripe.

Umfiki Sauvignon Blanc 1996

Very fresh and perky.

Vergelegen Chardonnay, Stellenbosch 1995

Warmth and depth of flavour, complexity, great charm and a lengthy presence on the palate.

Waterside White Colombard/Chardonnay 1996

Delightful, fresh apple/pear/melon fruit – lip-smackin' fresh.

SPANISH WINE RED

Agramont Tempranillo/Cabernet, Navarra 1990

Glorious lingering finish. Lots of flavour to the fruit, which hangs on for grimly delicious death.

Carinena 1988 Safeway

Castilla de Sierra Rioja Crianza 1992, Safeway

Lovely, creamy, vanilla edge to the fruit. Sinfully gluggable.

Don Darias

Brilliant with curry, just brilliant.

Stowells of Chelsea Tempranillo (3-litre box)

Great glugging flavour and texture.

Valdepenas Reserva 1991, Safeway   15   C

Has a herby warmth of fruit and a depth of flavour which never becomes overripe or lush because soft tannins intrude and give it weight, texture and balance.

Vina Albali Tempranillo, Valdepenas 1995   15   B

Lovely, rich, rounded, polished fruit.

Young Vatted Tempranillo, La Mancha 1995, Safeway   14   C

Dry yet young and risky and leaping with fresh fruit.

SPANISH WINE   WHITE

Agramont Viura/Chardonnay, Navarra 1994   14.5   C

Lashings of flavour, gently buttered.

Berberana Viura Crianza, Rioja 1992   12   C

Good with fish stew.

Monopole Barrel-fermented Rioja 1993   14   D

Expensive and purely for food (the wood is weighty but it overpowers the fruit). Grilled chicken great!

Somontano Chardonnay 1995   15.5   C

Who on earth needs to go near expensive white burgundy when there's this under £4?

Vina Malea Oaked Viura 1995   15.5   B

Brilliant value here: gently woody fruit with verve.

USA WINE RED

Brook Hollow Californian Red

Perfectly formed and fruity. Stylish, not over-rich or brutal.

Fetzer Zinfandel 1993

Big, bouncy, blissful – soft, sweet (in the most delightfully fruity way) yet dry to finish with controlled spiciness. Gently exotic and lithe, this is a delicious wine.

Glen Ellen Merlot Proprietor's Reserve 1994

Lovely value for money. Real class in a glass.

FORTIFIED WINE

Cream Sherry, Safeway

Fruity and thick.

Fino Sherry, Safeway

An oily, nervously fruity fino not of such austere dryness that it comes across as mean. Good with grilled prawns and ham.

Fonseca Guimaraens 1978

Hugely expensive and too much so considering the less than heavyweight fruit.

Gonzales Byass Matusalem Muy Viejo Oloroso

Like boot polish and brandy.

LBV 1987, Safeway

Lustau Manzanilla Sherry (half bottle)

Very dry and camomile tinged. Aperitif (of course) – for lovers of the stuff.

Lustau Mature Cream Sherry (half bottle)

A wonderfully rich, treacly tipple to set alight family reunions.

Lustau Old Amontillado Sherry (half bottle)

Goes with unlit pipes, Hush Puppies and unreadable Greek love poetry. If you can supply these props, this wine is delicious.

Lustau Old Dry Oloroso Sherry (half bottle)

To be drunk with nuts.

Ruby Port, Safeway

Sound, very sound.

Safeway LBV 1988

Depth, flavour, alcohol and fruit. A recipe for fruit cake (which you dunk in this wine).

Taylors LBV 1989

Flavour, yes – but not as fulsome as it has been.

10 Year Old Tawny Port, Safeway

Rather sweet and one-dimensional.

Vintage Character Port, Safeway

Dry, rich.

SPARKLING WINE/CHAMPAGNE

Albert Etienne Brut, Safeway `12` `G`

Albert Etienne Rose, Safeway `13` `F`

Asti Spumante, Safeway `11` `C`

Sweet and unadventurous – but then some women marry men like that.

Australian Sparkling, Safeway `15` `D`

Firmly fruity and keen. Excellent value.

Bollinger Special Cuvee Brut `12` `H`

Over twenty quid, is it worth it? I wish I could provide a whole-hearted yes in spite of Bollinger's very particular dry charms.

Cava Brut, Safeway `13` `F`

Buy it for the style and the big fat magnum.

Chartogne-Taillet Champagne Brut Cuvee Sainte-Anne `12` `G`

Cremant de Bourgogne Brut, Safeway `13` `D`

Cuvee Napa, USA `13.5` `E`

Freixenet Cordon Negro Brut Cava `13` `D`

Graham Beck Brut (South Africa) `13.5` `E`

Rather suffers value-for-money-wise, compared to Cava.

J. Bourgeois Pere et Fils Champagne Brut `12.5` `F`

Lindauer Brut `13.5` `D`

Delicate hint of lemon. A lovely little bubbly at a reasonable price.

Moscato Spumante, Safeway `12` `C`

Very fruity and sweet-edged.

Pol Acker Chardonnay Brut (France) `14` `C`

Soft and elegant. Very good value.

Saumur Brut, Safeway `14` `D`

Has a depth of flavour of some class.

Veuve Clicquot Champagne Yellow
Label Brut `12` `H`

SAINSBURY'S

Don't let the bastards grind you down

Superplonk is always interested to hear from readers who have found wines being sold at different prices from those they were led to expect by a write-up in the column. In most cases, the retailer can smoothly come up with some reason or other to explain – satisfactorily or otherwise – such discrepancies. But I think the wine team at J Sainsbury would be hard-pressed to account for the knockdown price Clare Gordon of south London was quoted for a bottle of its Bulgarian Merlot.

> I thought you might be interested to know that I have found a source of Sainsbury's Bulgarian Merlot considerably cheaper than J Sainsbury!
>
> It is on sale, complete with Sainsbury's label, in a night club at the Park Hotel Moskva in Sofia for $2 a bottle.
>
> I doubt whether Mr Sainsbury would be as amused as I was.

Price discrepancies are rarely greeted with such mirth. It is most frustrating for readers to arrive at a supermarket to find that a wine that has been recommended in the column will cost them more than they had been led to believe; it is very rarely the other way around. Like most retailers, J Sainsbury is not immune from this problem. Oonagh Hyndman of Boughton Monchelsea near Maidstone in Kent was so incensed she even suggested that there were sinister forces at work when she was scuppered in an attempt to purchase Sicilian Red. She wrote in June 1994.

> Please spare 1 column cm of shame for Sainsbury's who are clearly under the influence of the Mafia.
>
> Store at Quarrywood Maidstone had shelves groaning with Sicilian Red on 23.6.94, at normal price of £2.69. Enquiry elicited that 'supply problems' negated the £1.99 offer which will allegedly be available next week. Phone call to store rambled with usual excuses – Head Office decision, nothing to do with us, etc., etc.
>
> Meanwhile I am sans Sicilian Red at offer price, £11.00 poorer on bus and taxi fares to purchase same, and thoroughly disgruntled.

I was appalled by Ms Hyndman's letter and, as I always do, forwarded the complaint on to Sainsbury's head office. It was Sainsbury's director of off-licence buying at the time, Mike Conolly, who had the unfortunate task of explaining such an aberration. Possessed of a charming manner, Mr Conolly is in many ways the perfect person to pour oil on troubled waters. For instance, back in 1993, Sue Warren of Halifax had written to complain about a Carcassonne wine badly tainted by a duff cork. Mike replied at length and in some detail on the problems of cork taint, enclosing a £10 voucher for Ms Warren's trouble, which she subsequently vowed only to spend on *Superplonk* recommendations. That he did not beat around the bush and was prepared to say that supermarkets and the wine trade as a whole still have a problem with corks was most refreshing.

His frank and honest account of the Sicilian Red incident, which Ms Hyndman received in July 1994, gives an interesting insight into how the Sainsbury's pricing strategy works – or doesn't in this case. Moreover, it suggests that thanks to Ms Hyndman's letter, the supermarket may do things differently next time – which is heartening. I quote:

I thought it would be helpful to give you the background to the problems we encountered on our recent Sicilian wine promotion although I recognise that the account I shall give you may not entirely satisfy your complaint.

We purchased what we believed was an absolutely huge quantity of red and white and on the basis of past experience we felt that we had more than enough to cover a two-week offer, and probably sufficient to last up to 4 weeks at £1.99. In the event the degree of press coverage and a belated decision to feature the red wine in TV advertising led to a demand way above what we had expected and by the middle of the second week our depot stocks of red wine were virtually exhausted. We had to take a decision on whether to let the stock run through at £1.99 in which case we would have been out of stock for three to four weeks until new supplies could be bottled and shipped from Sicily, or dampen the demand by reverting to the normal price of £2.69. As you know we chose the latter course.

This was not an easy or comfortable decision and I think in retrospect we did not give sufficient weight to the amount of publicity the offer had produced from journalists. Should this situation recur I think we might well take a different view and I am grateful to you for bringing this to our attention as it is clearly an issue of principle which we need to address.

I am enclosing £10.00 worth of JS vouchers which I hope will act as a small recompense for your disappointment and will allow you to buy some further bottles of Sicilian wine albeit at the higher price.

I am sending a copy of this letter to Malcolm Gluck and I trust that it will help you to at least understand our thinking on this matter. I am grateful to you for having brought this issue to my attention via Malcolm.

Mr A.R. Steven of Bakewell encountered a similar problem with a bottle of Minervois back in early 1992, and believed he had the solution.

> I have been a regular reader of your column since it started and have enjoyed your recommendations, as many as I have been able to afford.
>
> I called in at Sainsbury's in Macclesfield yesterday to purchase some of the Minervois. It wasn't priced at £1.99 but £2.69. When I enquired the staff were very helpful and explained it had been on special offer but wasn't now and the dates quoted in the article were incorrect. They pointed out the current special offer and I did buy some of that and some Minervois too.
>
> The reason I am writing is not to complain but to suggest that maybe you could review wines coming up on special offer in advance by working with the supermarkets, as book and film reviewers must do to prepare their reviews.

As a matter of fact, *Superplonk* reviews will often coincide with attractive promotions, as it is then that the retailers bring the wines to my attention. It is for this reason I am generally baffled when I hear from readers that the wines are not available at the prices I have been told. Mike Conolly's letter about the Sicilian Red is a comparatively rare example of a rational and intelligible explanation for one of these incidents, even if the idea that such a sophisticated retailer as Sainsbury's could be so caught out seems rather hard to believe.

As I pointed out in my reply to Mr G.L. Everett of Hatch End, I ring supermarkets to check on the stock situation with such wines when I recommend them. When a Saturday morning dash to his local Sainsbury's proved fruitless, the disappointment was almost too much.

> At 8.30 a.m. I was reading your column in my *Guardian* and at 10.45 I was in my local Sainsbury's at Pinner

looking for your 17 points-rating Les Langues Rousses 1992 Chardonnay. They had not seen or heard of it!! I was deflated . . .

When you publicise a rattling good buy as I am sure this must have been would you please ensure when it is going to be available in which stores. The disappointment is unbearable!!

I was puzzled that Mr Everett had not been able to buy a wine I believed to be in plenteous supply, and replied thus.

Thanks for your card of 8 October, and I hope that by now Sainsbury's wine department have rung to explain the position regarding Les Langues Rousses Chardonnay. I believe they still have a great many bottles in stock and you should have no trouble acquiring as many of them as you like. If this turns out not to be the case, and you experience something else, please let me know.

I was surprised to get your card because I always do check the stock position on all the wines I write and rave about, to ensure that readers will not be disappointed.

Many thanks for writing.

Sure enough, in a later letter, Mr Everett informed me that he did find the Les Langues Rousses Chardonnay in stock in the same store a week later.

Regarding the availability of special offers mentioned in the column, readers have also discovered there is an additional snag with Sainsbury's as it effectively has two trading formats, J Sainsbury and Savacentre. As Dr G. Thackray of Edinburgh found out, special offers advertised for Sainsbury's are not necessarily available in Savacentre. He wrote in March 1993:

Armed with your article for Saturday, 29 February I went today to Sainsbury's Savacentre, Cameron Toll, Edinburgh. My intention was to buy Valpolicella Classico

Negarine at £6.08 for two bottles. However it was only on sale at £3.39 per bottle. I complained to the Grocery Manager, and showed him your article. He had two comments to make, neither of which was very convincing.

1. 'Malcolm Gluck is always getting it wrong – this is the second time in two months. This wine has never been on special promotion.'

2. 'Sainsbury's is not the same as Savacentre. They have offers which we don't.'

I would appreciate your comments, and, if you hear from Sainsbury's, a copy of their comments also.

I replied to the effect that the grocery manager was part right and part wrong. It is true that Savacentre does not always have the same offers as J Sainsbury, but his contention that *Superplonk* 'is always getting it wrong' is of course a gross distortion.

Fiona Lewry of Bolton reported more misinformation from J Sainsbury shop staff when she wrote in 1994.

Re: Romanian Pinot Noir NV (Sainsbury's)

Today I was unceremoniously informed that Sainsbury's is no longer stocking this wine. The man in the grey suit who told me this said he didn't know where this gorgeous bargain is now available. Perhaps you could help?

P.S. The bastards also no longer do the Auslese half-bottles, so could you recommend a new supermarket?!

Unfortunately for Ms Lewry, the gentleman was partly right, but he was extremely wide of the mark with regard to the highly rated Romanian Pinot Noir. I could at least put Ms Lewry at ease on that matter.

The grey-suited gentleman who told you that Sainsbury's are no longer stocking Romanian Pinot Noir is talking through that portion of his apparel which he uses to sit on. I can assure you that Sainsbury's will be stocking Romanian Pinot Noir for some time to come.

However, it is true that the bastards are no longer stocking the Auslese in half-bottles. But there is a lovely half-bottle of a more concentrated sweet wine, the Muscat de Rivesaltes, and you might look out for that. As far as I know no other supermarket stocks half-bottles of Auslese.

When I last heard from Fiona in July 1995, she informed me that she was still enjoying the Romanian Pinot Noir. Incidentally, I once offered to redesign the label of this wine in return for a lifetime's supply, but Sainsbury's never took up the offer. That fact alone, says Ms Lewry, ensures that there are always plenty of bottles waiting for her on the shelves!

Unfortunately, I could not offer the same solace to Diana Parry who wrote to me in 1992, with a similar tale to tell about her favourite Sainsbury's tipple which she had first encountered through *Superplonk*.

A cry for help! Since you interested me in Jurancon Sec white wine I have become addicted to it – on my last visit to the Vauxhall Sainsbury's to stock up they told me they no longer sold it. They once said that some years ago and it reappeared. What is the current situation? If it has indeed been discontinued at Sainsbury's can one find it elsewhere? I do hope so. Your *Superplonk* book is invaluable.

Having referred to my Sainsbury's wine list, I confirmed in my reply that the Jurancon Sec had indeed been removed. All I could do for the inconsolable Ms Parry was make her comfortable by suggesting some alternatives such as the Vin de Pays du Gers, Domaine Bordes 1991, Vin de Pays de Cotes de Gascogne (£3.59) or their South African Chenin Blanc. However, none of these rather more fruity alternatives could really be an adequate replacement for the Jurancon Sec which had a racy sort of acidity underpinning it which was delicious and unusual.

In finding the Jurancon Sec in the first place, Ms Parry had given a textbook demonstration on how to use a *Superplonk* recommendation. I was grateful to Mr David Beatt, a Sainsbury's customer from Middlesex, for pointing out a rather basic error in the use of the guide. He wrote in April 1995.

> I have just used your book the wrong way round!!
>
> Let me explain. I went into Sainsbury's and bought a couple of bottles – one a 1989 Madiran – Chateau de Crouseilles. It was undrinkable. Whether that is because it is corked or just bad I am not experienced enough to know. I will be taking it back to the shop tomorrow. Then – belatedly – I decided to see what you thought of it. It was not mentioned. Next time, I will look first – and not buy anything that is not mentioned and recommended in your book.
>
> The other one was a 'Sainsbury's Claret'. I have not yet drunk it, but when I do, I will know what a mark of 13 tastes like.

I was delighted that Mr Beatt has converted to the more conventional way of using the *Superplonk* guide, and trust that his 13-pointer lived up to his expectations.

J Sainsbury plc
Stamford House
Stamford Street
London
SE1 9LL

Tel 0171 921 6000
Fax 0171 921 7925
Internet order http://www.j-sainsbury.co.uk

SEE STOP PRESS SECTION AT END OF BOOK FOR LAST-MINUTE ADDITIONS TO THIS RETAILER'S RANGE.

ARGENTINIAN WINE   RED

Bright Brothers Malbec, Las Palmas 1992   `16` `D`
A big, rich, soupy wine with lots of berried fruit flavour.
Out-Cahors Cahors. Very impressive and broad-shouldered.

**Mendoza Cabernet Sauvignon/Malbec
Peter Bright, Sainsbury's**   `15` `B`
Bargain. Great big soft fruity bargain, with an edge of serious
dryness and haute couture styling.

Mendoza Country Red, Sainsbury's   `15.5` `B`
Delicious fruit with a lovely bright touch on the finish – like
shine on an apple. But this wine is no hard fruit. It is all plums.
Lovely throat-charming liquid.

**Mendoza Pinot Noir & Syrah 1995,
Sainsbury's**   `13.5` `C`
Top seventy-five stores. Interesting revolution suggested here: an
amalgam of the Cote d'Or and the Rhone. Do the Burgundians
a favour if nothing else and resurrect traditional practices.

**Mendoza Sangiovese & Cabernet 1995,
Sainsbury's**   `13.5` `B`
Top seventy-five stores. The sangiovese softens the blow of the
cabernet to nice, leathery effect. Great with offal.

ARGENTINIAN WINE   WHITE

Mendoza Country Rose Wine, Sainsbury's   `11` `B`
Selected stores.

Mendoza Country White Wine, Sainsbury's `15` `B`

Lots of rich fruit, comfortingly well packaged and smooth.

Tupungato Chenin Chardonnay Peter Bright, Sainsbury's `14.5` `C`

Lovely refreshing wine with balanced fruit. Delicious with rich fish dishes.

AUSTRALIAN WINE RED

Australian Cabernet Sauvignon 1994, Sainsbury's `14` `C`

Gently soupy wine which turns fresh and fruity on the finish.

Australian Red Wine, Sainsbury's `16` `B`

Nice touch of dusty drawers on the aroma of the fruit, which is full and plummy, sunny and ripe. Lovely rich fruit with gentle tannins. Good with roasts and cheeses.

Eileen Hardy Shiraz 1990 `13.5` `E`

Expensive toy for jaded executives who enjoy keeping a picture of an old lady locked in their cellars whilst the tannins develop. Big wine to see in the year AD 2000.

Hardys Nottage Hill Cabernet Sauvignon/ Shiraz 1994 `15` `C`

Classic rich Aussie with an insouciant touch of dry fruit.

Hardys Stamp Series Shiraz/Cabernet Sauvignon 1995 `14` `C`

Rich and soft – slightly soupy. A good glug.

Jacob's Creek Shiraz Cabernet 1994   `15` `C`

Delicious – as good as it's ever been and well worth the price –
rich, deep, softly textured.

Lindemans Bin 45 Cabernet Sauvignon 1994   `15` `D`

Seems more insistently rich than previous vintages. Quite
deliciously cheeky. This Aussie classic offers excellent value
for under a fiver.

Orlando RF Cabernet Sauvignon 1992   `14.5` `C`

Touch of beefiness here and velvet tannins. Too soft? For claret
die-hards yes. Not for me.

Penfolds Bin 2 Shiraz/Mourvedre 1994   `15.5` `C`

Penfolds Bin 389 Cabernet/Shiraz 1993   `15` `E`

Husky fruit which will develop better over the next eighteen
months.

Penfolds Kalimna Shiraz Bin 28 1993   `16` `E`

Typical Penfolds red. That is, modelled on Bordeaux for
dryness, Rhone for flavour, Chianti for earthiness and Navarre
for richness. This geographical tour-de-fruit equals one Barossa
Valley. Top sixty stores only.

Penfolds Koonunga Hill Shiraz Cabernet 1993   `13.5` `D`

Peter Lehmann Vine Vale Shiraz 1994   `16` `C`

Rivetingly rich flavour – it nails the tongue to the roof until it
screams with pleasure. Selected stores.

Pewsey Vale Cabernet Sauvignon, Eden Valley 1994   `12.5` `E`

Rosemount Estate Cabernet Sauvignon 1994   `14` `D`

Smooth, perhaps too smooth – it has flavour and polish but lacks character and verve. But it must rate 14 because of its soupy richess.

Rosemount Estate Cabernet/Shiraz 1994   `15.5` `D`

Almost totally brilliant. It's a lovely wine from the start (smell) through the middle layers of soft rich fruit and only fails by a whisker to produce a grandstand finish.

Rosemount Shiraz/Cabernet 1995   `15` `C`

Such smoothness and velvet-textured fruit. A gentility of fruit which surprises and delights.

Rothbury Estate South East Australian Cabernet Sauvignon 1993   `13.5` `D`

The ripeness of the fruit is restrained by the drying, softening tannins. Finishes a touch diffidently. Pricey.

St Hallett Cabernet Sauvignon/Cabernet Franc/Merlot 1992   `16` `D`

Echoes of mint and licorice to the rich edge of the fruit, which is seductively soft.

Tarrawingee Grenache, Barossa Valley, Sainsbury's   `16` `C`

Top seventy-five stores only. Wonderful rich flavour. Raspberry-tinged and delicious.

Tarrawingee Shiraz Cabernet, Sainsbury's   `13` `B`

Sweet, soft fruit.

Tarrawingee Shiraz Mourvedre, Sainsburys `12` `C`

Hints at excitement then throws it away with indecisive balance and muted fruit.

Tim Knappstein Cabernet Merlot 1991, Clare Valley `16` `D`

Lovely chocolatey finish on this soft, rich, fruity wine. Has complexity, flavour and forceful style.

Tyrrells Cabernet Merlot, South Australia 1994 `14` `D`

Selected stores. Flavoursomeness of the kind which reminds the well-travelled boozer of odd parts of Bordeaux rather than Oz – but it does have a softness on the finish uncharacteristic of the former region.

Wynns Cabernet Sauvignon, Coonawarra 1991 `14.5` `E`

Elegant, nicely textured (fruit and tannins come thick but not fast), flavourful. Top sixty-nine stores only.

AUSTRALIAN WINE WHITE

Australian Chardonnay, Sainsbury's `14.5` `C`

Only a suggestion of the bruising Aussie fruit of yesteryear. Has elegance and refined bite.

Australian Semillon Sauvignon 1995, Sainsbury's `13.5` `C`

Selected stores.

Australian White Wine, Sainsbury's `12` `B`

Mean on the fruit a bit.

245

Barramundi SE Australian Semillon/Chardonnay

Rich, fruit-salad nose. Lots of pineapple acidity and great, swinging melon/mango fruit. Smashing wine to let the heart soar.

Hill-Smith Estate Chardonnay 1994 14 D

Lovely aroma. It demands you at least sip it. But you want to quaff it rather. And this leads to ripe melon fruit with a smoky edge.

Hunter Valley Chardonnay Denman Estate 1994

Balanced, flavourful, classy. The fruit has depth without drowning the tastebuds.

Jacob's Creek Dry Riesling 1994 13 C

Pleasant fish 'n' chips wine.

Jacob's Creek Semillon/Chardonnay 1994

Jacob's Creek Chardonnay 1994

A reliable performer. No tricks. No gimmicks. Good fruit.

Lindemans Bin 65 Chardonnay 1994

Good as ever it was. Oily, ripe, balanced, very fruity. Lovely with grilled chicken.

Lindemans Padthaway Chardonnay 1994 15 E

Lovely woody, fruity wine. Lots of flavour and personality. Top fifty stores only.

Mick Morris Liqueur Muscat, Rutherglen (half bottle)

Top thirty-six stores only. Liquid corduroy impregnated with honey and soft fruits. a textured miracle of thickness and deep deep flavour.

Penfolds Barrel Fermented Chardonnay, South Australia 1993 `16` `D`

Superb wood/fruit/acid harmony. Selected stores.

Penfolds Koonunga Hill Chardonnay 1994 `14.5` `C`

Still one of the best branded Aussie chardonnays in spite of the fearsome fiver staring it in the face.

Rosemount Estate Chardonnay 1995 `16` `D`

Beautiful controlled fruit with vivacity and restraint. This paradox is Rosemount's hallmark.

Rosemount Estate Chardonnay/Semillon 1994 `15.5` `D`

Wonderful accompaniment to smoked salmon.

Rosemount Show Reserve Chardonnay 1994 `15.5` `E`

An elegant wood/fruit combo which pulsates with subdued fruit without even becoming too livid or lush. Very classy stuff.

Sainsbury's Australian White Wine Box (3-litre box) `12` `F`

57p a glass for an Australian white wine? Fair do's – although a wine this quiet and controlled is a tame one.

Saltram Chardonnay 1995 `15.5` `C`

Big, generous, warm, sunny wine bursting with flavour. Has a wonderful saucy (i.e. cheeky) finish on rich, melony, semi-tropical fruit. Great with chicken or Thai food. Has an eccentricity of flavour which would horrify white burgundy drinkers. Lovely!

Saltram Classic Semillon 1994

Flavoursome fruit which finishes soft. Rather a restrained, comforting wine. Selected stores.

Tarrawingee Riesling/Gewurztraminer

Musky, rich, soft to finish with a gentle, exotic spiciness, this is a terrific bottle for mildly spiced oriental food. Great fun.

Tarrawingee Semillon/Chardonnay, Sainsbury's

Lots of deep, rich, peach, pawpaw and melon fruit.

Wynns Coonawarra Chardonnay 1993

Top eighty stores only. Not a rich wine but a fruity one in a quiet but determined way. Touch expensive.

Wynns Coonawarra Riesling 1993

Try it and dare say 'I don't like riesling' afterwards. Only a faint mineral tinge on the finish of rich fruit hints at its grape variety.

AUSTRIAN WINE — WHITE

Lenz Moser Gruner Veltliner 1994

Not hugely fruity or demonstrative (it's rather restrained and Viennese, to be precise) but it is attractively crisp and clean – and very well priced. Selected stores.

Lenz Moser Selection Gruner Veltliner 1995 [13] C

Selected stores.

BULGARIAN WINE RED

Bulgarian Cabernet Sauvignon 1993, Oak Aged, Russe Region, Sainsbury's
15 B

Oodles of tastebud-lashing soft fruit. A pasta wine and a huge bargain.

Bulgarian Cabernet Sauvignon, Sainsbury's (3-litre box)
15.5 F

Young fruit with lots of vim and gusto allied to polished, smooth, flavour-filled depth of fruit which is both intense, gluggable, and very good with food. A delicious clean red.

Bulgarian Merlot 1993, Oak Aged, Liubimetz Region, Sainsbury's
16 B

Seriously dry-finishing fruit (plummy and soft). Terrific flavour and class for the money.

Bulgarian Merlot, Iambol Region 1995
14.5 C

Lovely plummy fruit with a chewy outer texture. Charming wine. Selected stores.

Bulgarian Reserve Gamza, Lovico Suhindol Region 1990
15 B

Soft plums, rich and drily edged.

Bulgarian Reserve Merlot, Lovico Suhindol 1991
14 B

Dry and outstanding with rich, savoury foods.

Bulgarian Vintners Yantra Valley Cabernet Sauvignon 1990
15.5 B

Real flavour and style here with the dry coating nicely counterpointing the soft rich middle fruitiness. Selected stores.

249

Country Red Russe Cabernet Sauvignon/ Cinsault, Sainsbury's (1.5 litres) | 15.5 | D

Brilliant: dry, textured, chewy, savoury, firm, fruity.

Country Wine, Suhindol Merlot/Gamza Sainsbury's | 12 | B

Reserve Cabernet Sauvignon Iambol Region 1991, Sainsbury's | 15 | C

Dark, rich, well-structured, fully flavoured, dry yet rounded and very smooth to finish – this is some wine for the money.

Special Reserve Cabernet Sauvignon Iambol Region 1991, Sainsbury's | 15.5 | C

Vivid fruit with a dry, savoury edge. Classy, balanced, terrific value.

Special Reserve Cabernet Sauvignon, Suhindol 1991 | 14 | C

Fresh-edged but dry. Brisk fruit, good with pastas.

Svischtov Special Reserve Cabernet Sauvignon 1988 | 16 | C

Gentle mintiness on the nose, rich fruit with dark, swirling cherry and blackcurrant flavours and a soft finish. An elegant, flavourful wine of restrained class and no little style.

Vintage Blend Oriachovitza Merlot and Cabernet Sauvignon Reserve 1990 | 16.5 | B

Vibrantly rich fruit mingling soft blackcurrants and dried raspberry with firm-edged acids. Terrific bargain.

Zlatovrach Reserve Mavrud, 1991 | 16.5 | B

Amazing richness and style for the money. Has a delightful

tannic shroud cloaking the fruit giving it texture and real style. Selected stores.

BULGARIAN WINE WHITE

Bulgarian Chardonnay, Lyaskovets, Sainsbury's

Terrific value. Lots of rich fruit and style. Superb fish wine which is classier than many a feeble chablis.

Bulgarian Country Wine Muskat and Ugni Blanc, Sainsbury's

Very attractive, powder-compact soft fruit undercut by a tingling freshness. Good value.

Bulgarian Misket, Slaviantzi 1993

Bulgarian Oak-fermented Chardonnay, Slaviantzi 1994

Selected stores.

Chardonnay Reserve Khan Krum 1993, Sainsbury's

Gentle opulence, subtle fatness, soft flesh. A comforting cannibalistic bottle. Selected stores.

Rousse Rikat Special Selection 1994

Selected stores. Clean, fresh, fruity and fulfilling as a quaffable aperitif.

Vintage Blend Khan Krum Chardonnay and Sauvignon Blanc Reserve 1992

Bargain richness and flavour. Versatile with food – from fish to fowl. Not at all stores.

CHILEAN WINE RED

Chilean Cabernet Sauvignon, Sainsbury's

Serious hints of class here, with its vegetal, minty undertones. These are very subtle but they do give the soft fruit complexity and style.

Chilean Cabernet Sauvignon/Merlot, Sainsbury's 23/3/97

Bargain. Elegant, soft, fruitily benign and satisfying.

Chilean Merlot, Sainsbury's

Rich and rampant, very dry and will soften quickly in bottle over the next few months.

Chilean Merlot San Fernando 1994, Sainsbury's

Has a hint of mint to go with your grilled lamb chops.

Chilean Red, Sainsbury's

Ripe plums, fresh and yielding. Lots of flavour here with a shroud of characterful dryness. Delicious food wine.

Santa Carolina Cabernet Sauvignon Reserva, Maipo 1991

Top seventy-five stores. Quietly stylish and nicely fruity.

Santa Carolina Merlot Reserva, Maipo Valley 1993

Humdinging fruitiness of the quietly impactful sort. Top seventy stores only.

Santa Rita '120' Pinot Noir, Casablanca 1994

Top seventy-five stores. Better flavour and value here for pinot freaks than in any of the store's pricey burgundies.

Villa Montes Oak-Aged Cabernet Sauvignon Gran Reserva, Curico 1992

Impressively soft, finely woven and classy. Complex deliciousness.

CHILEAN WINE WHITE

Caliterra Chardonnay 1992

Lovely melon/lemon style. Again, not huge. A touch expensive but it has got style.

Chilean Chardonnay 1993, Sainsbury's

Brilliant potency of woody rich fruit and acidity. Polished, cheap, complex, flavourful, striking – this is a great chardonnay for under £4.

Chilean Sauvignon Blanc, Maipo Valley, Sainsbury's

Creamy, nutty quality to the fruit here. Very attractive.

Chilean Sauvignon Semillon, Sainsbury's

Chilean White, Sainsbury's 21/3/97

So simple! Take rich fruit and elegant acidity and weld them firmly together. Here you have this bargain bottle of elegant wine.

Santa Carolina Sauvignon Blanc Reserva 1994 `15.5` `C`

Clean, with a lovely rich oily texture on the fruit. Lovely wine. Impressive balance. Top ten stores only.

Santa Rita Chardonnay, Estate Reserve 1994 `16` `D`

Demurely rich and fine with an aristocratic feel. Easy to drink, extremely elegant and fruity.

ENGLISH WINE RED

Denbies Surrey Red 1992 `10` `C`

Surprisingly fruity for an English red wine, but poor value. If it was £1.99 it might be acceptable but even at this price it would only score 13. Sentiment has bought it, and sentiment will move it off the shelf. To compare it, say, with the store's 1991 Copertino Riserva at 5p less is to compare Kiri Te Kanawa with a bookie shouting the odds.

ENGLISH WINE WHITE

Denbies Estate English Table Wine, 1992 `10` `C`

Hastings, Carr Taylor Medium Dry 1993 `14` `B`

Lamberhurst Sovereign Medium Dry `10` `B`

Three Choirs 1992, English Table Wine `14` `C`

Has a fat touch of off-dryness that I'm less convinced about than I was.

Wootton Trinity, English Wine, Somerset

Nothing wrong with this: flavour, balance, style. Delicious.

FRENCH WINE

Beaujolais, Sainsbury's 11 B

Beaujolais-Villages, Les Roches Grillees 1995 12 C

Beaune 1er Cru 'Clos de la Feguine' Domaine J. Prieur 1992 14 G

This has class, weight and style. But the price is high – even for this attractive level of gamy fruit. Top forty-four Fine Wine stores only.

Bergerac Rouge, Sainsbury's 12 B

Bergerie de l'Arbous, Coteaux du Languedoc 1993

The richness of this wine is soft and textured like velvet with flashes of denim. It's beautiful, deep and very sexy.

Bordeaux Rouge, Sainsbury's

Light, cheap, decent.

Bourgogne Hautes Cotes de Nuits, Les Dames Huguettes 1993

Expensive but tasty. Hammy, smoky fruit. Selected stores.

Bush Vine Grenache, Coteaux du Languedoc 1995

Has a lovely dry edge to raunchily flavoursome fruit of character. Selected stores.

Cabernet Sauvignon Syrah VdP d'Oc, Sainsbury's

A fruity yet dry pizza plonk.

Cabernet Sauvignon VdP d'Oc 1995, Sainsbury's

Good solid stuff. Selected stores.

Cahors, Sainsbury's

14 B

Bargain price for a rich dark wine which is brilliant with grilled food. Chewy like coal, but a lot softer to swallow. Excellent.

Chais Baumiere Cabernet Sauvignon Vin de Pays d'Oc 1993

Again, not as richly compelling as the previous vintage. What's going on? Are the yields too high?

Chais Baumiere Merlot 1993

13 C

Chais Baumiere Syrah, VdP d'Oc 1994

Dry, tobacco-ey, rich-edged yet dry, and has real southern character and warmth. Classy bottle of food-friendly fruit.

Chateau Beychevelle, 4e Cru Classe St Julien 1991

Glorious aroma of old books and wood. Classic structure and real weight. Will drink splendidly for seven to eight years. Top six Fine Wine stores only.

Chateau Bois de la Clide, Bordeaux 1994

Classic claret: dry, touch austere and proud, a hint of charcoal. Fruity? Not a lot. But with roast meat, it bursts into life. Selected stores.

Chateau Carsin, Premieres Cotes de Bordeaux 1993

Has evolving tannins yet to ripen fully and make this a more exciting wine. I do not know why the back label should say drink this wine within two years as I would think it better in three.

Chateau Chasse-Spleen, Moulis en Medoc 1990

14 G

At only six stores, this wine will be superb in five to seven years. It is impressive, with its herby, cherry-plum fruit, but very expensive.

Chateau Coutelin-Merville St Estephe 1990

14 F

Dry and rich with real depth to the tannic richness – but this is ready to drink with roast, herb-drenched lamb and most rewarding it would prove so partnered. Expensive.

Chateau d'Aigueville, Cotes du Rhone 1994

Soft, rich, deep, yet lively and characterful.

Chateau de Gourgazaud, Minervois 1992

Chateau de la Tour, Bordeaux Rouge 1994

14 D

Selected stores. Real frisky claret with lingering fruit.

Chateau de Roquetaillade la Grange, Graves 1988

16 D

Serious stuff – leathery, rich, concentrated. Dry, textured, perfect with a steak au poivre.

Chateau de Rully Rouge, Rodet 1993

12 E

Top forty-four stores only.

Chateau des Capitans, Julienas 1994

11 D

Chateau du Quint, Puisseguin 1994 `15` `D`

Has a hint of chocolate on its dry tannic edge. The fruit is friendly, considering the wine's youth. Classy and elegant, it will carry itself well for a few years yet. Selected stores.

Chateau Ducluzeau, Listrac 1992 `13.5` `E`

A rich, dry, earthy merlot which should be cellared for at least two years more to put on more points.

Chateau Ferriere 3e Cru Margaux 1993 `11` `G`

Adequate. Adequate? £15 is a lot for adequacy. Top nineteen Fine Wine stores only.

Chateau Fournas Bernadotte, Haut-Medoc 1990 `16` `D`

A very smooth package with enough personality from the wood and the tannins to provide complexity and flavour. Classy.

Chateau Grand Bourdieu, Bordeaux Superieur 1992 `12` `C`

Pleasant soft savoury tannins to the fruit.

Chateau Grand Puy Ducasse, 5e Cru Classe Pauillac 1991 `13.5` `G`

Like it – to drink. But to buy? Maybe in 2001. Top forty-four Fine Wine stores only.

Chateau Haut Faugeres, Grand Cru St Emilion 1990 `14` `E`

Fancy fruit – soft, smooth, polite. Decant for one and a half hours before drinking.

Chateau Hauterive le Haut, Corbieres 1992 `15` `C`

A wine to keep for five years and also to drink now with roast foods. It has great acid/fruit balance. Not at all stores.

Chateau la Gurgue, Margaux 1990   `12` `E`

Chateau la Louviere, Pessac-Leognan 1993   `13` `G`

Top nineteen Fine Wine stores only.

Chateau La Rose Coulon, Bordeaux 1990   `14` `D`

Excellent, dry, soundly constructed fruit. Has spiciness, style and some depth.

Chateau La Vieille Cure, Fronsac 1992   `15.5` `E`

Rich, savoury, lovely soft tannins.

Chateau la Voulte Gasparets, Corbieres 1991, Sainsbury's   `14` `C`

Aromatically wonderful (like an aged, hammy beaujolais), soft fruit, rather a flattish finish.

Chateau Lagrange, 3e Cru Classe St Julien 1988   `12.5` `G`

Top six Fine Wine stores only.

Chateau Lagrange 3e Cru Classe St Julien 1992   `13` `G`

Give it two to three more years at least. Top forty-four Fine Wine stores.

Chateau Lalande d'Auvion, Medoc 1990   `14.5` `D`

A mature claret perfectly full and fruity with the serious dryness of the Medoc.

Chateau Le Boscq Les Vieilles Vignes, Medoc Cru Bourgeois 1990   `14` `E`

Dry, deep, flavourful and expressive. Top 100 stores only.

Chateau Lynch Bages, 5e Cru Classe
Pauillac 1991   14.5 | G

Has that superb Pauillac combination of mature, rich dry fruit which is beautifully textured, bold, striking. Top ten Fine Wine stores only.

Chateau Marquis de Terme, 4e Cru Classe
Margaux 1992   13 | F

Classy, yet too pricey. Top forty-four Fine Wine stores only.

Chateau Marsau, Bordeaux Cotes de
Francs 1994   15 | C

A 100% merlot, from a hamlet near St Emilion, which puts to shame many clarets costing three times more. It is dry, rich, very savoury, and with the potential to age well for two years more, will attain greater softness and complexity. Selected stores.

Chateau Maucaillou, Moulis 1989   13 | F

Chateau Poujeaux, Moulis-en-Medoc 1990   15 | G

Chateau Roc de Grimon, Cotes de
Castillon 1993   12.5 | C

Selected stores.

Chateau Rolland, Bordeaux 1992   14 | C

Has fruit and flavour and real Bordeaux style for not a lot of money. Superb roast food wine.

Chateau Saint Bonnet, Medoc 1990   14 | E

Selected stores. Real hints of class here. Will improve for a few years yet or drink now with roast lamb.

Chateau Salvanhiac, St Chinan 1993,
Sainsbury's   13.5 | C

Chateau Segonzac, Premieres Cotes de Blaye, Cuvee Barrique 1991 | 15 | C

Structured, tannic (yet soft), lots of purposeful fruit. Excellent fruit wine (and cheese). Lush yet savoury edge. Good value from Bordeaux!

Chateau Suduiraut, Premier Cru Classe 1990 (half bottle) | 13 | F

Chateau Vieux Chevrol, Lalande de Pomerol 1990 | 12.5 | E

Top twenty-five stores only.

Chateauneuf-du-Pape, Les Galets Blancs 1993 | 13 | E

Chinon, Domaine du Colombier 1993 | 14 | D

A sleeper. It's only just waking up and shaking the fruit into action.

Claret Cuvee Prestige, Sainsbury's | 13.5 | C

Good tannins and fruit. Good with roast meats.

Claret, Sainsbury's | 13.5 | C

Some richness, some smoothness. Some.

Classic Selection Brouilly 1994, Sainsbury's | 13 | E

Not bad chilled. But not, at nigh on eight quid, great either. Top seventy-five stores only.

Classic Selection Margaux 1993, Sainsbury's | 13 | D

Soft – too soft? Selected stores.

Classic Selection Saint Emilion 1993, Sainsbury's `14` `E`

Exactly what it says it is. A classic St Emilion. Top sixty-nine stores only.

Clos Magne Figeac, Saint Emilion 1993 `14` `E`

An expressive bottle of dry, earthy fruit with an imperious reminder of its rich pedigree as it finishes in the throat. Delicious with roast lamb.

Comte de Signargues, Cotes du Rhone Villages 1993 `15` `C`

Rich, rounded, polished, soft – lush and firm at the same time in that unique Rhone way, with just an echo of earthiness.

Corbieres Chateau Bories-Azeau 1994 `15.5` `C`

Delicious, dark, dry fruit with plum and cherry undertones and a spicy finish. Excellent value. Great with rich food. Not a heavy wine, but robust, muscled and characterful. Selected stores.

Corbieres, Sainsbury's (3-litre box) `13.5` `F`

Young, fresh, fruity.

Cornas Les Serres 1990 `15` `F`

Has a lovely dried cherry/plum touch on the finish. Top thirty stores only.

Costieres de Nimes Les Garrigues 1994 `15.5` `C`

A rather light hearted Nimois, this one. But this gentility of richness and smoothness of manner is dry without austerity, fruity without being flabby, and earthy without being cloddish. The soft fruit centre is well held by the tannins.

Cote Rotie Brune et Blonde 1994 `18` `G`

Top twenty-five Fine Wine stores only. A great wine which is worth £18. Few bottles left.

Cotes du Luberon Rouge, Sainsbury's `12.5` `B`

Better than a lot of beaujolais.

Cotes du Rhone, Sainsbury's `14` `B`

Outstanding value for a soft, earthy fruit wine of some character.

Cotes du Rhone Villages, Beaumes de Venise `13` `C`

Cotes du Rhone Villages Saint Gervais, Laurent Charles Brotte 1990 `14` `C`

Fruity, soft, simple.

Cotes du Roussillon Villages, Saint Vincent 1990, Sainsbury's `14` `B`

Very dark rich fruit on display here with an admirably balanced overall style. Dry, full, very good with roasts and grills. Almost vies with Australia for softness and depth of colour. Not a drink for the faint-hearted, needs food, etc.

Crozes-Hermitage, Sainsbury's `13` `C`

Dry and slatey – like slurping blackcurrant juice off a roof tile.

Crozes-Hermitage Les Jalets, Jaboulet Aine 1994 `13.5` `E`

Pricey, a touch too accommodatingly phoney on the finish. Top fifty stores only.

Cuvee Prestige Bordeaux Rouge, Sainsbury's `11` `C`

Selected stores.

Cuvee Prestige Cotes du Rhone, Sainsbury's

Selected stores.

Domaine de la Baume Estate Merlot, VdP d'Oc 1994

Has such strident, deeply committed complexity for the money it almost defies belief. Massive flavour.

Domaine de la Cessane Grenache/Syrah, St Chinian 1993

Lovely chewy texture which keeps the fruit long on the palate and in the throat. The fruit is handsomely rich, not hugely deep but impactful, and the dusting of tannins is the exciting element.

Domaine de la Grangerie Mercurey 1991

Some rich-edged fruit, meaty and fulfilled – helped by soft tannins. Expensive idea but keep till the end of the century.

Domaine de Pujol Minervois, Cave de la Cessanne 1993

Good savoury shroud to the vaguely blackcurrant fruit. Has rustic character but is well-mannered and charmingly direct.

Domaine de Sours Rouge 1993

Selected stores.

Domaine Dury Millot, Paul Dugenais Meursault 1992

Too much! Too much!! Too much!!! (And not enough fruit or complexity in return.)

Domaine Joseph de Bel Air Pinot Noir, VdP d'Oc 1994

Top forty stores only.

Domaine le Cazal Minervois 1992   15.5   B

Really deliciously polished plummy fruit of great smoothness.

Domaine Rio Magno Pinot Noir, VdP l'Ile
de Beaute 1994   12   C

Pleasant, inoffensive, not rude in the least. Selected stores.

Domaine Saint Apollinaire Cotes du Rhone
1991, Sainsbury's   13   D

Domaine Sainte Anne, St Chinian 1992   11   B

Domaine St Marc, Syrah VdP d'Oc 1995   16   C

Rich, plummy undertones, ripe cassis overtones – this is a corker
of a syrah. Stylish, deep, soft, velvet-textured. Selected stores.

Echezeaux Grand Cru, Dagenais 1993   12.5   G

Some flavour and depth here.

Faugeres   14   B

A healthily fruity red wine from southern France, perfect with
sausage and mash. Some excellent on-form fruit here.

Fitou Chateau de Segure 1993   15   C

Soft, elegant, rich, superbly well polished. A stylish bottle of
Fitou. Selected stores.

Fitou, Les Gueches 1994   15.5   C

Has a delightful tannic edge (superbly rustic) yet the fruit is soft
and deliciously willing to please.

Fleurie Auguste Berthilies 1994   13   D

Fleurie, Georges Duboeuf 1994   10.5   D

Fleurie La Madone, 1995 `13` `E`

Soft and fruity. Some style here – but the price! Selected stores.

Gevrey-Chambertin, Burguet 1992 `12` `G`

Vague hints of what a decent burgundy should be.

Gevrey-Chambertin, Maurice Chenu 1993 `12` `F`

Top forty-five stores only.

Gigondas Tour du Queyron, 1990 `15` `E`

Expensive but expansive. Big, hearty, huge, smoky fruit. Concentrated soft centre. Lovely wine.

Graves Selection Sainsbury's, Louis Vialard `13` `C`

Good, soft fruit.

Hermitage Monier de 'La Sizeranne' 1991 `14.5` `G`

Worth £20? Well, it is delicious, complex, individual and cleverly flavoured. Top six Fine Wine stores only.

James Herrick Cuvee Simone VdP d'Oc 1995 `17.5` `C`

Superb classy stuff. Has texture, weight, balance, length and an overall feel of great natural rich hedgerow fruitiness. Top 100 stores only.

La Baume Syrah VdP d'Oc 1995, Sainsbury's `16.5` `C`

Superbly sunny and rich, warmly fruity and deeply inviting. This is a wonderful bottle of exciting Southern fruit and great charm and class. Selected stores.

La Source de Vignelaure 1994 `14` `C`

Better than previous vintages. Good rich fruit dusted by gentle tannins; excellent balance and a firm, fruity finish.

Les Forts de la Tour, Pauillac 1985 `10` `H`

A complete rich idiot's folly. Top six Fine Wine stores only.

Madiran, Chateau de Crouseilles 1990 `15` `D`

Rich, soft, rewardingly fruity, gently rustic, this has great charm and bite. Selected stores.

Meursault Rouge Clos de Mazeray 1992 `13` `G`

Hugely expensive for the meagreness of vegetal fruit on offer but having said that the texture does preside well over food. Top forty-four stores only.

Minervois, Sainsbury's `13` `B`

Soft fruit with a good smack of acidic freshness on the finish.

Morgon G. Duboeuf 1994 `13` `C`

Has a juicy edge to its richness.

Moulin a Vent, Cave Kuhnel 1994 `10` `E`

Nuits St Georges Premier Cru Les Damodes 1993 `10` `F`

Top twenty stores only.

Peter Sichel Selection, Oak Aged Bordeaux 1990 `14.5` `C`

Red Burgundy Pinot Noir, Sainsbury's `11` `C`

Sainsbury's Red Burgundy `12` `C`

Saint Joseph, Prieure Beaulieu 1991 `13` `D`

Selected stores. Some dark fruity substance here, at a price. But the fruit is simple for the money.

Santenay Premier Cru, Clos Rousseaux 1989

St Chinian Les Mourgues 1993

Handsome ruggedness without rattling the gently earthy, softly spicy fruit. Selected stores.

Vacqueyras, Paul Jaboulet-Isnard 1990

Has delicious texture but it's somewhat expensive.

Valencia Oak Aged, Sainsbury's

I've tasted fruit-drops with more character (to begin with) but then this bottle suddenly whacks it to you on the finish. Fun glugging.

Valreas Domaine de la Bellane, Cotes du Rhone Villages 1993 (Organic)

Delicious depth and flavour and its earthiness and warmth are controlled, never fierce, and most attractive. Top sixty stores only.

Vieux Chateau Landon, Medoc 1990

A 'bas' medoc it must be said, not an 'haut'. And so much the better. This is a totally mature, light wine with aroma, body and afterburn – but it is dry fruit which burns and it is a most caressing flame.

Vin de Pays de l'Ardeche, Sainsbury's

Simple, dry, cherry-edged. Good chilled.

Vin de Pays de l'Aude Rouge, Sainsbury's

A full-flavoured meaty red plonk.

Vin de Pays de la Cite de Carcassonne Merlot 1995, Sainsbury's

Has a dry charcoal edge to the brambly fruit.

Vin de Pays des Bouches du Rhone, Sainsbury's

Dry but fruity, simply gluggable but seriously good with roast lamb, this is a rustic character with smooth manners and some charm.

Vin de Pays du Gard Red, Sainsbury's (25 cl)

A quarter-litre can. Good fruit for picnics (and excellent chilled).

Vin Rouge de France, Sainsbury's (1.5 litres)

Plastic-bottled but far from plastic-fruited – good, simple, rustic glugging.

Vosne Romanee, Georges Noellat 1989

Greatly wrinkled but amusing – especially in the arrogance of its price.

FRENCH WINE WHITE

Alsace Gewurztraminer, Sainsbury's

Alsace Pinot Blanc, Sainsbury's

Not a bad price for the real thing: rich-edged, peach/apricot fruit, good acidic background, sound structure.

Bergerac Blanc, Sainsbury's `13` `B`

Blanc Anjou Medium Dry, Sainsbury's `12` `B`

Bordeaux Blanc Cuvee Prestige, Sainsbury's `11` `C`

Selected stores.

Bordeaux Blanc, Sainsbury's `12` `C`

Bordeaux Clairet (Rose) `12` `C`

Some dry, attractive fruit here. Selected stores.

Cabernet Rose de Loire, VdP du Jardin de la France 1995 `11.5` `C`

Selected stores.

Chablis 1er Cru Montee de Tonnerre, Brocard 1993 `13.5` `E`

One of the better chablis – even at a tenner. Top fifty stores only.

Chablis Domaine Sainte Celine, Brocard 1993, Sainsbury's `10` `D`

Chablis Grand Cru, Preuses, Jeanne Paule Filippi 1990 `15` `G`

More in the mersault style than pure chablis.

Chais Baumiere Sauvignon Blanc Vin de Pays d'Oc 1994 `15.5` `C`

Elegant, firm, poised – a balanced s.b. of decisively modern wine-making techniques but with a touch of good old-fashioned softness and French 'country' character.

Chardonnay VdP d'Oc, Cave de la Cessane 1995　16　C

So firm in its purpose and positively rich depth of flavour, never overdone, nicely poised, that it is a surprise for the money. Selected stores.

Chardonnay VdP d'Oc, Sainsbury's (3-litre box)　12.5　G

Chardonnay Vin de Pays d'Oc, Ryman 1994　16　C

A roast fowl chardonnay. By which I mean there is a lovely gamy edge to the fruit which chimes with chicken.

Chateau Carbonnieux Blanc, AC Pessac-Leognan 1993　12　G

Silly price – even if it is mildly impressive. Top nineteen Fine Wine stores only.

Chateau Carsin, Bordeaux Blanc 1994　16　D

Only fails by a whisker, due to a slight lack of emphasis on the finish, to rate even higher. Has aroma, depth, style, great class and a lovely woody flavour. Selected stores.

Chateau de Davenay, Montagny Premier Cru 1993　12.5　D

Chateau de la Chartreuse Sauternes 1990 (half bottle)　15　E

Gorgeous, unctuously fruity, hugely honeyed beauty of a bottle. Exceptional fruit. Top thirty-eight stores only.

Chateau de Rully Blanc, 1990　10　E

Chateau l'Ortolan, Bordeaux Blanc 1994　14　C

Solid and distinctive by virtue of what it is not rather than what it is. If that sounds a rather backhanded compliment I can only add it is a wine of quiet class, decent fruit and good balance. Also, the price is good.

Chateau Les Bouhets, Bordeaux Blanc Sec 1994

Solid rather than exciting. Selected stores.

Chateauneuf-du-Pape, Domaine Andre Brunel 1993

14 E

Expensive but very fine. Very soupy and rich and very deeply attractive. Selected stores.

Chenin Blanc VdP du Jardin de la France 1995

15.5 C

Has all the flashing, metallic finishing fruit of the grape. Selected stores.

Classic Selection Chablis 1994, Sainsbury's

13.5 E

Expensive.

Classic Selection Muscadet de Sevre et Maine Sur Lie 1995, Sainsbury's

10 D

Selected stores.

Classic Selection Pouilly Fuisse 1994, Sainsbury's

13 E

Attractive fruit here. But I don't like £9.95 on the price tag. Selected stores.

Classic Selection Pouilly Fume 1995, Sainsbury's

13 D

Expensive but extremely palatable. Rich, full, energetic, playful – it's a pleasant tipple.

Classic Selection Sancerre 1995, Sainsbury's

Classic Selection Sauternes, Sainsbury's (half bottle)

Not bad, but lousy value when Moscatel de Valencia pitches in at three quid or so. Top seventy-five stores only.

Classic Selection White Burgundy 1993, Sainsbury's

Has decent oily fruit but not eight quid's worth. Selected stores.

Clos St Georges Graves Superieures 1990/91

Try this as an aperitif. It's wonderful even though it's honeyed and toffeed.

Corbieres Blanc, Sainsbury's

Domaine d'Aubian Chardonnay, Fortant de France 1994

Beautifully textured, deep, balanced, handsomely well finished off (and even a bit luxurious), this is a scrumptious chardonnay for the money.

Domaine de Grandchamp Sauvignon Blanc, Bergerac 1994

Classy, vivid, cool. Hints of rich fruit but the freshness is controlled and impressive. Lovely stuff. Top 100 stores only.

Domaine de la Tuilerie Merlot Rose, 1995

The second-best rose in the store. (See p. 284 for the number one.)

Domaine de Sours Rose 1995 `11` `C`

Selected stores.

Domaine St Marc Sauvignon Blanc, VdP d'Oc 1995 `15.5` `C`

Brilliant, characterful bottle of balanced fruit and acid. Fresh, vigorous, charming, fish-friendly, delicious. Selected stores.

Enclos des Lilas Blanc VdP de l'Aude 1995 `14` `B`

Great citric fish wine. Fruity tippling. Selected stores.

Four Terroirs Chardonnay VdP d'Oc 1993 `14.5` `D`

Gaillac Blanc, Sainsbury's `15` `C`

Crisp, nutty, fruity – full of style and flavour. Very well-structured and built. Selected stores.

Gentil 'Hugel', Alsace 1994 `13` `D`

Selected stores.

Grenache Rose VdP de l'Ardeche, Sainsbury's `12` `B`

Gustave Lorentz Riesling Reserve, Alsace 1994 `13.5` `E`

Lemony and fresh – but needs another year on bottle to show of its best. Top seventy stores only.

Hardys Bordeaux Vin Blanc Sec, 1995 `14.5` `C`

A delicious, uncommonly delicious, bordeaux blanc sec. Has a soft undertone of ripe melon. New World in dress, Old World in manners.

Hardys Gaillac Blanc 1995 `13` `C`

Nutty, balanced, perfectly respectable.

Le Lizet Colombard Chardonnay, VdP des Comtes de Tolosan 1994

An excellent clean fish wine. Pert, fresh, demurely fruity.

Macon Blanc Villages, Domaine les Chenevieres 1993

Some depth of flavour here.

Macon Chardonnay, Domaines les Ecuyers 1993

A modest white burgundy of not totally inoffensive price or flavour.

Menetou Salon, Domaine Henri Pelle 1993

Meursault 1er Cru 'Goutte d'Or', Paul Dagenais 1992

Top forty-four Fine Wine stores only.

Meursault Les Perrieres, Premier Cru 1987

Selected stores.

Mme Gary's Block Chardonnay, VdP d'Oc 1994

A most individual yet impressively New World in feel chardonnay with superb balanced, rich fruit. Has a lovely baked touch on the finish. Top sixty-nine stores only.

Montagny Antonin Rodet

Not bad for such an arrogant assumption that the words on the label imply great quality and craftsmanship. Has fruit and flavour and some style. I said some.

Moulin des Groyes, Cotes de Duras
Blanc 1994
`15` `C`

Top 100 stores. What a terrific fish-stew wine we have here. Ripples with melony flavour which is never overdone or too adolescent in feel.

Mouton Cadet Bordeaux Blanc 1994
`12` `D`

Has some flavour.

Muscadet de Sevre et Maine, Sainsbury's
(3-litre box)
`13` `B`

A decent muscadet! In a cardboard box! Shiver my timbers – a double miracle.

Muscadet de Sevres et Maine sur Lie,
Premiere Jean Drouillard, 1995
`14.5` `D`

The best muscadet I've tasted for twenty years. Has full fruit attack and a delicious lemony finish. Great shellfish wine. Top twenty stores only.

Muscadet Sur Lie la Goelette 1994
`11` `C`

Really, compared with the other wines that are currently available, these people should pack up and grow carrots.

Muscat de Beaumes de Venise 1995,
Sainsbury's (half bottle)
`14` `C`

A highly sweet, complex wine of great charm. Selected stores.

Muscat de Saint Jean de Minervois
(half bottle)
`14` `B`

Sweet satin.

Oak Aged Chablis, Madeleine Matthieu
1993, Sainsbury's
`15` `D`

Lots of flavoursome woody fruit. Class act.

Pouilly Fume Figeat 1993   `10` `D`

Premieres Cotes de Bordeaux NV   `11` `C`

**Puligny Montrachet 1er Cru Hameau de
Blagny 1993**   `10` `G`

Top six Fine Wine stores only.

**Puligny Montrachet 1er Cru
'Les Chalumeaux', Paul Dagenais 1992**   `11` `G`

Top forty-four Fine Wine stores only.

**Puligny Montrachet, Domaine Gerard
Chavy 1992**   `14` `F`

Difficult to rate. It is fine, solid, well made, even a touch classy,
but at three times the price of other French chardonnays at
Sainsbury's is it even twice as good? It's only 50 per cent better
than some.

**Rose d'Anjou, VdP du Jardin de la
France 1995**   `12` `C`

Has a faint sweet edge to the crisp acidity. Good with grilled
mackerel.

**Roussanne Barrique Reserve, Galet
Vineyards 1995**   `14` `C`

Has the softness yet roughness of underripe peach. Yet it's a dry
wine. Top 100 stores only.

Sancerre 1993, Sainsbury's   `13.5` `D`

Expensive but not at all bad considering the silly price of so
many underfruited sancerres nowadays. This isn't a bad wine
by any means.

Sancerre Henry Pelle 1994, Sainsbury's `13.5` `E`

New vintage. Drinkable, modern, clean, pricey.

Sancerre, Les Celliers de Ceres 1993 `16` `C`

A miracle! Sound sancerre under a fiver! Indeed, it's better than sound, it's terrific. Few bottles left, though.

Saumur Blanc, Domaine des Hauts de Sanziers 1991 `12` `C`

Lip-puckering curiosity of interest to live shellfish eaters.

Sauvignon Blanc Cave de la Cessanne 1995 `15.5` `C`

A delicious, classically style s.b. of deftly interwoven fruit and acid. Well priced. Top 100 stores only.

Sauvignon Blanc VdP du Jardin de la France 1995 `14` `C`

A most attractive fruity wine – from the 'jardin' indeed. Selected stores.

Sauvignon de St Bris, Bersan 1995, Sainsbury's `13.5` `D`

Classy, austere, a touch unfriendly.

Tokay Pinot Gris, Cave de Ribeauville 1989 `16` `E`

Brilliant apricot aroma. Captivating fruit of great concentration of flavour and complexity and firmness of finish. A superb bottle of wine.

Touraine Sauvignon Blanc, Sainsbury's `10` `B`

Rather fleshless fruit here.

Vin Blanc Medium Dry, Sainsbury's   12.5   B

Excellent step-on-the-way-up to drier styles for the Liebfraumilch fresher.

Vin Blanc Dry, Sainsbury's   13.5   B

Old-fashioned in feel but modern in fruit. Tasty, fresh, simple, good to glug or with fish dishes.

Vin de Pays d'Oc, Sainsbury's   13   B

Good-value clean wine.

Vin de Pays de Gascogne, Domaine Bordes 1995   15   C

Delightful soft fruit with vivacious acidity. Lovely tickle down the throat.

Vin de Pays des Cotes de Gascogne, Sainsbury's   14   B

One of the most attractive white Gascons on sale: lush fruit, fresh and flint-edged. Lovely style for the money.

Vin de Pays du Gard Blanc, Sainsbury's (25 cl)   11   A

Picnic can with a rounded finish – both can and fruit.

Vin de Pays du Gers, Sainsbury's   14   B

A lovely refreshing mouthful. Terrific price for this quality of fruit and structure.

Viognier VdP de l'Ardeche, Duboeuf 1995   14.5   D

Soft apricot-edged fruit with a fresh edge. A delightful viognier of style and class. Top fifty stores only.

Viognier VdP d'Oc, Pere Anselme 1994   14   C

Top seventy-five stores. Dry, polished, hinting at apricot

fruit without fully grasping, but a poised mouthful of fruit nevertheless.

Vouvray, La Couronne des Plantagenets 1994

Pot-pourri on the nostril with an echo of dry honey which is picked up by the rich fruit. Not fully dry, but never sweet, this is a lovely aperitif. Selected stores.

Vouvray, Sainsbury's

Yes, it's sweet but it is delicious and an interesting aperitif. Lovely controlled waxy honeyed fruit.

White Burgundy, Sainsbury's

Touch dull – especially compared with other JS chardonnays at the same price.

GERMAN WINE WHITE

Baden Dry, Sainsbury's

This has a curious woolly aroma but the fruit is delightful and delicious with poached fish.

Bereich Bernkastel, Sainsbury's `11` `B`

Bernkasteler Badstube Riesling Spatlese Von Kesselstatt 1988 `14` `D`

Selected stores. Rich hints of fruit, vivid acidity, good balance and finish. Expensive but classy aperitif.

Binger St Rochuskapelle Spatlese 1993 `12.5` `B`

Dexheimer Doktor Spatlese 1994, Sainsbury's 15 C

Sweet, all right, sweet, yes it's sweet. But the acidity is slightly minerally, so it isn't unbalanced and the fruit has a subtle toffeed crispness. Keep it for five to six years. It'll only get better and rate higher. Or enjoy it as a fruity, rich aperitif, with mild blue cheese. Selected stores.

Erdener Treppchen, Riesling Spatlese 1985 12 D

Not in the class of the previous vintage. Lost its complexity. Selected stores.

Graacher Himmelreich Riesling Spatlese Von Kesselstatt 1988 15 D

Fine fruit and acidity. Lovely delicate balance. Great with aperitif. Good with prawn toast!

Hock, Sainsbury's 10 A

Musty fruit, sharp edge. Also available in a quarter-litre can.

Kabinett Sainsbury's, Dalsheimer Berg Rodenstein 1992 12 B

Kim Milne Riesling 1993, Sainsbury's 14.5 C

Has a hint of the steeliness that this grape in its moselle guise offers but this counterpoints the fruit which, whilst never full, is restrained and most becoming as an aperitif.

Liebfraumilch, Sainsbury's 10 B

Also available in litre bottles.

Morio-Muskat St Georg, Pfalz 11 B

Mosel, Sainsbury's 12 B

Do try it as a summer aperitif or in a spritzer.

Niersteiner Gutes Domtal, Sainsbury's `11` `B`

Reasonable aperitif. Also available in 1.5-litre bottles.

Oppenheimer Krotenbrunnen Kabinett `12` `B`

Good with smoked fish.

Peter Nicolay Bernkasteler
Johannisbrunnchen Rivaner 1992 `11` `C`

Piesporter Goldtropfchen Riesling Spatlese
1990 `16` `E`

Petrol, honey, lime, melon – this is a classic aperitif moselle of
extreme elegance, available only in the top ten stores.

Piesporter Michelsberg, Sainsbury's `12` `B`

Aperitif.

Spatlese Mosel-Saar-Ruwer, Bernkasteler
Kurfurstlay 1992, Sainsbury's `11` `C`

St Ursula Devil's Rock Riesling 1994/5 `15.5` `C`

Delicate true-riesling aroma, delicate acidity and good fruit,
and fresh, mineral-edged finish. Excellent smoked fish wine.
Developing very subtle petrolly undertones. Will improve for
eighteen months or more. Selected stores.

Trocken Rheinhessen, Sainsbury's `11` `B`

Weisenheimer Mandelgarten Ortega
Trockenbeerenauslese 1994 `15` `E`

Sweet molasses and baked apples. Sip it carefully. Top ten
stores only.

Wiltinger Scharzberg Riesling Kabinett,
Moselle 1993 `14` `B`

Light, summer aperitif – good, rich yet subtle. Just undercut by firm, balancing acidity. Has a good peasant elegance about it.

Wormser Liebfrauenmorgen Beerenauslese 1994 `13` `D`

Lay it down for seven to ten years. Wonderful things will result! Available in just the top ten stores.

GREEK WINE RED

Kourtaki VdP de Crete Red `13` `B`

A very bright and eager wine. Good with pastas.

GREEK WINE WHITE

Kourtaki VdP de Crete White `12.5` `B`

Retsina `13` `B`

Resinated and fruity, but also clean to finish and under £3 I find this wine both a bargain and excellent with grilled fish as well as, of course, Greek starters.

HUNGARIAN WINE WHITE

Chapel Hill Estate Barrique Aged Chardonnay 1993 `14.5` `C`

Rich, woody (but gently so), slightly oily-textured wine. Delicious. Selected stores only.

Gyongyos Estate Chardonnay 1994 `12` **B**

Not as lively as previous vintages.

Gyongyos Estate Sauvignon Blanc 1995 `14` **C**

Back to something of its old racy zippiness. A simple sauvignon, but crisp and gently fruity and firmly authentic. Selected stores.

Hungarian Cabernet Sauvignon Rose, Nagyrede Region, Sainsbury's `16` **B**

The best rose for the money I've tasted in ages. Apple-cheeked, raspberry/cherry fruit, soft yet fresh – it's brilliant.

Hungarian Chardonnay, Balaton Boglar `13` **B**

Hungarian Irsai Oliver, Balaton Boglar `14` **B**

Floral fruit of gentility and warmth. Drink it before food or with fish and fennel.

Hungarian Pinot Gris, Nagyrede Region, Sainsbury's `13` **B**

Hungarian Zenit, Nagyrede Estate 1995 `14` **C**

Clean, crisp, with a lemony finish. Can you say as much for your habitual aperitif tipple? Selected stores.

Pinot Blanc, Nagyrede 1992 `12` **B**

Tries hard, but its softly, softly approach to the acidity does not balance out the fruit, so while it is a cheap, drinkable wine it has no hugely attractive features.

ITALIAN WINE RED

Bardolino Classico, Sainsbury's `13` `B`

Cherries and white chocolate.

Barolo, Giordano 1988 `14` `E`

Expensive but possessing great length of flavour (which is fruit of a soft berried nature enhanced by a faint licorice echo).

Barrique Aged Cabernet Sauvignon, Atesino 1993 `16` `C`

Cabernet Sauvignon delle Tre Venezie Geoff Merrill, Sainsbury's `13` `C`

Campomarino Biferno `15` `C`

Has the earthy richness of montepulciano with the mineralised fruit and acid of aglianico. Very good value. Selected stores.

Castelgreve Chianti Classico Reserva 1991 `15.5` `D`

Lovely maturity here. Deeply flavoured and rich. Great food wine. Selected stores.

Chianti 1994, Sainsbury's `14` `C`

Soft, edgily dry, very well-balanced.

Chianti Classico, Briante 1994 `15` `D`

Quite delicious – full and rich, vigorous and deep, yet with a gentle restrained acidic bite.

Chianti Classico Riserva Castello di San Polo in Rosso 1990 `16` `E`

A dark, rich, very dry chianti of classic weight, style and fruit. Very classy. Top forty stores only.

Chianti Classico, Villa Antinori 1990 `12` `D`

Fleshy but not as fulsome as it might be.

Copertino Riserva 1992, Sainsbury's `16` `C`

Brilliant coffee-edged fruit, fully ripe and mature. Lovely texture and fruit.

Lambrusco Rosso, Sainsbury's `12` `B`

Sweet fruity fun with bubbles. For wakes.

Lambrusco Secco Ross 'Vecchia-Modena' `14` `B`

Apple-skin fruit of subdued plumpy charm. It fizzes on the tongue. Great with first-course charcuterie. Top sixty-nine stores only.

Merlot Atesino, K. Milne 1994 `12` `C`

Top seventy-five stores.

Merlot Corvina Vino da Tavola del Veneto, Sainsbury's `14.5` `B`

Delicious drinking. Has gentle quaffing charms, rich fruit bolstered by good acidity.

Montepulciano d'Abruzzo, Sainsbury's `15` `B`

Wonderful soft, zippy, cherry/plum fruit of lush style and drinkability.

Morago Cabernet Sauvignon, VdT del Veneto 1993 `14` `C`

Has a serious side (politically correct cabernet, dry and peppery) and a make-yourself-at-home affability (soft fruit which weeps with flavour).

Negroamaro del Salento   14   B

Fresh, biting red. Selected stores.

Rosso del Salento Puglia, Colucci   14   B

Definite hints of light, civilised, cigar fumes on the bouquet. The fruit is all friendly plums. Selected stores.

Rosso di Verona, Sainsbury's   11   B

Sangiovese di Romagna, Sainsbury's   13.5   B

Juicy as a fresh squeezed plum.

Sangiovese di Toscana, Cecchi 1995   13.5   C

Sicilian Nero d'Avola & Merlot, Sainsbury's   15   C

Incredibly polished savouriness and smooth, well-turned-out depth here. Lovely.

Sicilian Red, Sainsbury's   14   B

Brilliant pasta-eaters' bargain. Soft, touch of sunny earth – good finish. Excellent stuff for the money.

Squinzano Mottura 1994   14   B

Selected stores.

Teroldego Rotaliano Geoff Merrill, Sainsbury's   12   C

Top 115 stores only.

Terre del Sole Sardinian Red Wine   14   B

Selected stores. Serious fruit here which never descends into farce – though it is great fun to drink with rich Italian dishes.

Valpolicella Classico Amarone, Sartori 1989   13.5   D

Valpolicella Classico Negarine 1994, Sainsbury's
`14.5` `C`

Very juicy and dark cherry ripe. Selected stores.

Valpolicella Classico, Sartori 1994
`13` `B`

Valpolicella, Sainsbury's
`11.5` `B`

Vino Nobile di Montepulciano, Cecchi 1991
`14` `D`

A dry one, this. Top thirty stores only.

ITALIAN WINE
WHITE

Barrique Aged Chardonnay Atesino Geoff Merrill, 1994
`15` `C`

Delicious underlying richness and flavour to the freshness.

Bianco di Custoza, Geoff Merrill 1995
`14` `C`

A lemonic fish wine. Great with spaghetti alla vongole.

Bianco di Verona, Sainsbury's
`13` `B`

Some profundity to the flavour – not a lot but enough to tickle the palate.

Chardonnay del Salento, Sainsbury's
`14.5` `B`

Nutty, crisp, flavoursome. Great-value fruit here – clean as a virgin policeman's whistle.

Chardonnay del Salento, Vigneto di Caramia 1994
`15.5` `D`

Not cheap but then nothing about the wine is. It is more elegant and silky, more appropriate to the grape than many a meursault at four times the price.

Chardonnay delle Tre Venezie Geoff Merrill, Sainsbury's
14 | C

Some flavour and style here.

Cortese del Piemonte 1995
15 | C

Deep and flavourful, almost brimming with flavour, yet finishes brisk and fresh. Delightful wine. Top eighty stores only.

Frascati Secco Superiore 1995, Sainsbury's
14 | C

Bite and flavour. A worthy frascati.

Frascati Superiore, Cantine San Marco 1994
16 | C

Stupendously tasty frascati. Complex fruit, fine balance. Quite delicious.

Gavi Bersano 1993
13 | D

Expensive curiosity – with a nod, fruit-wise, to Chateauneuf-du-Pape Blanc.

Grechetto dell'Umbria 1995, Sainsbury's
13.5 | C

Selected stores.

Inzolia & Chardonnay (Sicily), Sainsbury's
14 | C

Tasty, very tasty. Bright and breezy.

Lambrusco Rosato, Sainsbury's
10 | B

Le Trulle Chardonnay del Salento 1994
15.5 | C

Lots of flavour here but not of the peasant 'take-me-as-you-find-me' variety. This is a controlled, gorgeously fluent wine of style, complexity and thirst-quenching crispness yet fruitiness.

Lugana San Benedetto, Zenato 1994 `14` `D`

Delicious.

**Orvieto Classico Secco Geoff Merrill,
Sainsbury's** `13` `C`

Fair enough.

Pinot Grigio Atesino 1994, Sainsbury's `13.5` `B`

All right.

Rosato del Salento `11` `B`

Ho, hum. Selected stores.

**Sauvignon Blanc delle Tre Venezie 1995,
Sainsbury's** `14.5` `C`

Has some vigour and personality. A solid, crisp glug or to drink
with shellfish. Selected stores.

Sicilian White, Sainsbury's `12` `B`

Some echoes of richness to the fruit.

**Soave Classico Costalunga Pasqua 1994,
Sainsbury's** `11` `C`

Soave, Sainsbury's `11` `B`

Soave Superiore, Sartori 1994 `12` `B`

Some evidence of fruit here.

Terre del Sole Sardinian White Wine `14` `B`

Selected stores. Very clean, crisp and refreshing.

Tocai del Veneto (3-litre box) `11` `E`

Trebbiano di Romagna Sainsbury's　14.5　B

Superb value here. An engaging white wine, clean and untroubled by anything remotely like a bad conscience, which has firm flavoured fruit with a nutty finish.

Trebbiano Garganega Vino da Tavola del Veneto, Sainsbury's　13.5　B

A pleasant, edgily fruity aperitif. Rather simple but refreshing.

Tuscan White, Cecchi　13　B

Selected stores.

LEBANESE WINE　RED

Chateau Musar 1988　13　E

MOROCCAN WINE　RED

Moroccan Red, Sainsbury's　14　B

Very classy dry edge to the fruit which has depth and richness. Great with casseroles.

MOROCCAN WINE　WHITE

Moroccan White, Sainsbury's　14　B

Plenty of flavour and a fair degree of depth here.

NEW ZEALAND WINE · RED

Matua Valley Pinot Noir Waimauku Estate 1994 · 13 · D

Tastes like a pinot for sure. But not quite a seven-quid one. Top sixty stores only.

NEW ZEALAND WINE · WHITE

Grove Mill Sauvignon Blanc, Marlborough 1995 · 15.5 · E

A complex, handsomely finished, prettily integrated fruit/acid double act of great style and class like first-class old-style sancerre in its zippy infancy. Top fifty stores only.

Matua Chardonnay, Hawkes Bay 1994 · 15 · D

Impressively deep and rich but not as impudent as some New Zealand chardonnays, and so will please palates with classical inclinations and tastes. Top twenty-five stores only.

Montana Sauvignon Blanc, Marlborough 1995 · 13.5 · C

Grassy, blurred.

New Zealand Dry White, Sainsbury's · 14 · C

Delicious, with a restrained richness of tone and a gentle citric touch. It aches to release its temperamental grassy undertone of acidity but the fruit won't let go. The result? Wine of charm.

Nobilo Chardonnay, Poverty Bay 1994 · 13 · C

Fresh and striking. Top fifty stores only.

Nobilo White Cloud, 1994 `13.5` `C`

Not as exciting as the 1993 but still among the cheapest NZ wines on the market and sound, fruity drinking.

Stoneleigh Vineyard Sauvignon Blanc, Marlborough 1995 `15.5` `D`

Lovely! A real fresh tastebud zapper.

Timara Dry White 1994 `14` `C`

Villa Maria Chardonnay 1995 `14.5` `D`

An elegant, slightly wishful chardonnay. It has an admirable restraint without being supine.

Villa Maria Private Bin Sauvignon Blanc, Marlborough 1995 `15` `D`

From the tang of crushed grass which greets the nostrils, to the racy fruit which slides over the tastebuds so slickly, to the final sigh of acidity as it quits the throat, this is a New Zealand sauvignon in fine fettle.

PORTUGUESE WINE RED

Arruda, Sainsbury's `14` `B`

Burly fruit yet balanced and dry. One of this book's long-term favourite reds which is now beginning to be a little overshadowed by the rest of the JS Portuguese red range.

Cabernet Sauvignon Ribatejo, Sainsbury's `13` `C`

Top seventy-five stores.

Do Campo Tinto, Sainsbury's `14.5` `B`

Excellent, serious structure resulting in highly quaffable fruit –
has bite and briskness and good flavour.

Portuguese Red Wine, Sainsbury's `13` `B`

Cheap and cheerful.

Quinta da Bacalhoa Cabernet Sauvignon 1993 `16.5` `D`

Ripe and gravy-like with flavours of game and blackcurrant –
a feral, slightly spicy, very rich wine of high aromatic charms
and deep rich fruit. Selected stores.

PORTUGUESE WINE — WHITE

Do Campo Branco Peter Bright, Sainsbury's `14` `B`

Pleasant freshness and lilting fruitiness. Agreeably priced and
flavoured.

Do Campo Rosado, Sainsbury's `12` `B`

Selected stores.

Portuguese Rose, Sainsbury's `8` `B`

Santa Sara 1993 `15` `C`

Fresh and nutty. Lovely style of balanced fruit.

Sauvignon Blanc Ribatejo 1995, Sainsbury's `13.5` `C`

Only the flabby finish spoils the otherwise excellent structure.
Selected stores.

Vinho Verde, Sainsbury's

ROMANIAN WINE RED

**River Route Selection Pinot Noir, Recas
1994**

Selected stores.

**Romanian Pinot Noir Dealul Mare,
Sainsbury's** *25-3-97*

Still one of the tastiest pinots around for the money.

SOUTH AFRICAN WINE RED

**Bellingham Cabernet Sauvignon, Paarl
1994**

Slips down easier than most cabernets. Top twenty-five stores
only.

Bellingham Merlot, Paarl 1994

Rather a nail-biting performance, this, to rate 14. Broad to begin
with, it gets fresh on the finish where it should be bloody. Top
twenty-five stores only.

Fairview Cabernet Sauvignon, Paarl 1994 14 D

Tongue- and teeth-hugging tannins which should soften well
over another year in bottle to reveal real classy fruit. Top
twenty-five stores only.

Fairview Pinotage, Paarl 1995

Rubbery fruit of high polish, flavour and depth. Great food wine – casseroles, roasts, risottos. Top seventy-five stores only.

Kanonkop, Paul Sauer, Stellenbosch 1990

A rich and very potently berried wine.

Pinotage, Coastal Region, Sainsbury's

A brilliant alternative to overpriced beaujolais. Just as soft and fruity but with a lovely dry edge.

Rustenberg Cabernet Sauvignon, Stellenbosch 1991

Old-style South African wine which is oxidised and dirty. Must have rich food to be remotely palatable. Top twenty-five stores only.

South African Cabernet Merlot Reserve Selection 1994, Sainsbury's

Superb balance of elements, dryness and fruitiness, persistence and real classy flavoursomeness. Lovely polished wine of great fruit and class. Top seventy-five stores only.

South African Cabernet Merlot, Sainsbury's 14.5 B

Soft, slightly smoky and plummy, this is an attractive food wine. Suits cheese and grilled vegetable dishes.

South African Cabernet Sauvignon, Sainsbury's 16 C

A wonderfully soft, sweet-finishing yet tannic, fruity wine – not hugely complex but superbly drinkable.

South African Cape Red Wine, Sainsbury's 13.5 B

Soft but never gooey. Strawberry on the finish.

South African Pinot Noir Reserve Selection
1995, Sainsbury's `12` `C`

Has a smell like an expensive volnay. But it finishes like cheap valpolicella. Selected stores.

South African Pinotage/Cinsault,
Sainsbury's `15` `B`

Still up to snuff, this richly rounded, satisfyingly priced wine. Selected stores.

South African Pinotage Reserve Selection
1995, Sainsbury's `15.5` `C`

Ripe, rolling, running with quaffable rubbery fruit with enough depth and fullness to go with food. Top sixty-nine stores only.

South African Pinotage, Sainsbury's `14` `C`

Swirling fruit which never gets giddy or out of balance. Great pasta plonk.

South African Shiraz/Cabernet Sauvignon,
Sainsbury's `13` `C`

Sweet finish to the fruit. Top seventy-five stores only.

Thelema Cabernet Sauvignon 1992 `16` `E`

Lovely, unhurried, berried fruit which is perfectly mature, deliciously fruit-sweet, and dry and teeth-huggingly vigorous on the finish. A delicious roast lamb wine of considerable aplomb. Selected stores.

SOUTH AFRICAN WINE WHITE

Boschendal Chardonnay, Paarl 1994 `12.5` `D`

Disappointing at this price. Was once a 15/16-point wine.

Cape Dry White Wine, Sainsburys `14` `B`

Mildly entertaining.

Cape Medium White Wine `14` `B`

A brilliant and easily scaleable ladder for those on their way up from Liebfraumilch. Excellent with Peking Duck.

Cape Sweet White Wine, Sainsbury's `13` `C`

For Auntie Flo, this flows with avuncularly friendly and sweet fruit.

Chardonnay Vergelegen 1993 `15` `C`

Chenin Blanc, Sainsbury's `15` `B`

Gets to be a fruitier bargain every vintage. Pear-drops and sticky-toffee to finish – oodles of fruit and great with fish and chips.

Danie de Wet Grey Label Chardonnay 1995 `14` `D`

Not as thrilling or as positively elegantly citric as previous vintages. It will mature over the year. Selected stores.

Fairview Estate Semillon/Chardonnay, Paarl 1994 `17` `C`

Almost a medicinal malt whisky edge to the lovely rounded fruit. But it finishes beautifully.

Neil Ellis Sauvignon Blanc, Groenekloof 1994 `14.5` `C`

One for the sancerre lover disillusioned with poor fruit and wicked prices. Neil's wine is aromatic, gently nutty, restrained and whistle-clean. Very good value for the sheer class on offer here.

South African Colombard, Sainsbury's · 14 · B

Starts fruity and full, finishes fresh and wild. Very African.

South African Fume Blanc Reserve 1995, Sainsbury's · 14 · C

A good fruity glug which only fails to score more because of a somewhat lack-lustre finish.

South African Reserve Selection Chardonnay 1995, Sainsbury's · 16 · C

Lovely complex medley of competing flavours. They are constructed around a melony softness, a touch of creaminess and a firm acidic side which is never too intrusive. Truly delicious.

South African Sauvignon Blanc Reserve Selection 1995 Sainsbury's · 16 · C

Terrific price for such flavoursome elegance and rich-edged style. Great class here. Top seventy stores only.

South African Sauvignon Blanc, Sainsbury's · 13 · B

South African Sauvignon Blanc/ Chardonnay, Sainsbury's · 15 · C

The marriage of grapes pits the robust, open-hearted melony fruit of the chardonnay against the pithy, laconic acidity of the sauvignon. It works very well.

Thelema Chardonnay 1994 · 16 · E

Now, this wood is delicious! And nourishing. It gives the bouquet beauty, the fruit depth, the acidity elegance and a fine framework, and its overall effect is very classy. Selected stores.

Thelema Sauvignon Blanc 1995 · 15.5 · E

Delicate, delicious, will improve over the next year in bottle. Expensive but individual; a well-crafted wine. Selected stores.

Vergelegen Sauvignon Blanc, Stellenbosch 1994

Nuts under the deep fruit which is not laid on thick but still has a lovely rich, rolling feel in the mouth. A wine to unwind with.

SPANISH WINE   RED

Classic Selection Rioja 1990, Sainsbury's

'Classic' meaning high-priced in Sainsbury's parlance. This high price is almost worth paying.

El Conde Oak-Aged Vino da Mesa, Sainsbury's

Still a dry, fruity bargain.

JS Rioja Crianza Bodegas Olarra 1993

Fruity and soft with a ripe raisiny edge. Leathery interior. Great food wine.

Jumilla, Sainsbury's
15.5   C

Brilliant fruity value. Lovely structure, weight, flavour, richness and balanced tannins, acid and fruit. Selected stores.

La Mancha Castillo de Alhambra 1994, Sainsbury's
15.5   B

Bargain, and the best vintage yet. Full, rich, ripe, soft, flavoursome.

Marques de Caceres Rioja, 1991 (1.5 litres)
14   E

Mont Marcal Cabernet Sauvignon Reserva, Penedes 1990 [15] C

Surprisingly vigorous for half a decade old. Lovely mature fruit with solid ripe edge of flavour and depth. Great food wine. Top sixty-five stores only.

Navarra, Sainsbury's [11] B

Navarra Tempranillo/Cabernet Sauvignon 1991, Sainsbury's [15] C

Orobio Rioja Reserva 1990 [14] D

Smooth, atypical. Not a vanilla or wood touch in view. Top 100 stores only.

Ribera del Duero Crianza, Conde de Siruela 1989 [14] D

A reluctant 14, I must admit. It is expensive though the fruit is polished, deep and attractive, but it lacks acidity to give real balance, which a wine at nearly £7 must have to partner food.

Rioja Reserva, Vina Ardanza 1987 [12] E

Old, crotchety, bad-tempered – good for octogenarians who need winter warmth.

Rioja, Sainsbury's [15] B

Bargain fruit and flavour. Light, unwoody, very fresh and delicious yet with hints of depth.

Santara Cabernet Merlot, Conca de Barbera 1993 [17] C

Magnificent fruit! Has richness and depth of great warmth.

Sierra del Sol Tinto Vino de Mesa, Sainsbury's [10] B

Stowells of Chelsea Tempranillo (3-litre box) 14 F

Great glugging flavour and texture.

Valencia Red, Sainsbury's 13 B

Vina Herminia, Reserva Rioja, 1985, Bodegas Lagunilla 14 D

Lush, raunchy stuff – delicious cheese wine.

Vino de la Tierra Tinto Peter Bright, Sainsbury's 15 B

Lovely sunshine-filled, fruity wine of softness and flavour.

SPANISH WINE WHITE

Marques de Caceres Rioja Blanco Crianza 1993 13 C

A subtle Bounty Bar of a wine. For Thai food only. Top sixty-five stores only.

Moscatel de Valencia, Sainsbury's 16 B

Brilliant honeyed wine with a finish like marmalade. Superb pudding wine for a song.

Navarra Barrel Fermented Viura Chardonnay 1994, Sainsbury's 14 C

Clash of vibrancy and calmness. The acid is vibrant, the fruit is solid and unruffled. Top fifty stores only.

Navarra Blanco, Sainsbury's 14 B

Bargain nuttiness and subtle depth and flavour.

**Navarra Cabernet Sauvignon Rosado 1995,
Sainsbury's** `12` `C`

Rioja Blanco, Sainsbury's `13` `B`

Milky, coconutty, but also fresh and light. Good salad wine.

Santara Chardonnay 1995 `15.5` `C`

Well-crafted chardonnay in the modern, food-friendly, fleshy
manner.

**Santara Conca de Barbera Hugh Ryman
1994** `14.5` `B`

Dry but soft-edged with always a hint of crispness about it. A
most agreeable aperitif or first-course soup and salad wine.

**Vino de la Tierra Blanco Peter Bright,
Sainsbury's** `15` `B`

Simple good value here – for fish and chips parties.

**Vino de la Tierra Medium, Extremadura,
Sainsbury's** `13` `B`

**Vino de la Tierra Sweet, Extremadura,
Sainsbury's** `13` `B`

Do try it! It's tastier than any amount of Liebfraumilch.

USA WINE   RED

Californian Red, Sainsbury's `13` `B`

**E. & J. Gallo Turning Leaf Cabernet
Sauvignon 1994** `13.5` `D`

Warm and possessing some depth but uncompetitively priced
compared with Chile or South Africa. But you're getting better,

Gallo, so stick at it! You might just make a terrific wine at a dirt-cheap price one day.

E. & J. Gallo Turning Leaf Zinfandel 1994 `12` `D`

Not bad, but very overpriced at nigh on six quid. Anodyne and characterless, it lacks the oomph of real red zin. It fails to finish with £6 worth of vivacity. If it was £3.29 it would be a good buy. A partially turned new leaf.

Gallo Sonoma Cabernet Sauvignon 1992 `13.5` `E`

Only just fails to make 14. It is expensive – but it is gently impressive, if rather ripe.

South Bay Vineyards Californian Pinot Noir `13.5` `C`

Sweet fruit maturity. Expensive for the complexity on offer.

South Bay Vineyards Zinfandel `17` `C`

Delicious soft, riotous fruit with leathery richness, soft spices and a lovely black cherry and spice finish. Lingering and lovely.

USA WINE WHITE

Californian White, Sainsbury's `12` `B`

If you like fruit juice you'll like this.

Canelones Chardonnay Semillon, Sainsbury's `12` `C`

E. & J. Gallo Turning Leaf Chardonnay 1994 `14` `D`

Classy and rich. Not especially elegant or finely balanced as great Californian chardonnays are but it's good with chicken.

Gallo White Grenache 1993

Sheer rhubarb crumble. It seems absurd to go to the trouble of growing grapes to make wine so gauche – if wine gums could be persuaded to ferment into alcohol this is the wine they would make.

Sauvignon Blanc, Firestone 1993, Sainsbury's

Curiously delicious and idiosyncratic. Fat fruit with a mellow finish but vibrant acidity stops it cloying. Rather impressive. Top 110 stores only.

South Bay Vineyards Californian Chardonnay

Sutter Home White Zinfandel 1995

Sweet, but not agonisingly so.

Washington Hills Chardonnay, Columbia Hills 1992

FORTIFIED WINE

Aged Amontillado, Sainsbury's (half bottle)

Aperitif. Top ninety stores only.

Blandy's Duke of Clarence Malmsey Madeira

An expensive companion for fruit cake. Top twenty stores only.

Cantine Pellegrino Superiore Garibaldi Dolce Marsala (half bottle) `14` `D`

Enjoy it with a large slab of Christmas cake. Selected stores.

Cockburns Anno 1988 LBV `17` `E`

Resoundingly rich fruit with a chocolate and cherry liqueur ripeness to its edge. Lovely stuff for blue cheese.

Cream Montilla, Sainsbury's `14` `B`

Drink it with creme caramel and ice cream.

Dow's Extra Dry White Port `14` `E`

An expensive but interesting and robust (19% alcohol) aperitif. It is a real gutsy pick-me-up at sundown time, though. Has a delicious nuttiness.

Dow's Single Quinta Bomfim 1984 `15` `G`

Lovely figgy, raisiny fruit which is like velvet (stretched). Top twenty stores only.

Fonseca Guimaraens Vintage Port 1978 `17` `G`

Rich spiced plums plus a cassis-like concentration and ripeness of fruit which is always, magically, dry.

Fonseca Vintage Port 1982 `16.5` `G`

Holy cow! This is a port to make you disbelieve in Santa Claus. Top forty stores only.

Manzanilla, Sainsbury's `12` `C`

Matusalem Sherry (half bottle) `14` `E`

Extraordinary old rich hag of a wine which weaves magic spells over the tongue. Particularly well suited to fruit cakes. Top twenty-four stores only.

Medium Dry Amontillado, Sainsbury's `12` `C`

Medium Dry Montilla, Sainsbury's `14` `B`

A cheap alternative to sherry – not sweet exactly but great with hard cheese and hard fruit.

Medium Sweet Oloroso, Sainsbury's `13.5` `C`

Excellent with fruit cake.

Moscatel Pale Cream, Sainsbury's `15` `C`

The ultimate ice-cream wine.

Moscato di Pantelleria Marsala 1994 (half bottle) `13.5` `D`

Blue cheese wine. Selected stores.

Old Oloroso, Sainsbury's (half bottle) `14` `B`

Very dry and stuffy. Drink with a volume of odes (Greek). Top 100 stores only.

Pale Cream Montilla, Sainsbury's `13` `B`

Sweet aperitif, well chilled.

Pale Cream Sherry, Sainsbury's `14` `C`

Superb sweet aperitif.

Pale Dry Amontillado, Sainsbury's `15` `C`

Brilliant. Drink it well chilled.

Pale Dry Fino Sherry, Sainsbury's `15.5` `C`

A superb grilled prawn wine. Also a dry, uplifting aperitif.

Pale Dry Montilla, Sainsbury's `13.5` `B`

Drink chilled with ham dishes. A dry, sherry-like wine of excellent value.

Palo Cortado, Sainsbury's (half bottle) `14` `B`

Aperitif. Top eighty stores only.

Pedro Ximenez Montilla (half bottle) `16` `D`

Like ingesting diesel oil used to lubricate a celestial chariot. Ambrosiacally rich, deep and sweet, it is strictly for cooking and rich cake eaters.

Pellegrino Marsala `14` `B`

Brilliant gravy enhancer and also a great sinew-stiffener prior to dull dinner parties.

Rich Cream Sherry, Sainsbury's `14.5` `C`

Have it with a helping of flaming Christmas pudding.

Sainsbury's 5 Year Old Sercial (half bottle) `14.5` `E`

A curious dry yet raisiny rich wine. Good with fruit cake, nuts and old woman novelists. Top sixty stores only.

Sainsbury's LBV 1989 `13.5` `E`

A sweet warm port with a friendly disposition but not as gripping as previous vintages.

Sainsbury's Madeira (half bottle) `14` `C`

Great to add to gravies (five minutes' cooking minimum). Not at all stores.

Sainsbury's Ruby `13.5` `D`

Good basic stuff.

Sainsbury's Tawny `14` `D`

Rich yet not too rich for cheese.

Taylors LBV, 1989 `14.5` `E`

A delicious rich full-bodied beauty.

10 Year Old Tawny Port, Sainsbury's [16] [F]

Magnificent, raisiny fruit which starts basso profundo and finishes mezzo soprano. Great cheese wine and also worth trying with fruit cake.

Warre's Traditional LBV 1982 [14] [G]

Pricey but luxurious. Selected stores.

Warres Warrior Vintage Character Port [16] [E]

Rich ripe fruit with a lovely rounded flavour. Very attractive depth with vinosity. Delicious.

SPARKLING WINE/CHAMPAGNE

Angas Brut Rose (Australia) [15] [D]

Deliciously incisive.

Asti, Sainsbury's [11] [C]

Australian Sparkling Wine, Sainsbury's [14] [C]

Excellent stuff for cheap wedding givers.

Blanc de Noirs Champagne, Sainsbury's [16] [F]

Elegant, so very elegant.

Cava, Sainsbury's [15] [C]

Delicious as ever. And very good value.

Champagne Extra Dry, Sainsbury's [15.5] [G]

Subtle richness. Available in half bottles as well.

Champagne Rose, Sainsbury's [13] [F]

Chardonnay Brut Methode Traditionelle, Sainsbury's (France) | 14.5 | D

Selected stores. Elegant yet with hints of richness. As drinkable as many a champagne priced three times more.

Cockatoo Ridge Sparkling Wine | 13 | D

Cuvee Napa, Mumm California | 13.5 | E

Quiet, not explosive, and rather like a reasonably made champagne.

Gallo Brut NV | 10 | D

Good for dinners when no one has any reason to celebrate.

Green Point Vineyard Domaine Chandon 1991 | 12 | F

Lambrusco Bianco Medium Sweet, Sainsbury's | 10 | B

Lambrusco Secco, Sainsbury's | 8 | B

Louis Kremer Champagne Brut | 16 | E

Creamy Kremer! Lovely rich champagne (but not too rich) with good balance.

Madeba Brut, Robertson (South Africa) | 12.5 | D

Mercier Brut | 11 | G

Mercier Demi Sec | 12 | G

Sainsbury's Cava Rosado | 15 | C

Delicious dry rose. Good with food, too.

Sainsbury's Demi Sec Champagne
Drink cava. Don't drink this sweet thing at over £12.

Saumur, Sainsbury's
Bargain. Pleasant dry fruit of some distinction for the price.

Seaview Pinot Noir Chardonnay 1992 (Australian)
A massively satisfying, elegant bottle at the peak of its maturity yet with fresh, clean fruitiness. Can only be compared to really fine bubblies costing lots more.

Sekt, Sainsbury's

Veuve Clicquot Vintage Champagne 1988
Not worth five times the price of a £4.99 bottle of JS Cava.

Vin Mousseux Brut, Sainsbury's

Vintage Cava, Mont Marcal 1991
Deep, richly attractive aroma of compelling quality. The fruit tends towards fatness but is not blowsy. Good with smoked fish.

Vintage Champagne Blanc de Blancs 1990, Sainsbury's
Exceedingly elegant and well-flavoured champagne – it contrives to be warm and welcoming yet classic, gently fruity and finely wrought. Good price for such effusive charm.

Yalumba Pinot Noir/Chardonnay, Australia
Absolutely stunner for the money: rich and biscuity, great balancing acidity and an overall style hinting refinement and class. Rheims quakes in its Gucci boots!

SOMERFIELD/ GATEWAY

Richard, toffeed fruit

As a wine writer for the *Grauniad*, one learns not to be too critical of the typographical slips of others. Nevertheless, when Mr Ross Jones of Kingston-upon-Thames brought to my attention a shelf-sticker from Gateway which read: 'What the experts say: Vina Albali Gran Reserva – Richard, toffeed fruit, extremely mature, Malcolm Gluck, the *Guardian*, 4 July 1992', I could not resist a smirk. Sending me the shelf-sticker, Mr Jones enclosed his missive:

> I purloined this from a Gateway supermarket and thought you might like it for your scrapbook. Perhaps in your next article you will let us know what or who is Richard and are the *Grauniad* proof-readers alive and well and living at Gateway.

I was happy to clarify the matter with this reply:

> Thanks for your card and enclosure which you sent way back. I'm sorry I've only just got around to replying but I've been so busy touring the nation's bookshops signing copies of the new *Superplonk* paperback that the kids are beginning to wonder who the strange man is who

313

rushes off every afternoon to endure British Rail services to far-flung centres of literacy.

Your card was most amusing and the sub-editors at the paper had a good, but nervous, laugh about it. The mistake is the store's completely and they are embarrassed as hell about making a *Grauniad* error and they are desperately reprinting (so they say).

Most of the other omissions and errors on the part of Gateway and Somerfield stores, reported in readers' letters, were of a rather more mundane and less hilarious nature. But the volume of correspondence I received when readers could not find the wines that I had reviewed underlines just how frustrating this experience can be for drinkers. In May 1996, a particularly irksome chapter of events took place concerning the timing of a £1.99 promotion for Argentinian Country Red. Having reported in my column what the retailer had told me, that the offer was to run until 28 May, I received a letter from Gateway informing me of an error on its part. The promotion was in fact scheduled for the first two weeks of May. I included an explanation in my next *Guardian* column, urging all disappointed customers to write personally to the Gateway chairman, David Simmons.

Usually, I pass on complaints and queries from Gateway customers to the company's buying controller for wine, Angela Mount, who to her credit is always ready to smoothe ruffled feathers. When Mr Ed Fancourt of Lincolnshire found the Chateau de Valoussiere to be out of stock at his local Somerfield in November 1994, he wrote:

Having relatively recently started reading your *Superplonk* column, and having just purchased the book by the same name and *Gluck's Guide '95*, I feel I should thank you for the sound, pragmatic, and, above all, cost-conscious advice on wine which has provided me with many a bargain.

There are of course a few problems that I have experienced along the way.

My local Somerfields (both quite large) seem to know nothing whatsoever about either the Chateau de la Valoussiere red or the Merlot from the Minervois ('93). Their only Vin de Pays d'Oc Merlot is the Voraine de la Magdelaine which, having tried it, is surely not the wine you were referring to.

As I do when all such problems arise, I passed on Mr Fancourt's letter to Angela Mount and was pleased to hear that she had addressed his query. There had, apparently, been a delay in the shipment from the supplier. Demonstrating sound PR practice, she sent him a complementary bottle of Chateau de Valoussiere and advised him which stores would eventually be carrying the wine.

However, Somerfield's record on customer care is not entirely unblemished, as Mr Graham Perkins' letter of February 1995 bears witness.

I have only very recently become a 'follower of Gluck' and in spite of the somewhat mixed verdict on Somerfield in *Superplonk* made the trip to Malvern today in search of the Domaine de St Julien Pays de l'Herault. On consulting a supervisor (found with difficulty) I was told that this had totally sold out of all Somerfields on the first day it appeared. I then asked about the massive display of Cabernet Sauvignon marked special offer but unpriced. These apparently were to go on sale tomorrow at £1.99 (if I had read your column with care I would have known, but there was nothing to say so in the store).

I left Somerfield feeling rather frustrated and irritated by the offhand attitude and went straight to Safeway where I spent rather more than I had intended on reliable bottles of Bulgarian and where I found the staff helpful and efficient.

Somerfield needs reminding of the need to send customers away happy and satisfied – I trust you will see that the message is hammered home.

Once more, I passed on the complaint and the amazing Ms Mount was again mobilised to calming effect. According to a subsequent letter from Mr Perkins, profuse apologies had been made and a free bottle of Vin de Pays de Gascogne dispatched.

Angela Mount was also extremely helpful with an enquiry from Mr J.B.H. Gardiner of Odiham, Hampshire who had been led to believe by staff at his local store in Alton that all the Gateway stores operated independently of one another in terms of assortment selection and pricing. Angela assured Mr Gardiner that pricing and wine selection for all Gateway stores was her responsibility and that the information he had been given was incorrect. She also sent him a bottle each of the Chateau Le Clairiot and Gyongyos Sauvignon Blanc, the quest for which had originally taken Mr Gardiner to the Alton store. A few months later, in October 1994, I received the following update from Mr Gardiner:

Ref. Gateway Alton Hants. They have now been 'retrained'.

The Australian Dry White at £1.99 was being unloaded and displayed on the day of your report.

Last Saturday 1.10.94 I went to Somerfield in Farnham. The wines listed as being special offer until 15.10.94 were all there excepting Chateau de Belesta 1992 which was 'sold out'.

I checked with the wine 'checker' and showed him your article. He was not apologetic and said more or less, 'We cannot work in conjunction with newspaper wine reporters to make supplies coincide with their articles.' *'We do not work like that!'* His words.

Another outfit requiring retraining.

It is clear from these letters that Gateway head office has its house in order PR-wise, but as is so often the case with supermarkets it is a lack of customer care on the shop floor itself which can let a retailer down.

Of course, the whole point of supermarkets is that the emphasis is on self-service and personal customer care is by necessity kept to a minimum, theoretically to reduce costs and therefore keep prices at their most competitive. But it is interesting to note that supermarkets have recently begun to pay more attention to personal customer service – offering to carry shopping to cars or increasing the numbers of 'packers' working at checkouts – as competition between the rival chains reaches fever pitch.

Somerfield
Gateway House
Hawkfield Business Park
Whitchurch Lane
Bristol
BS14 0TJ

Tel 0117 9359359
Fax 0117 9780629

SEE STOP PRESS SECTION AT END OF BOOK FOR LAST-MINUTE ADDITIONS TO THIS RETAILER'S RANGE.

ARGENTINIAN WINE   RED

**Argentine Country Red San Juan,
Somerfield**   `14` `B`

Juicy, fruity and full of itself, and this self is great company.

ARGENTINIAN WINE   WHITE

Argentine Country White, Somerfield   `13` `B`

AUSTRALIAN WINE   RED

**Australian Cabernet Sauvignon 1996,
Somerfield**   `14` `C`

Delicious quality of quaffing cabernet with sufficient dryness, fruit and character to enhance food.

Australian Dry Red, Somerfield   `13` `B`

Fruity, honest.

Australian Shiraz   `13` `C`

Cabernet Sauvignon, Somerfield   `13.5` `C`

Dry and most agreeable.

Hardys Bankside Shiraz 1992 `15` `D`

Elegant, thrusting style of fruit which persists on the tongue.

Penfolds Bin 407 Cabernet Sauvignon 1991 `14` `E`

Terrifically smooth, perfectly mature and, curiously, lively and juicy.

Penfolds Koonunga Hill Shiraz Cabernet 1994 `15` `D`

Like a minor bordeaux but more warmly fruity. Excellent grilled chop bottle.

Penfolds Rawson's Retreat Bin 35 Cabernet/Shiraz 1994 `15.5` `C`

Excellent value. Has lovely texture and warm spicy fruit of depth, flavour, balance and finish. Great roast food wine.

Somerfield Cabernet Shiraz `13.5` `C`

Extra zing here.

Stowells of Chelsea Shiraz Cabernet (3-litre box) `14` `G`

Rich fruit with earthy undertones. Has a long, meaty finish with a firm, purposeful balance of fruit and acid.

AUSTRALIAN WINE WHITE

Australian Chardonnay, Somerfield `13.5` `C`

Extraordinarily richly flavoured. Almost unbalanced and quite madly fruity. Needs to be drunk with a grilled salmon steak or pasta with tomato sauce.

Berri Estates Unwooded Chardonnay 1995 | 15 | D

Rich, unctuous, oily, full, deep and a profound companion to chicken and fish.

Chardonnay, Somerfield | 13 | C

Church Hill Chardonnay 1995 | 14 | D

A certain elegance here. Charming fruit, but it does cost.

Hardys Nottage Hill Chardonnay 1995 | 15.5 | C

Quietly impressive.

Jacob's Creek Chardonnay 1994 | 14.5 | C

Lots of the usual rich fruity attack underpinned by a delicious freshness. Good, balanced, goes well with food.

Jacob's Creek Chardonnay 1995 | 14.5 | C

A richly inviting wine. Good flavour, balance and depth – and price.

Jacob's Creek Dry White | 12 | C

Jacob's Creek Semillon Chardonnay 1995 | 13.5 | C

Jamiesons Run Coonawarra Chardonnay 1993 | 14 | E

On the exuberant side but lithe with it. Moves stylishly with grilled flatfish.

Lindemans Bin 65 Chardonnay 1995 | 15.5 | C

Still batting well and positively under a fiver.

Moondah Brook 1993 | 16 | D

A melange of fruit: full, ripe, quirky, oddly delicious. A luxuriously exotic wine with lots of personality.

Penfolds Australian Dry White 1996, Somerfield
`14.5` `B`

Lovely musky flavour. Handsome depth of fruit. The 1996 vintage is excellent.

Penfolds Barrel Fermented Chardonnay 1994
`14.5` `D`

Handsomely built with a hint of ruggedness and woody depth.

Penfolds Organic Chardonnay/Sauvignon Blanc, Clare Valley 1995
`14.5` `D`

Delicious – if a touch expensive.

Penfolds Rawson's Retreat Bin 21 Semillon/Chardonnay 1995
`15.5` `C`

Apples, walnuts, pineapple, melon – quite an impressive medley here. The acidity is pure, crisp Golden Delicious.

Rosemount Estate Semillon 1995
`14` `D`

A racy, well-bred beast – runs well with seafood.

Stowells of Chelsea Semillon Chardonnay (3-litre box)
`14` `G`

Presence and lift, style and purpose – this fruit knows where it's going. Good with food and mood.

BULGARIAN WINE RED

Bulgarian Cabernet Sauvignon, 1989 Somerfield
`15` `B`

Rough-edged but bruisingly fruity and deep. With roast meat and vegetables it's brilliant.

Country Red Merlot/Pinot Noir, Somerfield   15   B

Cardboard and old socks to smell but on the palate a solid whack of rich, deep, dry fruit hits you. Terrific pasta plonk.

Stambolovo Merlot Reserve 1990   15.5   C

Rich, deep, full of vigour and still lively but tasty tannins, this is a thundering bargain. Has complexity and class.

BULGARIAN WINE   WHITE

Bulgarian Chardonnay Sliven Region, Somerfield   13.5   B

A better blend than previously.

Somerfield Bulgarian Country White   14.5   B

Fresh, gently lemony, very pert and appealing. A delicious garden guzzle.

CHILEAN WINE   RED

Chilean Cabernet Sauvignon Segu Olle, Somerfield   14.5   C

Firmly fruity, dry, impressively polished and smooth.

Stowells of Chelsea Chilean Merlot Cabernet (3-litre box)   10   G

This wine is soft yet with an agreeably gentle level of proud tannins. Why don't I rate it higher? I simply find the aroma off-puttingly ripe and rubbery. It really ought to be better put together than this.

CHILEAN WINE
WHITE

Caliterra Chardonnay, Curico 1995
16 C

Nuttiness under the fruit gives it an added layer of complexity. The fruit is dry and rich, the structure poised and fine. The texture is perfect.

Caliterra Sauvignon Blanc 1995
14 C

Nutty, with a coating of lemon.

Chilean Sauvignon Blanc, Somerfield
14 C

Elegant fruit here to tease a palate into shape and prepare it for food.

ENGLISH WINE
WHITE

Denbies Engilsh
12 C

Lamberhurst Sovereign
13 B

Apply and sweet melon fruit. Some freshness. Good aperitif and garden party wine.

Lamberhurst Sovereign Medium Dry
10 B

FRENCH WINE
RED

Beaujolais Pierre Dupond 1995
10 C

Beaujolais-Villages, Duboeuf `12` `C`

Bergerac Rouge 1993, Somerfield `11` `B`

Bourgogne, Hautes Cotes de Beaune 1993 `11` `D`

Cabernet Sauvignon VdP d'Oc Val d'Orbieu, Somerfield `13` `B`

Jammy.

Chateau Baron Segur Montagne-St-Emilion 1993 `13` `D`

A pleasant enough, authentic St Emilion: fruity, dry, firmly structured – but it is not a six-quid wine.

Chateau Carbonel Cotes du Rhone 1994 `14.5` `C`

Juicy coating of fruit masking dry, brisk fruit.

Chateau de Caraguilhes, Corbieres 1993 `16` `C`

Brilliant, organic red: full, deep, rich, earthy (but never crude), fruity, balanced, integrated, food-friendly, well-priced.

Chateau de la Valoussiere, Coteaux du Languedoc Jeanjean, 1993 `13` `C`

Chateau de Montmal Fitou, Jeanjean 1993 `14` `C`

Soft, spicy, dry, plummy. An excellent casserole bottle.

Chateau La Chapelle Baradis, Cotes de Castillon 1989 `14` `C`

Nice, mature, deep, dry fruit.

Chateau Latour Segure Lussac St Emilion 1992 `15` `D`

Big-shouldered, husky, very dry. But lots of flavour and woody undertones. Terrific with roast vegetables.

Chateau Le Clairiot Bordeaux 1995 `15` `C`

Brilliant value – stylish, dry, savoury, excellent with food.

Chateau Montmal Fitou, Jeanjean 1993 `14` `C`

Very attractive, earthy, soft fruit.

Chateau Saint Robert, Graves 1993 `14` `D`

Dry, deeply flavoured, will develop well for two to three years in bottle.

Chateau Talence, Premier Cotes de Bordeaux 1993 `13.5` `D`

Firm, dry savouriness.

Chateauneuf-du-Pape La Solitude, 1993 `13` `E`

The fruit is OK. But the price tag isn't.

Claret, Somerfield `14.5` `B`

Approachably soft and supple, it has flavour, fruit and an edge of dry tannic savouriness.

Corbieres Val d'Orbieu, Somerfield `12.5` `B`

Good earthy character.

Cotes de Duras 1994 `13.5` `B`

Ah! Tannins! (Good, gravy-like fruit.)

Cotes de Gascogne Red 1995, Somerfield `13` `B`

Friendly.

Cotes de Rhone Celliers de l'Enclave des Papes 1995 `12` `B`

Intensely juicy fruit.

Cotes de Roussillon Jeanjean `13` **B**

Cotes de Ventoux, Somerfield `12` **B**

Cotes du Marmandais 1993 `12.5` **B**

Crozes Hermitage, Celliers de Nobleus 1993 `13` **C**

Slight cigar-smoke edge to the jammy fruit.

Domaine d'Abrens Minervois, Jeanjean 1993 `12.5` **B**

Very soft. Almost a whisper compared to some raucous minervois. Touch young.

Domaine de Rivoyre Cabernet Sauvignon, VdP d'Oc 1993 `14` **C**

Good-looking beast. Almost TOO good-looking. Wouldn't mind a cauliflower ear or a bent nose here to give it some character. But smooth? Yes. Limited distribution.

Domaine de Saint Julien VdP l'Herault, les Chais Beaucairois `13.5` **B**

Domaine des Salaises, Saumur Remy Pannier 1993 `15` **C**

Terrific Loire red which oozes dry, raspberry fruit yet has that touch of slatey tannicity which distinguishes it. Balanced and stylish, this is a great price. Not available in all stores.

Domaine St Paul VdP de l'Herault `13` **B**

Fitou Caves de Mont Tauch, Somerfield `14` **B**

Dry, but the plummy fruit shines through.

Fitou Cuvee Rocher-d'Embree — 13 C
Simple, dry, good for bangers 'n' mash.

Hautes Cotes de Beaune Rouge, Cottin 1994 — 12.5 D

Macon Rouge Cottin Freres 1994 — 12 C
Bit austere.

Mas Segala Cotes du Roussillon Villages 1994 — 16.5 C
Wonderful. Characterful, yet distinguished. Huge bargain.

Medoc P. Sichel — 12 C
Has claret character, but at nigh on a fiver it is poor value.

Merlot VdP d'Oc Jeanjean — 14.5 B
Brilliant value. Lovely tannins, hint of leather and wrap-around soft blackcurrant fruit. Attractively textured.

Minervois Jeanjean — 13.5 B
Fresh and perky.

Oak Aged Claret — 13 C
Very soft and savoury.

Red Burgundy 1994, Somerfield — 10 D

Saint-Joseph, Cuvee Medaille d'Or, Caves de Saint Desiderat 1991 — 15 E
Lashings of flavour, depth, style, muscle and fluidity.

St Emilion P. Sichel — 13.5 C
Typicity, flavour, A hint of class.

Stowells of Chelsea Claret Bordeaux Rouge (3-litre box) `13` `G`

A good simple quaffing claret with an agreeable echo of the dry, tannic heritage of the region.

Stowells of Chelsea Vin de Pays du Gard (3-litre box) `14` `F`

Delightful smooth fruit with flavour and balance. A lovely touch – a distant echo, really – of earth.

Syrah VdP d'Oc `13` `B`

Good with soups and salads.

Vacqueyras Vieux Clocher, Arnoux 1993 `14` `C`

A resounding tinkle of good firm fruit from this old bell.

VdP des Bouches du Rhone Rouge `12` `B`

Smells like the rubber handle of an old gardening implement. But the fruit is less off-putting and drinkable.

VdP des Coteaux de l'Ardeche, Somerfield `13.5` `B`

Character, flavour, good price.

FRENCH WINE   WHITE

Bordeaux Sauvignon Blanc, Somerfield `12` `B`

Chablis Premier Cru, Grande Cuvee, La Chablisienne 1990 `11` `F`

The best-selling wine in the store's fine wine range. Doesn't excite me hugely.

Chardonnay VdP d'Oc 1994, Somerfield — 14 | C

Buttery, lemony, softly fruity. Forthrightly stylish and well priced.

Chardonnay VdP Jardin de la France 1995 — 14.5 | B

Has soft fruit typical of chardonnay gently pressed plus a lemony finish. Excellent value.

Domaine de Bordeneuve VdP des Cotes de Gascogne Blanc, 1995 — 14 | B

Pineapple and melon – a refreshing fruit salad of a wine.

Domaine de la Tuilerie Chardonnay, Hugh Ryman 1995 — 15 | C

Excellent price for such classy fruit.

Domaine de Rivoyre Chardonnay, VdP d'Oc 1993 — 16 | C

Full ripeness of melons in the mouth. Quite superb and polished with tongue-tingling acidity. Stylish, explicit, fine. Limited distribution.

Entre Deux Mers 1995, Somerfield — 12 | C

Gewurztraminer d'Alsace Turckheim 1995, Somerfield — 14 | D

Needs a couple of years to age to be at its best.

Hautes Cotes de Beaune Cottin Freres 1995 — 11 | D

James Herrick Chardonnay VdP d'Oc 1995 — 15 | C

An elegant, comfortingly accommodating wine. A bottle to relax with.

Macon Blanc Villages 1995, Somerfield `13` `C`

Muscat a Petits Grains, VdP des Collines de la Moure 1993 (half bottle) `14` `B`

Treat for days when you're all alone and all you want to do is tackle the newest Loretta Lawson mystery with fresh fruit and cheese for company.

Oak Aged Bordeaux Blanc 1994, Somerfield `13` `C`

Touch pricey.

Pinot Blanc d'Alsace Turckheim 1995, Somerfield `12` `C`

Better in late 1997.

Sancerre Domaine Les Grands Groux, 1995 `11` `E`

Stowells of Chelsea Vin de Pays du Tarn (3-litre box) `12` `F`

Sound but dullish – not a lot of fruit.

Syrah Rose Val d'Orbieu, VdP d'Oc 1995 `12` `B`

Dry, good with fish.

Val d'Orbieu Viognier Chais Cuxac, VdP d'Oc 1995 `14` `B`

The cheapest viognier in the country?

VdP de Cotes des Gascogne Blanc 1995, Somerfield `13` `B`

Fresh, keen, fruity and appealing. Great with fish 'n' chips.

VdP des Bouches du Rhone Blanc `13` `B`

Curious toffeed fruit with sweet/sour finish. Odd.

VdP des Coteaux de l'Ardeche Blanc 1994, Somerfield `13.5` `B`

Fresh, clean, good value.

White Burgundy 1995, Somerfield `12` `D`

GERMAN WINE — WHITE

Baden Dry NV, Somerfield `12.5` `B`

Bodenheimer Burgweg Juwel Beerenauslese 1989 (half bottle) `14` `D`

With a slice of fruit tart or an apple and a hunk of cheese this wine is a jewel indeed. Alas, it's over a fiver for the half bottle which is an angelic size for such a wine but a devilish price tag, though it is beautifully stratified sipping, with layers of herby honey-tinged fruit wound around subtle orange and lime peel flavouring.

Gewurztraminer Halbtrocken Rietburg Co-op, Pfalz NV, Somerfield `12` `C`

Hock Rudolf Muller, Somerfield `13` `A`

A bargain aperitif. Not unpleasant in its lightness.

Morio Muskat St Ursula 1994 `14` `B`

Perfect back-garden tipple.

Mosel Riesling Halbtrocken, Somerfield `14` `B`

Interesting, spiky aperitif. Delicious mineral acidity and lemony fruit.

Mosel Rudolf Muller, Somerfield `13.5` `B`

Brilliantly priced alternative to Lieb – drier too.

Niersteiner Spiegelberg Kabinett, Rudolf Muller, Somerfield `14` `B`

The sweet-seeming honey edge is saved from full-blown sugariness by the fineness of the acidity. Delicious aperitif.

Oberemmeler Rosenberg Riesling 1989 `10` `E`

Pfalz Riesling Trocken Rietburg 1989, Somerfield `12.5` `C`

I suspect many readers will find this dry riesling, with its curious kerosene aroma and austere fruit, nigh undrinkable. But with Chinese food it might be a revelation.

Pinot Blanc Trocken, St Ursula 1993, Somerfield `12` `C`

Rheingau Riesling, St Ursula 1994, Somerfield `12` `C`

Rheinhessen Auslese, Rheinberg Kellerei 1994, Somerfield `13.5` `C`

Terrific aperitif.

Rheinhessen Spatlese, Rheinberg Kellerei 1994, Somerfield `11` `B`

Rudesheimer Rosengarten, Somerfield `12` `B`

Scharzhofberger Riesling Kabinett, Rudolf Muller 1990 `13.5` `C`

Expensive a little, but a pretty aperitif all the same.

St Johanner Abtei Kabinett, Rudolf Muller 1993, Somerfield `13` `B`

Bright and fruity.

HUNGARIAN WINE   RED

Bulls Blood, St Ursula 1993 `10` `B`

I suppose with a goulash this German-bottled Magyar might work, but it is not a hugely exciting wine in other respects.

HUNGARIAN WINE   WHITE

Chardonnay, Somerfield `13` `B`

Good fruit up front but not hugely effectively round right to the finish. But for all that, very attractive and excellent value.

Gyongyos Chardonnay 1995 `13.5` `C`

Lemony and bright.

Gyongyos Sauvignon Blanc 1995 `14` `C`

Back to something of its old racy zippiness. A simple sauvignon, but crisp and gently fruity and firmly authentic.

ITALIAN WINE   RED

Bardolino Fratelli Pasqua, Somerfield `11` `B`

Cabernet Sauvignon del Veneto 1994 | 12 | C

Chianti 1994, Somerfield | 10 | C

Sweet and rather dull. Lost its vigour in the past six months.

Chianti Classico Montecchio 1994 | 14.5 | C

Terrific price for such Tuscan charm. Real earthy style yet very polished.

Chianti Classico Rocca della Macie 1990 | 13.5 | E

Expensive for the style.

Chianti Classico Serristori 1994, Somerfield | 13 | D

Soft, sweet-finishing, very faintly earthy specimen which seems a touch characterless and expensive.

Chianti Conti Serristori 1995, Somerfield | 11 | C

Copertino 1991 | 14 | C

Smooth, juicy, ripe.

I Grilli di Villa Thalia, Calatrasi 1993 | 15 | C

Brilliant value with dry, deeply rich fruit.

Lazio Red, Casale San Giglio 1994 | 14 | B

Character and bite. Good pizza party wine.

Merlot del Veneto Fratelli Pasqua, Somerfield | 12.5 | B

Some plumpness of flavour in the fruit.

Montepulciano d'Abruzzo 1994 | 13.5 | C

Tasty – has dryness yet a soft polish to the fruit.

Montereale Sicilian Red, Calatrasi 1995 | 13 | B |

Good party wine.

Valpolicella Fratelli Pasqua 1995 | 10 | B |

ITALIAN WINE — WHITE

Bianco del Monferrato, Araldica 1995 | 13 | B |

Nice little wine for the money.

Chardonnay del Piemonte Araldica 1995, Somerfield | 12.5 | C |

Frascati Pallavicini 1995, Somerfield | 12 | C |

Expensive for the simplicity of the style.

Le Trulle Chardonnay del Salento 1994 | 16 | B |

Butters the tongue with highly civilised fruit at a very reasonable price. Good southern Italian fruit vivified by New World oneological whizz kids.

Orvieto Classico Conti Serristori 1995 | 12 | C |

Pricey.

Pinot Grigio Fratelli Pasqua 1995, Somerfield | 12 | C |

Soave Fratelli Pasqua 1995, Somerfield | 12.5 | B |

Somerfield Montereale Sicilian White, Calatrasi | 15 | B |

Lots of astonishingly well-integrated flavour here. Has an almond touch on the finish.

Verdicchio Classico Bianchi 1994

MOLDOVAN WINE — WHITE

Kirkwood Moldovan Chardonnay 1995 14 C

Fresh hint of pineapple, clean – not as varietally impactful as it might be but very attractive.

NEW ZEALAND WINE — RED

Montana Cabernet Sauvignon 1994 14 C

Juicy edge to dry, serious fruit. Needs food to come fully alive.

NEW ZEALAND WINE — WHITE

Montana Sauvignon Blanc 1995 13.5 C

Nobilo White Cloud 1995 13 C

Fish 'n' chips wine. Selected stores.

Stoneleigh Sauvignon Blanc 1995 15.5 D

Lovely! A real fresh tastebud-zapper.

**Stowells of Chelsea New Zealand
Sauvignon Blanc (3-litre box)** 13.5 G

Keen, grassy aromas, good fruit, rather a quiet finish.

Timara Dry White 1995

Cut-grass edge.

PORTUGUESE WINE RED

Alta Mesa Estremadura 1994

Simple, soft, ripe, very fruity, delicious chilled and poured over parched tongues.

Dao Reserva, Caves Alianca 1990

Bargain rich, dry fruit. Husky voices but sweet notes intrude and with rich food it's a wonderful bargain.

Douro Foral, Caves Alianca 1991

Delicious – there is no other word for it. It's dry to finish but fruity to kick off and it's thoroughly attractive and soft.

Estorila, Benfica Co-op

Dry and nutty with excellent flavour and fruit.

Foral Tinto Douro Reserva, Caves Alianca 1991

Dry, richly edged, full of flavour.

Leziria Tinto Almeirim

Quinta da Pancas Cabernet Sauvignon 1995 16 C

This wine has long been a favourite of mine, and the '95 vintage is better than ever, justifying a near six quid price tag. Lovely rich fruit abetted by perfectly evolved tannins.

PORTUGUESE WINE WHITE

Bairrada Branco, Caves Alianca, Somerfield

Rather soft and giving.

Estorila Vinho Branco

Delicious. Has crispness yet there on the finish lurks an undertone of creamy nuttiness. Great with smoked fish.

SOUTH AFRICAN WINE RED

Huguenot Hill South African Dry Red

Ripe, polished, deeply flavoured, has nice tannins and it's handsomely built. Very good value for casseroles.

Kumala Cinsault Pinotage 1995

Wallow in soft fruit yet get a degree of thoughtful complexity, lots of rich flavour and a depth which offers style and huge thirst-quenching possibilities. A sunny wine!

Landema Falls South African Cabernet Sauvignon

Gently peppery and spryly fruity. Delicious with roast meats.

South African Pinotage 1996, Somerfield

Juicy and ripe.

SOUTH AFRICAN WINE WHITE

Bellingham Sauvignon Blanc 1995 14 C

Gently grassy and lemony. Great with grilled sardines.

Clearsprings Cape White 15 B

Wonderful medium-sweet, pear-drop fruit of great interest as a chilled aperitif and for people who don't like bone-dry wine.

Huguenot Hills South African Chardonnay 1995 12.5 B

Kumala Colombard/Chardonnay 1995 14 B

Getting to the end of its freshness register but still a good, firmly fruity tipple.

South African Chenin Blanc, Somerfield 13 B

South African Dry White, Somerfield 15.5 B

Lovely fruit here – rounded ogen melon with a slightly musky edge. Superb quaffing bottle.

SPANISH WINE RED

Berberana Tempranillo, Rioja 1994 15 C

Rich, ready, gently vanilla-edged and perfectly well-formed.

Don Hugo Tinto, Somerfield 13.5 B

A good solid fruity battler with an earthy edge. Has character and food-friendliness.

339

Rioja Tinto, Bodegas Almenar Crianza 1992, Somerfield   `15` `C`

Delicious richness with coarseness.

Santara Dry Red Conca de Barbera 1995   `14` `B`

Dry, fruity, with a hint of a smile.

Senorio de Agos, Rioja Reserva 1989   `13` `D`

Torres Sangredetoro 1992   `12` `C`

Not as rich or thrilling as previous vintages. But the '94 is 16 points!

Valencia Red Vincente Gandia, Somerfield   `14` `B`

Nice juicy finish on the fruit which is firm and well structured. Bargain pasta bottle.

Vina Albali Gran Riserva 1984   `13` `C`

Lacks the weight to score more at nigh on a fiver.

SPANISH WINE   WHITE

Castillo Imperial, Somerfield   `14` `B`

Dead simple party plonk with a great flourish on the finish.

Don Hugo Blanco NV, Somerfield   `15` `B`

Banana, vanilla, coconut – terrific breezy fruit just packed with flavour. Great with fish curries!

Gandia Hoya Valley Chardonnay 1994   `14.5` `B`

Hardly one for the purist, but it is a mightily effective, firmly fruity wine with a bruised edge. It goes well with chicken dishes.

Moscatel de Valencia V. Gandia, Somerfield   16   B

Great stuff for the money. Honeyed with soft marmalade undertones.

Rioja Mariscol Crianza 1992   14.5   C

Terrific bottle for tarragon chicken or rich fish dishes. A lovely shape to the gentle vanilla fruit which is smooth, never hoarse or broken-backed. An elegant wine.

Santara Dry White Conca de Barbera 1995   14   B

Decent, if not hugely thrilling, tippling.

Somerfield Valencia Dry White, Vincente Gandia NV   14.5   B

A superbly quaffable party wine and fish-stew wine: dry, firm, fruity-edged, positive, balanced. Brilliant value.

USA WINE   RED

Californian Dry Red, Somerfield   13.5   B

Solid fruit rather than deeply exciting.

Redwood Trail Pinot Noir 1994   14   C

Real pinot – of character, gaminess and with strawberry-scented fruit.

Sebastiani Californian Cabernet Franc 1994   14   C

Delicious smooth vanillaed fruitiness.

USA WINE WHITE

August Sebastiani's White Zinfandel 1994 `12.5` `C`

Sweetish fruit but fair flavour. Rated at £2.99 only. Not
worth £3.99.

Sebastiani Chardonnay 1994 `13` `C`

Sebastiani Sauvignon Blanc 1995 `13` `C`

FORTIFIED WINE

Luis Caballero Fino Sherry, Somerfield `14.5` `C`

A fino with fruit (dry) but not as bone-dry or as saline as
aficionados demand – but a good first step for oloroso fans
looking to develop their palates.

Manzanilla Gonzales Byass, Somerfield `15` `C`

Chilled with grilled prawns or slices of mountain ham, this wine
is the business – THE business.

SPARKLING WINE/CHAMPAGNE

Angas Brut Rose (Australia) `15.5` `D`

Like pleasantly acidic raspberries – dry ones.

Chardonnay Brut, Varichon (France) `15` `C`

A cool, elegant alternative to champagne. Not stocked in the majority of Somerfield stores.

Cordoniu Chardonnay Brut `14` `D`

Clean and sassy.

Cremant de Bourgogne 1991 `14.5` `D`

An elegant bubbly with a gently fruity edge to the final flourish of the fruit.

Louis Domcourt Champagne NV `14` `E`

If you must have champagne, this is well priced, well blended and good value for money. It is a well balanced blend.

Moscato Fizz `13` `A`

Mumm Cuvee Napa Brut (California) `13.5` `E`

Elegant, if a little pricey.

Prince William Blanc de Blancs Champagne `13.5` `G`

Deliciously correct and proper. But £15? Hmm . . .

Prince William Champagne NV `12` `F`

Prince William Rose Champagne, Henri Mandois NV `12` `G`

Seaview Brut `14` `D`

Seppelt Great Western Brut Reserve, Australia `15` `C`

Wonderful value. Gentle lemonic fruit with finesse and style.

Somerfield Cava NV
15 D

Terrific value for money: elegant, finesse-full fruit, gentle acidic finish of refreshing charm.

Touraine Rose Brut, Caves de Viticulteurs de Vouvray
13 D

TESCO

So much hot air

As Tesco is now the country's number one wine retailer, it is not surprising to see it well represented in the *Superplonk* mailbag. Sadly, it has to be said that enquiries about wines which have been reviewed but which customers have been unable to find in Tesco stores account for a significant percentage of the letters, but in that Tesco is certainly far from unique.

Early in 1996, I received just such a letter from Mr Graham Manning of Stratford St Mary near Colchester. In common with some other readers faced with this vexing problem, Mr Manning suspects the retailer may be guilty of sharp practice in submitting certain vintage wines for tasting, but then only stocking the following year's vintage. He wrote:

> For the third year running I have got your *Superplonk* guide. As usual, it's entertaining and informative and no doubt I shall use it all year and look forward to the 1997 version.
>
> This year as last I hotfoot it to Tesco with a shortlist of those wines you rate very highly, only to find them absent from the shelves. Last year I was disappointed. This year I believe it is more serious.
>
> It seems to me that Tesco are sending you the last couple of bottles of wines they know you will rate highly and are then stocking up on next year's vintage expecting customers not to notice or buy anyway. What do you think?

Can I suggest that wines which will not be available after the first week in January be omitted from your annual guide?

While many readers have written in complaining that they could not find certain wines on the shelves, few have raised this specific point about retailers substituting vintages. Of course, it is in the very nature of the wine business to move on to the next year's vintage, and at least demonstrates that a particular supplier has a consistent quality and the retailer a degree of fidelity to its suppliers.

A rather more frequent gripe from readers – not only with regard to Tesco – relates to the selective distribution of certain wines. It was this old chestnut which prompted Mr Dave Thomas of Coventry to write. He had bought a bottle of Domaine de Pigoudet at his local Tesco, only to find when he returned to purchase another bottle that the store did not in fact carry that line. The original bottle he had bought was in fact a 'rogue delivery'.

In his letter of June 1991, Mr Thomas asks: 'Perhaps through your column you could influence the big stores like Tescos to explain why they discriminate against some areas yet continue to advertise countrywide? This practice results in a great deal of time being wasted by both customer and staff which must be counter-productive and inefficient.'

For some, the frustration is too much to bear. I received the following letter from Mrs A.M. Kingston, 'Exasperated of Leeds', in May 1995:

Enough is enough! I am wasting no more of my life looking for wines that you recommend. Last Saturday, as usual, I read your article, made a note of the wines I fancied and on Monday went to my local Tesco for the Noble Oak Bulgarian Merlot/Cabernet.

No, they were sorry, they weren't going to get any of the Noble Oak because there wasn't enough to go round all their stores. This is the main Tesco in Leeds so I don't suppose it was the only store that had frustrated *Guardian* readers roaming the aisles and making their way to Safeway (which did have the Domaine Vieux Manoir de Maransan).

I can tolerate reading about wines I can't afford; I can tolerate reading about wines I could afford if there was an appropriate outlet near enough; what has me seething with rage is finding wines I would like to buy have disappeared down some black hole south of Sheffield before reaching my local stores. At the very least, will you please persuade Tesco (and Sainsbury's for that matter) to come clean about the availability of the wines they want you to plug in your column.

Not being able to find a wine which has been favourably and temptingly described in a wine column has to be one of the most frustrating experiences for the wine consumer. Having suffered this experience, Mr James Aston of Burgess Hill wrote on 12 July 1994 with some searching and pertinent questions:

> Your column is the first thing I turn to every Saturday morning when the *Guardian* is delivered, in addition to which I buy several copies each year of your excellent paperback, *Superplonk*, one to keep, the others as gifts to friends. Relying on such sure support, could I ask you to settle a point for me, which is whether the wines of which you write are sent to you by the shops, to review in the manner of publishers sending out books for review, or whether you yourself pick and choose the wines?
>
> The matter arises from the favourable comments you made about Tesco's Recioto Amarone della Valpolicella, Villa Cera 1986 at £5.49, in a column last March. I was so disappointed at my failure to find it after trips to the local Tesco that I wrote and told them so. I wrote more in sorrow than anger, on the basis that it was quite unfair for them to send out wines for review and then not stock

them at large new stores such as B. Hill, plus the fact that it is by no means the first time it has happened. I doubt if it will be the last, which is why I enquire.

You will see their (eventual) reply; I acted on it quickly, and so did Mr Beddow (wines and spirits manager at Burgess Hill) – he phoned exactly 25 hours later to say he had got two cases in. When I went to see him he insisted that wine correspondents go round doing their own selections, and that it often causes them embarrassment because of the supply position. If he is right, then my complaint was founded on the wrong basis, and in order to avoid making an ass of myself at some future date, will you be good enough to say what actually happens? No need for a formal reply if you're busy drinking and writing; a couple of lines on a compliments slip will do. Apologies for the errors; corkscrew time in an hour, when things will improve!

Tesco's offer of help to Mr Aston in this matter sadly lacked that most effective of palliatives – the gift voucher. Having dragged their feet rather in dealing with the problem, a free fiver's worth would not have done any harm. But Mr Aston's question about how and which wines come to be reviewed needed an answer. I wrote:

Firstly, to answer your question about the wines that are sent to me, it is a mixture of unsolicited bottles sent to me by all the high street wine retailers and supermarkets who think a particular wine will be of interest to me and also wines which I myself on perusing wine lists think that I would like to taste to see whether they are worth including in the column.

The fact is that Mr Beddow is not entirely correct when he says that wine correspondents go round making their own selections. As I say some of the time I do, but a lot of the time, and certainly in the case of Tesco's Recioto Amarone della Valpolicella, it is actually the retailer who sends me the wine, or invites me to a wine-tasting at which the wine features among many other bottles. And I taste it there and rate it accordingly. I always make sure that a wine I write about is widely stocked. Where it is in restricted supply, I always say so. I hope this answers the points you make.

I had had a similar letter from Mr M.R. Jones of Northampton back in 1990 who had been trying to buy a bottle of Forget Brimont champagne at the Tesco stores in Banbury and Leamington without success. On that particular occasion, Steven Wellard, Customer Services Director at Tesco, had replied to the enquiry, explaining that the champagne had been reviewed 'without our prior knowledge', causing an increase in demand. While Mr Wellard was extravagant in his explanation of how 'linear footage' dictates the assortment carried by any particular store, he also chose to eschew the tried and tested gift voucher approach.

Steve Browness of Peterborough had better luck. Having bought a bottle of Dolcetto d'Acqui 1990 from Tesco, he wrote to me with three questions about the wine and its packaging.

Re. Tesco's Dolcetto d'Acqui 1990
For the last two years I have been buying supermarket wines on the strength of your recommendations in *Superplonk*. Generally speaking I have been more than satisfied with my purchases. Last week, I purchased a bottle of the above Italian wine from Tesco. Three unusual features have caused me to write to you.

Firstly, upon pulling the cork I noticed that it bore the legend 'Espana'. Secondly, the bottle is brown – unusual for a red wine. And thirdly, while drinkable, the wine was highly unexceptional.

I was able to go some way to satisfying Mr Browness's curiosity on all three counts. I explained that Spain was a major cork producer and often supplies corks for other countries' wines. Red wine is often put in brown bottles, and the early production of this wine had been disappointing. I also passed on Mr Browness's letter to Tesco who wrote to him with their own explanation and a complimentary bottle of wine.

Aside from standing for public office or possibly moving into the field of political assassination, there was less I could do to help Mr M. Stanton of Liverpool. He wrote in February 1993 about a surge in the price of a wine recommended in my column at £1.99, and found in Tesco at £2.49:

> After having read your column on cheap wine bargains on 7 February in *Weekend Guardian* I decided to try a local Bulgarian Country Wine, at the price you quoted, £1.99 at Tesco. Having purchased a bottle (with the lady wrapping it up for me), low and behold 'Sorry to say you're wrong', its price was £2.49 a bottle. Surely it doesn't jump 50p overnight, or pardon my mistake, anything can happen under this government!
>
> P.S. I still like your column.

While the government is responsible for the unreasonably high excise duties charged on wine in this country, in this instance it was more likely to have been the retailer than Messrs Major and Lamont (Chancellor of the Exchequer at the time) who were behind the foul-up – for a change. However, when Ms JF Boyle of Meersbrook, Sheffield wrote to me complaining of hot air blowing throughout the wine department, I could not help but suspect further government interference.

Ms Boyle had observed that blowers in Tesco's Woodseats store were directing hot air directly on to the wines which might have affected their drinkability. I forwarded the letter on to Tesco who acted on it and replied to Ms Boyle in June 1994:

> Following your correspondence with Malcolm Gluck we have had all the systems at the store checked by heating and ventilation engineers. A number of changes have been implemented.

Above the wine shelving the direction of the air vent has been changed using a 'ventilation blind' system. Now the air is projected into the aisle instead of directly down on to the wine.

Checks have been made and we are pleased to say that the hot air no longer cooks the wine!

I hope that you continue to enjoy shopping at Tesco.

Tesco's PR department was also called into action when Mr Stanley Stamper of Angus was unable to buy a bottle of Tokay, reviewed in the column in October 1993. He first wrote to me on 13 November:

I have, with appreciation, your 1993 *Superplonk* paperback. Bought in Tesco – yet, despite unashamedly using your illustrious name when writing with a polite query to said supermarket and breaking all Scots-are-mean certainties by enclosing a stamped, self-addressed for a reply, nix.

All brought about by your fulsome praise of Tesco's Tokaji Aszu 5 Puttonyos, 1988, at £6.49 per 50cl bottle, in *Weekend Guardian* 16.10.93.

I phoned Riverside, Dundee, Tesco and was asked if Tokay was Japanese. Perhaps my accent. Discovered it was not in stock anyway, so wrote to the Stockbuying Manager, asking if the branch would be stocking the wine and, if not, could he make arrangements for me to buy a case.

No reply, so I have ceased at present from shopping at the store. Voting with my credit card so to speak.

Any advice? I really would like to get the 5 Puttonyos Tokay, as the only one I have found so far locally is in Asda – 3 Puttonyos, 1981/83 at £6.99.

The next week I replied to Mr Stamper with bad news. It is a long way from Angus to Blackpool.

The nearest branch of Tesco which stocks the Tokay is Blackpool!!!! However, I have spoken to Tesco's HQ and they tell me that you may order the wine if you ring your local branch. The branch, however, must order a case of it in order to sell you one bottle and I have asked that this happens but I cannot promise. Please tell your branch to speak to Ms Janet Lee at Tesco's wine-buying department in Cheshunt and she will expedite matters. I have had a word by phone with this department and they promise to do their best to help. If the problem still persists, please get back to me.

The minimum ordering requirement was of no concern to Mr Stamper, as he was quite prepared to buy the whole case. Not only did Tesco ensure that Mr Stamper could buy the Tokay at his local store, but I am delighted to report that Janet Lee of Tesco's wine department also sent him £10 of tokens which he put towards the purchase of six bottles of the Tokay. Finally satisfied, he wrote to me on 10 December:

Thanks to your silver tongue or golden writing, I have at last obtained the Tokay about which you wrote so glowingly in the *Guardian*. You were, of course, right. It is superb.

Ah, the power of the pen.

While Mr Stamper was eventually placated by some excellent PR work, I wonder whether Mr J. Jakers of Wyvern may represent more of a challenge for Janet Lee and her team.

Bugger Tesco's. I have been out of my way to visit a large Tesco store (in Worcester) and they do not stock 'Malcolm Gluck' and they do not have Randall Ridge, Noble Oak Bulgarian, Catalan Red – white or the . . .

What is the point of it all?

Over to you, Ms Lee.

Tesco
Tesco House
PO Box 18 Delamare Road
Cheshunt
EN8 9SL

Tel 01992 632222
Fax 01992 644235

SEE STOP PRESS SECTION AT END OF BOOK FOR LAST-MINUTE ADDITIONS TO THIS RETAILER'S RANGE.

ARGENTINIAN WINE WHITE

Picajuan Peak Chardonnay NV

Oh! What a pity! The weak finish mars the plot of this potential thriller.

AUSTRALIAN WINE RED

**Australian Cabernet Sauvignon,
SE Australia, Tesco**

Leathery, slightly exotic aroma. Full, soft, caressing fruit of a degree of complexity which is surprising at the price.

Australian Mataro, Tesco

Australian Ruby Cabernet, Tesco

**Australian Shiraz, McLaren Vale 1994,
Tesco**

Rich and very smoothly conceived. Perfect ripe Aussie shiraz – so easy to drink it's embarrassing. Not at all stores.

Barossa Merlot 1993, Tesco

A massively, richly fruity, yielding, sensual, deep wine of achingly delicious softness. Top seventy-seven stores only.

Barramundi Shiraz/Merlot

Vibrant, spicy, fun.

Bin 707 Cabernet Sauvignon, Penfolds 1992   18.5   G

Just a beautiful thing all round. Elegant tannins, perfect fruit, perfect construction, a man-made thing of perfect weight. Selected stores only.

Bleasdale Langhorne Creek Malbec 1990   13.5   D

Expensive for the style. Tasty and well developed but those extra pennies tell. Top seventy stores only.

Brown Brothers Tarrango 1995   13   C

Just a touch expensive for such fun-filled fruit. Juicier than beaujolais, though. Selected stores.

Chapel Hill McLaren Vale Cabernet Sauvignon 1993   15   E

Expensive but beautifully structured. Has lovely tannins and fruit. Will develop well in bottle for a couple of years. Top sixteen stores only.

Chapel Hill McLaren Vale Shiraz 1993   15   E

Has a mild coffee/chocolate touch on the finish. A subtle wine, then, but a well-endowed one to start off with. Not at all stores.

Coonawarra Cabernet Sauvignon 1994, Tesco   14   D

Hardys Nottage Hill Cabernet Sauvignon/ Shiraz 1994   15   C

Classic rich Aussie with an insouciant touch of dry fruit.

Ironstone Cabernet/Shiraz 1993   16.5   D

Stunning ripeness yet gloriously controlled length of tonality. The fruit stretches the length of the palate from tongue-tip to adenoids. It glides down gorgeously. A sensual wine. Selected stores.

Kingston Estate Mataro 1994

Expensive for the level of fruit on offer which although most attractive is not complex enough to merit a £6 price tag. Selected stores.

Kingston Estate Shiraz 1993

Lovely rich fruit and light tannins. A meaty wine of great softness and flavour and subdued spiciness. Selected stores.

Kingston Reserve Riverland Shiraz 1992

Top seventy-seven stores only.

Lindemans Bin 50 Shiraz 1993

Rich, very textured, deeply flavoured and great company. Selected stores.

Maglieri Shiraz, McLaren Vale 1993

A medium-weight shiraz of depth, flavour, soft tannins, savoury fruit and delicious richness. Smooth delivery of fruit. Top seventy-seven stores only.

McLaren Vale Grenache, Tesco

Just plain wonderful. Has rounded fruit with dry, gently tannic undertones and a sinfully soft, lingering finish. Brilliant fruit. Not at all stores.

McLaren Vale Merlot, Ryecroft 1993

Beautifully integrated fruit and acid. A very soft, rich wine of stand-alone class and vibrancy. Only food will make it wobble. Choose light dishes – not those overspiced or oversauced.

Mick Morris Durif 1991

Looks like ink, smells like port, textured like fresh tar, tastes like cassis (plus rich tannins of great depth), this is a very potent contender indeed. Try it with roast game (duck breast with cassis sauce would be wonderful). But be warned: a little goes a long way with this 15% alcohol wine. Top seventy stores only.

Old Penola Estate Coonawarra Cabernet Sauvignon 1991   13.5   D

Loses out a bit, at this price, because the finish is rather anodyne and oversoft. Top seventy-seven stores only.

Orlando RF Cabernet Sauvignon 1992   14.5   C

Touch of beefiness here and velvet tannins. Too soft? For claret die-hards yes. Not for me.

Penfolds Bin 128 Shiraz, Coonawarra 1992   14   E

Only just makes this rating. It's impressive to start but I'd like more heft on the finish for this kind of money. Selected stores.

Penfolds Bin 35 Shiraz Cabernet 1994   15.5   C

Excellent value. Has lovely texture and warm, spicy fruit of depth, flavour, balance and finish. Great roast food wine.

Penfolds Kalimna Bin 28 Shiraz 1993   16   E

Robustness yet poise and grace. Yes, it's got a bruiser's build and punch but it pirouettes perfectly on the tongue, like a blackberry bush (brambly, rich, dry, brackeny) on wooden stilts. Selected stores.

Rosemount Balmoral Syrah 1993   12   G

This is just too much money for this much fruit. Delicious at £6/£7 but not at £17. Top sixteen stores only.

Rosemount Shiraz/Cabernet 1995 `15` `C`

Such smoothness and velvet-textured fruit. A gentility of fruit which surprises and delights.

Shiraz, Tesco `13` `C`

Excellent value, demurely fruity.

St Halletts Old Block Shiraz 1993 `14` `E`

Ripe and very ready. Selected stores only.

Stirling Estate Shiraz 1992 `15` `D`

Vigorous yet softly gripping tannins give the fruit a firm attacking structure and smooth delivery.

Stowells of Chelsea Shiraz Cabernet (3-litre box) `14` `G`

Rich fruit with earthy undertones. Has a long, meaty finish with a firm, purposeful balance of fruit and acid.

Temple Bruer Cornucopia Grenache 1994 `15.5` `D`

This has come on nicely in bottle. Shrouded in dark, rich herby fruit, the soft centre is ripe and full, and so the overall effect is lots of flavour, dry yet bursting with energy and subdued spiciness. Selected stores.

Temple Bruer Shiraz/Malbec 1989 `14` `D`

Dry, mature, serious, with a beautifully developed tannic softness. Top seventy stores only.

Tesco Australian Red, Shiraz/Cabernet Sauvignon, S Australia `14` `B`

Brilliant value. The shiraz and cabernet sauvignon grape varieties combine most attractively and offer a tarry aroma, excellent fruit with some cherry and plum, and a dryness which is not too spicy or sweaty. Outstanding value.

Thomas Mitchell Cabernet/Shiraz/Cabernet Franc 1994 `15.5` `D`

Rhone meets Chinon in this rich, forceful, tasty wine.

Tim Adams Shiraz 1993 `14` `E`

This has character but the price is high. I suspect it might be better in a year. Top seventy-seven stores only.

Wynns John Riddoch Cabernet Sauvignon, Coonawarra 1992 `13.5` `G`

Intense mature blackcurrant aroma. Rather sweet fruit. Top seventy-seven stores only.

Yalumba Bushvine Grenache, 1993 `16.5` `D`

Aromatic, softly tannic, figgy, blackcurranty, plummy – this is a lot of wine. Tremendous partner for casseroles.

AUSTRALIAN WINE WHITE

Australian Chardonnay, SE Australia, Tesco `14` `C`

Has oodles of fruit and finishes with a sly wink of lemonic acidity.

Australian Colombard/Chardonnay, Tesco `15` `B`

Great combo of grapes offering zest, fruit and acid. Lovely glass of wine. Very tasty.

Australian Sauvignon Blanc, SE Australia, Tesco `14` `C`

Dry yet with lots of friendly fruit which makes the wine palatable with salads or on its own.

Australian White, Rhine Riesling, SE Australia, Tesco `14` `B`

Flavour and fruit. Ignore the riesling you may know and hate – this example has the sun in it.

Barramundi Semillon/Chardonnay `15` `C`

Rich, fruit-salad nose. Lots of pineapple acidity and great, swinging melon/mango fruit. Smashing wine to let the heart soar.

Best's Colombard 1995 `15.5` `C`

Just lie back and wallow in this wine's fruit. Or throw it at Chinese food. Lush, ripe, ravishing stuff!

Cape Mentelle Semillon/Sauvignon Blanc 1995 `16` `E`

It's a treat. One of Western Australia's classic wines. Beautifully structured, finely wrought, superbly easy yet complex. A lovely wine. Top sixteen stores only.

Chapel Hill Unwooded Chardonnay 1994 `15` `E`

Has the rich thrust of ripe melon with the cool, incisive thrust of a fresh acidity – all naked and unmasked by wood. A wine of elegance. Finely cut. Top seventy-seven stores only.

Chardonnay, Tesco `12` `C`

Clare Valley Riesling 1995, Tesco `14.5` `C`

An old favourite in a new vintage. Deliciously ripe, forward aperitif which is never coarse or blowsy. Not at all stores.

Delatite Dead Man's Hill Gewurztraminer 1992

An overpriced curiosity. Appealing rose-petal fruit but lacks bite and an easy-to-swallow price. Not at all stores.

Great White 1995

Fruity, simple, attractive – but not at £3.99.

Hardys Nottage Hill Chardonnay 1995

When a wine gets so close to a fiver, it must equally offer fiver fruit. This one succeeds.

Hunter Valley Semillon 1994, Tesco

Good at everything but the muted finish and the numbers on the price tag. Not at all stores.

Ironstone Semillon/Chardonnay 1995

Great wine for shellfish and Thai fish dishes. Not an exotic wine but a decisive one. Selected stores.

Krondorf Show Reserve Chardonnay 1993

15 E

Oily, nutty, tastebud-enveloping flavour. Expensive but a treat. Top sixteen stores only.

Lindemans Padthaway Chardonnay 1993

15.5 E

Worth the money for the beautifully integrated wood and fruit which is lengthy, fine, concentrated and quite delicious. Extremely elegant.

McLaren Vale Chardonnay 1995, Tesco

So easy to like. It's oily, rich, characterful, elegant and charming on the finish as it leaves the throat. Not at all stores.

Mick Morris Liqueur Muscat (half bottle) `15.5` `C`

Wonderful with Christmas pudding. Indeed, it seems vinified from Christmas pudding itself.

Noble Semillon, Riverina 1992, Tesco (half bottle) `15` `D`

Echoes of lemon curd and ginger marmalade here. Drink it with a black mood and watch it lift. Top seventy stores only.

Old Triangle Semillon/Chardonnay 1995 `13.5` `C`

Penfolds Semillon/Chardonnay 1995 `14` `D`

Poached chicken and this wine would be a marvellous union. Not at all stores.

Pewsey Vale Eden Vale Riesling 1995 `14.5` `D`

Always one of Australia's more biting and successful rieslings. Not at all stores.

Preece Chardonnay 1994 `15` `D`

As exotic and plump as a Turkish belly dancer. Not at all stores.

Rhine Riesling, Tesco `15` `B`

Rich, oily and most attractively fruity. Great aperitif and also with fish. Interesting accompaniment to complex salads.

Rosemount Estate Chardonnay 1995 `16` `D`

Beautiful controlled fruit with vivacity and restraint. This paradox is Rosemount's hallmark.

Rosemount Estate Sauvignon Blanc 1995 `16` `D`

Expensive but classy, clean, fruity and very fine with fish dishes.

Rosemount Roxburgh Chardonnay 1993 `17` `G`

Yes, 17 points, 17 quid. No justice, is there? This wine is simply one of the best chardonnays in the world. It is a perfect melding of wood, fruit and acid into a delicately rich, lingering, superbly textured work of huge charm and great finesse. Top sixteen stores only.

Sauvignon Blanc, Tesco `13` `C`

St Halletts Semillon/Sauvignon Blanc 1995 `14` `E`

Suave, gently rich, characterful fruit. Not at all stores.

Stirling Estate Chardonnay 1995 `15` `D`

New vintage, available at top fourteen stores. Lovely rich ripe fruit which careers off the tastebuds like liquid melon and slides down the pocket of the throat.

Stowells of Chelsea Semillon Chardonnay (3-litre box) `14` `G`

Presence and lift, style and purpose – this fruit knows where it's going. Good with food and mood.

Temple Bruer Botrytis Riesling (half bottle) `14.5` `D`

A blend of '92 and '93, this is a very rich wine which is good now with soft fruit desserts but kept for ten years will be dazzling.

Tim Adams Semillon 1994 `14` `E`

The sort of rich, luxurious semillon to appeal to lovers of old sauvignon blanc. Top seventy-seven stores only.

AUSTRIAN WINE   RED

Lenz Moser Blauer Zweigelt 1994 `15.5` `C`

The beaujolais of Vienna (but much better). A lovely supple, fruity wine of considerable charm and no little finesse. Great value and served chilled will please even those who say they prefer white to red. Top seventy stores only.

AUSTRIAN WINE WHITE

Lenz Moser Gruner Veltliner 1994

Not hugely fruity or demonstrative (it's rather restrained and Viennese, to be precise) but it is attractively crisp and clean – and very well priced. Selected stores.

Lenz Moser Selection Gruner Veltliner 1995 13 C

Selected stores.

BRAZILIAN WINE RED

Brazilian Cabernet Sauvignon/Merlot, Tesco

Moving forward to the exuberance of fruit you would expect from Brazil. Selected stores.

BRAZILIAN WINE WHITE

Brazilian Chardonnay/Semillon, Tesco 14 B

Brazilian Pinot Blanc, Tesco 12.5 C

BULGARIAN WINE RED

Bulgarian Cabernet Sauvignon Reserve
1989, Tesco

An aromatic, rich, bright-fruit edged wine of impressive weight and class for the money. Soupy, ripe (yet dry-finishing) and excellent with roasted and grilled meats and vegetables.

Bulgarian Country Red, Tesco `13` `A`

BULGARIAN WINE WHITE

Bear Ridge Aligote `14` `B`

Lots of flavour here. A more multi-layered aligote (grape variety) than ever emerged from Beaujolais. Not at all stores.

Bear Ridge Bulgarian White 1993 `13` `B`

Sound, fruity, drinkable, technically correct. But wears a bowler hat rather than a baseball cap.

Bear Ridge Dry White `12` `B`

Not at all stores.

Bear Ridge White Cabernet Sauvignon
1994

Well, it's not every day you drink the claret grape so wan but the fruit's all there – quirky and talcum-soft. Good with fish salads. Not in all stores.

Bulgarian Chardonnay Reserve, Tesco `14` `B`

Bulgarian Country White, Tesco `12` `A`

CANADIAN WINE — RED

Canadian Red, Tesco `10` `C`

CANADIAN WINE — WHITE

Canadian White, Tesco `13.5` `C`

Aromatic and tasty. The wine is a touch expensive at nigh on four quid.

CHILEAN WINE — RED

Caliterra Cabernet Merlot 1993 `15` `C`

Dry and rich-edged. Good balance, slightly restrained but ultimately very satisfyingly fruity and very good value.

Caliterra Cabernet Sauvignon Reserve 1992 `14.5` `D`

Classy feel here and some delivery of savoury fruit.

Canepa Oak Aged Cabernet Sauvignon 1992 `14` `C`

Not a pound better wine than the store's own-label Chilean cabernet. Selected stores.

Canepa Oak Aged Zinfandel 1994

Jammy yet very dry with touches of rich tannin. Top seventy stores only.

Chilean Cabernet Sauvignon, Tesco

Has a warm, brisk edge of no-nonsense fruitiness. It's sympathetic to the tastebuds, bold to the throat, agreeable with roast meats and grills.

Chilean Red, Tesco

Ridiculous price for such calm, classy richness and depth. Not hugely complex but decidedly delicious.

Don Maximo Cabernet Sauvignon 1993

Errazuriz Don Maximiano Cabernet
Sauvignon Reserva 1993

Lot of money for an admittedly highly drinkable wine. Nice perfume, soft fruit on the palate, but finishes with less vigour than I require to rate a wine over 14 at nigh on seven quid. Top seventy-seven stores only.

Errazuriz Merlot 1995

A bomb of a wine. The flavour fills the mouth (leathery, soft, blackcurranty ripe) and explodes with richness. Selected stores.

Stowells of Chelsea Chilean Merlot
Cabernet (3-litre box)

This wine is soft yet with an agreeably gentle level of proud tannins. Why don't I rate it higher? I simply find the aroma off-puttingly ripe and rubbery. It really ought to be better put together than this.

Undurraga Pinot Noir, Maipo 1995

Soft like peach-down though not so juicy nor so ripe. But it's the texture which makes the wine.

367

CHILEAN WINE WHITE

Caliterra Casablanca Chardonnay 1995 `16` `D`

Mature feel, youthful structure – a winningly delicious marriage of firm, subtly rich fruit, gentle acids and superb brilliance. A lovely wine. Top seventy-seven stores only.

Caliterra Sauvignon Blanc 1995 `14` `C`

Nutty, with a coating of lemon.

Canepa Oaked Chardonnay 1993 `16` `C`

Hints at rumbustiousness but doesn't, thankfully, quite pull it off. The punchy fruit (melon) is beautifully counterpointed by the acidity (pineapple) and the result is a lovely, good-value tipple. Great with all sorts of fish and light fowl dishes.

Chilean Sauvignon Blanc, Tesco `14.5` `C`

Excellent combination of elegant fruit and elegant acidity. A terrific sauvignon: class in a glass.

Chilean White, Tesco `16` `B`

Simply one of the tastiest own-label Chilean white wines on sale under £3.50. It is classy, elegant and refreshing.

Errazuriz Chardonnay 1995 `C`

Rolls around the tongue like creamy, melon-coated pebbles fresh from some Lewis Carroll stream. Delightful wine.

Errazuriz Chardonnay Reserva 1994 `16` `D`

Has the added chewiness genuine reserve wines have so it's more resilient and flavoursome with food. A richly elegant, fruity statement. Selected stores.

CYPRIOT WINE RED

Keo Othello `4` `B`

CYPRIOT WINE WHITE

Keo Aphrodite Dry White `11` `B`

ENGLISH WINE WHITE

Denbies English Table Wine NV `13` `B`

FRENCH WINE RED

Anjou Rouge, Tesco `13` `B`
Some amusing fruit. Best drunk chilled with grilled salmon.

Beaujolais, Tesco `13` `C`
Light and fruity, the label says, and this is no lie.

**Beaumes de Venise, Cotes du Rhone
Villages 1994** `14` `D`
I did hesitate about this rating but decided that in spite of being over a fiver this wine had the class and richness of flavour to merit joining Club 14-20. It is polished and lingering. Top seventy-seven stores only.

Bordeaux Rouge 1995   13.5   C

Good basic glugging claret.

Bourgeuil, La Huralaie, Caslot-Galbrun 1992   15   C

Black cherries and raspberries richly mixed, very dry, very chunky. Superb food wine. Coal-chewy, dark, and dank to taste; it is hard and tannic and softening nicely – if you can still find the odd bottle to try it.

Buzet 1991   13.5   C

Brisk fruit, edgily tannic.

Cabernet Sauvignon, Haute Vallee de l'Aude, Tesco   13   B

Excellent value for the family get-together with a roast on the table.

Cahors, Tesco   12.5   B

Selected stores.

Chartron La Fleur Bordeaux Rouge 1993   14.5   C

Bargain savoury fruit, dry and a touch sulky, but handsome tannins give it a final flourish of some style.

Chateau Bois Galant, Medoc 1990   13   D

Impressively well developed, the tannins in this wine. Very good with grilled lamb chops with rosemary.

Chateau Cantemerle Grand Cru Classe 1992   12   F

Silly price for such smug smoothness and softness. Selected stores.

Chateau Cote Montpezat, Cotes de Castillon 1993 | 14 | D |

Good, brambly fruit, good tannins. An austere wine but will age for several years and will go now with roast meats.

Chateau d'Arsac Haut-Medoc 1991 | 11 | G |

Chateau de Beaulieu Coteaux d'Aix en Provence 1994 | 11 | C |

Chateau de Goelane 1992 | 12 | D |

Weak finish to the performance lets it down a touch.

Chateau des Gondats 1992 | 13 | D |

Serious tannins. Must have food, roast or raw.

Chateau du Bluizard, Beaujolais Villages | 10 | C |

Almost charmless, but not quite. Top seventy stores only.

Chateau Haut Faugeres, St Emilion 1991 | 13.5 | E |

Grasps at being impressive and classic and doesn't quite achieve it with the effortlessness of previous vintages.

Chateau Labegorce Margaux 1989 | 13 | G |

Chateau Leon Bordeaux 1993 | 13 | C |

Hints of smoke and charcoal on the offhand fruit give it bite and flavour. But it comes across as unfriendly and rather bristly, which time may not necessarily mellow. Selected stores.

Chateau les Gravieres, St Emilion 1992 | 12 | E |

Light, dry, but will it repay cellaring? I think not.

Chateau les Valentines Bergerac 1989 | 14 | C |

Very dry and still developing flavour in bottle (will improve in two to three years). Has a meaty edge to blackberry fruit which is rather serious.

Chateau Lynch Moussas, Pauillac 1989   `11` `G`

Chateau Marquis-de-Terme, Margaux 1988   `13` `E`

There is a touch of beefiness about this grand margaux but I would prefer to wait a few years before I met it and it had softened.

Chateau Michelet, Bordeaux (2-litre box)   `14` `E`

A hugely approachable, soft, friendly claret. Very drinkable and very smooth.

Chateau Patache d'Aux, Cru Grand Bourgeois 1991   `15.5` `D`

Splendid little claret with depth of fruit and tannins, and of surprising class. Great roast lamb wine. Might be even better if you put it down for three years.

Chateau Pigoudet, Coteaux d'Aix en Provence 1991   `15` `C`

Delicious chocolate-coated (yet dry) brambly fruit. Very tasty.

Chateau St Georges, St. Emilion 1993   `12.5` `G`

Not as thrill-packed as previous vintages. Selected stores.

Chateau St Louis La Perdrix, Costieres de Nimes 1993, Tesco   `14`

A warm, southern food wine which has herbiness, a gentle spiciness and savoury fruitiness to enhance anything from sausages to chicken.

Chateau St Nicholas, Fronsac 1987   `10` `D`

Chateau Toutigeac 1992 `14` `C`

Good, rich, balanced, well-structured.

Chateau Vieux Castel Robin, Saint Emilion 1990 `15` `D`

Soft and very thick with such accessible fruit you can eat it . . .
I mean drink it . . . with a spoon.

Chateauneuf du Pape 1994, Tesco `13` `D`

Chateauneuf du Pape les Arnevels, Quiot 1992 `12` `E`

Touch flabby.

Chateauneuf-du-Pape Le Chemin des Mulets 1992 `14` `E`

Immediately soft-drinking wine of instant likeability.

Chinon, Baronnie Madeleine, 1990 `14` `D`

I think the time has come to drink all available bottles of
this wine.

Claret, Tesco `14` `B`

Lovely soft yet dry example of the genre. Excellent value for a
superbly approachable bottle.

Clos de Chenoves, Bourgogne Rouge 1990 `12` `D`

Corbieres, Tesco `13.5` `B`

A worthy, characterful food wine.

Cotes de Duras, 1993 `10` `B`

Cotes de Duras, Tesco `13` `B`

Soft with faintly savoury fruit. Very good value.

Cotes de Provence, Tesco — 13 | B

Relatively smooth rustic plonk.

Cotes de Roussillon Rouge, Tesco — 12.5 | B

Cotes du Frontonnais 1990 — 13 | B

Cotes du Marmandais Domaine Beaulieu-Saint Saveur 1992, Tesco — 13 | B

Cotes du Rhone, Tesco — 11 | B

Cotes du Rhone Villages 1993 — 11 | C

Cotes du Rhone Villages 1994, Tesco — 13 | C

Young and dry. Will soften in the months to come.

Couly Dutheuil Chinon, Baronnie Madeleine 1992 — 16 | D

Lovely maturity (which will develop for a further few years). The cherry and raspberry fruit has fully integrated with the slate-like tannins and the result is a lovely dry, food-friendly wine (all meats and vegetables) as well as being superbly drinkable by itself – chilled.

Crozes Hermitage 1992 — 13 | D

Domaine Cazelles-Verdier, Minervois 1990 — 15 | C

Dry, smoky, fruity, rich. A lovely wine. Available through Tesco mail order only – two bottles per mixed case.

Domaine de Conroy Brouilly, Jean St Charles 1994 — 11 | D

Juicy fruit of adolescent demeanour.

Domaine de la Doline Fitou 1992

Soft, supremely drinkable, and very briskly fruity. Not at all stores.

Domaine de la Source Syrah 1994, Tesco

Dry and fruity. More a town than a country mouse.

Domaine de Lanestousse Madiran 1990

Shows the Aussies a clean pair of fruity, leathery, dry-soled heels and even chucks in a genuine and unique rustic edge. A deeply savoury, tannic, velvety, lithe wine of superb character. Wonderful with all cheese dishes.

Domaine de Pauline Cotes du Rhone 1993

Good tannins here but well tamed by the frisky fruit which also offers excellent balancing acids. Good chilled, this wine. Selected stores.

Domaine de Prebayon, Cotes du Rhone Villages 1993

Some depth and flavour here.

Domaine de Trillol, Corbieres 1989

Lively and bright with a heavy hint of smoker's cough to the fruit. Available through Tesco mail order only – two bottles per mixed case.

Domaine des Baumelles, Cotes du Luberon 1993

Domaine du Soleil Vegan Merlot, VdP d'Oc 1994

Dry, leathery, very attractive.

Domaine Georges Bertrand Corbieres 1993

Soft chocolatey tannins. Almost too soft. Selected stores.

Domaine Maurel Fonsalade, Saint Chinian 1994

Whacks it to you on the finish rather belatedly – after you have wondered where the fruit has gone. It scores in the end but seems rather hesitant to kick off. Top seventy-seven stores only.

Escoubes Rouge, Vin de Pays de l'Aude, Grassa, Tesco

A pasta party plonk: dry, rich, earthy, fun. Selected stores.

French Cabernet Sauvignon, VdP de la Haute de l'Aude, Tesco

Anyone who says they find cabernet sauvignon too austere will find a friend in this wine.

French Country Red, Tesco (1 litre)

Fronton, Cotes du Frontonnais 1991

Nice baked fruit.

Gamay VdP du Jardin de France, Tesco

Light, bright, cherryish.

Gevrey Chambertin, Marchand 1992

Some savoury fruit, but the price? Absurd.

Grand Carat, Vin de Pays du Comte Tolosan 1994

Earthy as a gardener's welly-boot sole after an afternoon on the allotment.

Grenache, Tesco · `16` `B`

Terrific fruit, terrific price tag. Even Aussie wine-makers (who must remain anonymous) have raved about this dry yet vibrantly fruity wine. Rustic yet rich, smooth yet characterful, this is a stunning wine for the money.

Hautes Cotes de Beaune, Caves des Hautes Cotes 1992 `10` `D`

Top seventy stores only.

Hautes Cotes de Nuits, Caves des Hautes Cotes 1992 `12` `C`

La Vieille Ferme, Cotes du Rhone 1994 `14` `C`

Handsomely embodies ruggedness and soft fruity depth.

Le Bahans du Chateau Haut-Brion, Pessac-Leognan 1992 `12` `F`

Interesting! It bows so low and obsequiously you never see its face. Selected stores.

Les Domaines Buzet, Domaine de la Croix 1989, Tesco `13` `C`

Tannins in evidence, herby and baked, and maybe it will get even better over the next two to three years.

Les Domaines de Beaufort Minervois 1993, Tesco `13` `B`

Cheery cherries.

Les Domaines des Baumeilles, Cotes du Luberon 1992, Tesco `13` `C`

Les Forts de Latour, Pauillac 1986 `10` `H`

Les Vieux Cepages Carignan 1994 `12` `B`

Les Vieux Cepages Grenache 1994 `13` `B`
Probably at its best with spicy food.

Louis Jadot Beaune Premier Cru 1990 `10` `F`
Only in the top seventy stores.

Margaux 1992, Tesco `12` `E`

Medoc, Tesco `12` `C`

Merlot, Vin de Pays de la Haute Vallee de l'Aude, Tesco `13` `B`
Don't put pepper on your sausages. Drink this wine with them instead.

Minervois, Tesco `13` `B`
Pleasant cherry fruit.

Morgon, Arthur Barolet 1994 `11` `D`

Moulin de Saint-Francois Corbieres 1993 `13.5` `D`

Nature's Choice Organic Red, Bordeaux Superieur 1994 `13` `C`
Has some certainty of flavour and a soft, giving texture.

Pauillac 1990, Tesco `13.5` `D`
Dry, authentic claret.

Pavillon Rouge du Chateau Margaux 1990 `11` `G`

Red Burgundy, Tesco `11` `C`

Red Graves, Tesco `12` `C`
Bit weedy, but respectably weedy. Overpriced.

Saint Joseph, Verrier 1992 `10` `D`

Sancerre Rouge `12` `D`
Dull. Pricey. A pointless purchase. Top fifty-seven stores only.

Saumur 1991 `15` `C`

Saumur Rouge 1993 `13.5` `C`
An excellent bottle for those Spanish fish stews with chorizo.

St Emilion, Tesco `13` `C`
Attractive soft fruit finish to a stalwart British favourite.

St Estephe 1993, Tesco `15.5` `E`
Has ripe blackcurrant overtones, no crude tannins, and rich, warm, savoury fruit. Superb.

St Julien 1993, Tesco `15` `E`
A superbly well-balanced, fruity, delightfully dry claret of real class. Has a softness which is handsomely coated in good tannins. Delicious. Selected stores.

Vin de Pays de Cotes du Tarn, Tesco `14` `B`
Delicious, modern, soft fruit. Fresh finish. Slightly nutty. Very good value.

Vin de Pays de l'Aude Rouge, Tesco `13` `B`
Has a pleasing lilt to its voice which recalls sweet cherry.

Vin de Pays de la Cite de Carcassonne, Tesco `13.5` `B`
Lots of flavour here.

Vin de Pays de la Gironde, Tesco `10` `B`

Vin de Pays des Cotes de Perignan, Tesco `14` `B`
Worth buying just for the Darling Grapes of September label.

FRENCH WINE WHITE

Alsace Gewurztraminer 1994, Tesco `13.5` `D`
The usual rose-petal aroma and fruit but with more vigour to the acidity. This is an expensive wine, it must be admitted, but it will rate 15/16 in three to four years time.

Alsace Pinot Blanc, Tesco `11` `C`

Alsace Riesling Graffenreben 1995 `11` `D`
Expensive and somewhat muted by inexperience of the real world. Given a couple of years in bottle, however, to reflect and mature, this could be a terrific wine – even a £6.99 one.

Anjou Blanc, Tesco `12` `B`
Weird wet-wool-drying-in-front-of-a-one-bar-electric-fire fruit. Will be more gripping with rich fish dishes.

Beaujolais Blanc 1993 `10` `C`

Bordeaux Blanc de Blancs `13` `B`

Bordeaux Blanc, Tesco `15` `B`
Brilliant cheapie with lemon, lime and melon fruit softly and subtly put together.

Bordeaux Rose, Tesco `13.5` `C`
Excellent little wine for flirting with.

Bordeaux Sauvignon Blanc 1995

Seafood classic. Not a tart, tired sauvignon – this is all get-up-and-go.

Cabernet de Saumur, Caves des Vignerons de Saumur, Tesco

A good, firm rose with dryish cherry and raspberry fruit.

Chablis 1993, Tesco

Chablis Premier Cru, Montmain, La Chablisienne 1991

Chardonnay Reserve, Maurel Vedeau 1994

Good grilled fish wine with good depth of flavour. Top fourteen stores only.

Chardonnay Serge Dubois, Vin de Pays d'Oc 1992

Subtle, woody aroma with a gentle richness to the fruit. Classy in feel but not ultimately in the finish. Remarkable aperitif. Available through Tesco mail order only – two bottles per mixed case.

Chasan 1991, International Winemaker series

Some pleasant melon fruit to this Vin de Pays d'Oc.

Chateau de Beaulieu Coteaux d'Aix en Provence 1994

Chateau de Carles Sauternes 1993

Lot of money. Too much for this plonker. Top seventy stores only.

Chateau de la Colline Bergerac Blanc 1994 [14] [C]
Classy depth of fruit here with real flavour.

Chateau de la Colline Bergerac Rose 1994 [12] [C]
Pear-drop and cherry ripe.

Chateau la Foret St Hilaire Entre-Deux-Mers 1994 [12] [C]

Chateau les Marcottes St Croix du Mont 1990 [14.5] [E]
Superb honeyed fruit. Only at Wine Advisor stores.

Chateau Magneau, Graves 1990 [14] [F]
A hugely elegant, richly wooded wine of taste, flair and flavour. Marvellous with grilled fish with a complex sauce.

Chateau Malagar, Bordeaux Blanc 1994 [15] [C]
Classy and classic. Very serious, deep fruit, dry and haughty, but with a truly stylish finish. Great with grilled chicken and saucy fish dishes. Not at all stores.

Chateau Passavent Anjou Blanc 1994 [15.5] [C]
New vintage. Delicious aperitif and Chinese food wine – almost medium-sweet but not truly or madly or deeply. Delicious. Top fourteen stores only.

Chenin Blanc, VdP du Jardin de la France, Tesco [15] [B]
Has a delicious off-dry honey finish to a crisply conceived wine.

Cotes de Provence, Tesco [11] [B]

Cotes de Roussillon, Tesco   `12` `B`

Some pleasant fruit to this.

Cotes du Rhone Blanc 1994   `13` `C`

Severely earthy and bold and a touch underfruited. Not at all stores.

Cuvee Reserve Cotes du Rhone Blanc, Tesco   `14` `C`

Domaine Chancel Rose 1994   `13` `C`

Flavour here.

Domaine de la Done Rose Syrah 1994   `12` `B`

Selected stores.

Domaine de la Jalousie 1994, Tesco   `15` `C`

Exotic acids underpinning the round soft melon grapiness of the style. Terrific, punchy, refreshing glug. Not at all stores, but one of the most stylish Gascon whites on anyone's shelves.

Domaine de la Jalousie Late Harvest VdP des Cotes de Gascogne 1993   `14` `C`

An interesting alternative aperitif. Sure, it seems a little sweet (the grapes were very ripe when picked) but it has honeyed richness without being blowsy or sullen.

Domaine de Montauberon Marsanne, VdP d'Oc 1993   `12` `C`

Dry. Too dry.

Domaine du Soleil Chardonnay VdP d'Oc 1994   `13.5` `C`

Earthy fruit here.

Domaine Lapiarre Cotes de Duras 1993 `15` `C`

Attractive, almost NZ zest in the aroma of the wine which contrives to grassy herbiness. The fruit is soft and melon, not hugely bold but effective, and the finish is crisp and flavoursome. An excellent wine by itself or partnered with fish and salads. Not at all stores.

Domaine Sabagnere, VdP de Gascogne `13.5` `C`

Not at all stores.

Domaine Saint Alain, Vin de Pays des Cotes du Tarn 1993, Tesco `14` `B`

Excellent fruit (analogous to nothing yet grown). Mysteriously delicious.

Domaine Saint James Viognier, Vins de Pays d'Oc 1994 `14` `C`

Quirky fruit (that's fresh, young viognier for you) – which has flavour and style. Must be drunk with fish dishes or perhaps Thai food.

Domaine Saubagnere, VdP des Cotes de Gascogne 1994, Tesco `13.5` `C`

Some freshness and weight. Selected stores.

Domaines Saint Pierre Chardonnay, Vin de Pays d'Oc 1993 `12.5` `C`

Pleasant country flavour. What country? Oh, you know, a country far away where they speak drily and sunnily of rustic matters.

Dorgan White Vin de Pays de l'Aude `13` `B`

Dry Muscat, Vin de Pays des Pyrenees-Orientales 1993 `11` `B`

Entre Deux Mers, Tesco

Vividly fruity yet in the end a finely balanced specimen. Good with fish or a great quaffing wine. Perfect price.

Escoubes, VdP des Cotes de Gascogne, Grassa, Tesco

A delicious pineapple wine with firm fruit lurking behind a fresh face.

Fortant de France Grenache Blanc 1994

A truly flavoursome glug as well as a rich wine with great food-loving traits.

Fortant de France Sauvignon Blanc 1994

Lovely big wine with a subtly blistering attack of melon nicely subdued in the finish. Delicious.

French Chardonnay, VdP d'Oc, Tesco [12] [C]

Gaston Dorleans Vouvray Demi-Sec 1993 [12] [C]

Aperitif. Or try it with smoked oysters. Not at all stores.

Grenache Blanc, VdP de l'Herault, Tesco [12] [B]

Haut Poitou Sauvignon Blanc 1994 [13.5] [C]

Aromatic, fruity, fresh, gripping – good with grilled and poached fish dishes. Touch expensive for the style.

La Vieille Ferme Cotes du Rhone Blanc 1995 [12.5] [C]

Not available in all stores.

Le Porcil Chardonnay 1993 [15.5] [D]

Improved, this wine – now it's a real contender. The wood/fruit marriage is lovely to taste. Selected stores.

Les Domaines de la Source Muscat, Tesco `13` `C`

Pleasant aperitif.

Les Vieux Cepages Cinsault Rose 1994 `10` `B`

Louis Jadot Pouilly Fuisse 1994 `12` `F`

Macon Blanc Villages 1993, Tesco `12` `C`

Meursault 1992 `12` `F`

Has some flavour and edgy class, but what a price tag.

**Montagny Premier Cru Oak Aged,
Buxy 1991** `12` `D`

Muscadet de Sevres et Maine `13` `B`

Don't think of it as muscadet. Think of it as very pleasant, fruity, uncomplicated wine.

Muscat Cuvee Jose Sala, Tesco `15` `C`

Toffee-nosed and less than £4? Aristocratic sweetness never came so cheap.

Muscat de Beaumes de Venise (half bottle) `14` `C`

Useful half bottle. Has a waxy finish along with the usual honey. Top fourteen stores only.

Muscat de Rivesalte (half bottle) `14` `B`

A light pud wine with soft citrus and subtle marmalade undertones. Excellent with grapes and hard cheese to make a complete meal. Honey with a raisin undertone. Delightful with hard fruit tarts.

Oak Aged White Burgundy 1994, Tesco `13.5` `C`

This vintage is richer than previous ones but still not as exciting as I'd like for a fiver.

Organic White, Tesco `12` `C`

I wish I liked this wine more. It simply lacks vivacity for the money.

Pouilly Fume, Cuvee Jules 1994 `10` `D`

Premieres Cotes de Bordeaux, Tesco `11` `B`

Riesling, Tesco `14` `B`

True varietal vivacity of fruit and acid. Brilliant oyster wine.

Sancerre, Alphonse Mellot 1994, Tesco `13` `D`

Sancerre Les Ruettes 1995 `12` `D`

**Sauvignon Blanc Selection Jean-Marie
Johnston, VdP d'Oc 1995** `13` `C`

Good stab at a classic sauvignon but it doesn't quite make its mind up fast enough for me.

Sauvignon Blanc, Tesco `13` `B`

Has some richness of tone but is it quite as crisp as it might be?

Sauvignon de St Bris 1995, Tesco `14` `C`

Snips the palate nicely with its freshness and fruit. Has Old World tenacity of flavour. Top seventy-seven stores only.

Semillon Bordeaux, Tesco `13` `B`

A plain white, undemandingly fruity, which is a pleasure to drink with lightly dressed salads.

St Veran Les Monts, Co-Op Prisse 1993 `13.5` `D`

Not at all stores.

Touraine Sauvignon, Tesco | 13 | B

Delicious, fresh, gooseberry aroma, but then it fails to punch home the fruit on the finish. Quiet, understated fruit. Not shrieking with grassy overtones.

VdP de la Dordogne Co-Op Sigoules, Tesco | 15 | B

A modern, melony wine without being brash. Lots of fruit and flavour and balancing fresh acidity. Superbly drinkable.

Vouvray, Tesco | 14 | B

Touch of sweet fruit in an off-dry wine of great appeal. Supremely nice wine for the hock drinker looking for more finesse and food compatibility.

White Graves, Tesco | 13 | C

GERMAN WINE   RED

Echo Hill Baden Pinot Noir 1993 | 13 | B

Called Echo Hill, presumably, because if you shout loud enough the sound is faithfully returned. Therefore I shout: 'More Fruit Please!' I await its return with eager anticipation. Can't believe there are bottles still left.

GERMAN WINE   WHITE

Baden Dry, Tesco | 14 | B

There is a faint echo of sticky toffee in this dry fish 'n' chips wine. Good clean drinking.

Bernkasteler Kurfurstlay, Tesco ⬛13 ⬛ B

Try it instead of Lieb – much more of a generous wine. Not at all stores.

Bornheimer Adelberg Beerenauslese 1994 (half bottle) ⬛13 ⬛ C

Will taste at its best around AD 2010. Top seventy stores only.

Devil's Rock Riesling 1994/5 ⬛15.5 ⬛ B

Delicate true-riesling aroma, delicate acidity and good fruit, and fresh, mineral-edged finish. Excellent smoked fish wine. Developing very subtle petrolly undertones. Will improve for eighteen months or more.

Dry Hock, Tesco ⬛13 ⬛ B

Fresh and straightforward and good with fish dishes.

German Pinot Blanc, Tesco ⬛12 ⬛ C

Hock, Tesco ⬛11 ⬛ A

Kreuznacher Riesling Spatlese, Anheuser 1991 ⬛12 ⬛ C

Nice fruit. Needs a couple more years to develop. Everything my wife hates in a German wine. But in five years?

Lenz Moser Beerenauslese 1994 (half bottle) ⬛14 ⬛ D

A deliciously honeyed wine to put down for five years or so, when it will be thrilling. Selected stores.

Morio Muskat, Tesco ⬛15 ⬛ B

A brilliant thirst-quenching guzzle with a marzipan-dry finish to its fruit. Great solvent for end of the day blues.

Muller Thurgau, Tesco

12 B

Niersteiner Gutes Domtal, Tesco

12 B

Paulinshof Riesling Spatlese 1994

12 D

This might be a 15/16 point wine in three to five years but right now it is too one-dimensional. It's a baby. But a baby from one of my favourite wine-makers.

Rauenthaler Rothenberg Riesling Kabinett, Diefenhardt 1989

14 C

Remarkable value for the year, with the petal fruit beginning to emerge. Nice aperitif now but in three to four years will be even better.

Rheinpfalz Dry Riesling

12 B

Riesling Mosel, Tesco

13 B

A simple, pretty aperitif in the lightweight moselle tradition.

Scharzhofberger Van Volxem 1992

13.5 C

Needs even more time to develop.

St Johanner Abtei Kabinett 1994, Tesco

12 B

A delicate aperitif of limited appeal. Needs a hot garden to enjoy it in.

St Johanner Abtei Spatlese 1993, Tesco

12 B

Steinweiler Kloster Liebfrauenberg Auslese

13.5 C

Blue cheese wine (but not Roquefort). Not at all stores.

**Steinweiler Kloster Liebfrauenberg
Kabinett** `13.5` `C`

Delicious as a home-coming tipple – before you dive into something serious. Not at all stores.

**Steinweiler Kloster Liebfrauenberg
Spatlese** `13.5` `C`

Try it with a goat's cheese salad. Not at all stores.

GREEK WINE   RÉD

Nemea 1992 `13.5` `C`

The smell of sun-baked Hellenic isles in every sip? Not quite. But close. Very close. Top seventy stores only.

GREEK WINE   WHITE

Kretikos 1991 `12` `C`

HUNGARIAN WINE   RED

Merlot/Cabernet Sauvignon `10` `C`

Reka Valley Hungarian Merlot, Tesco `14` `B`

Touch old-sockish but great fun chilled with grilled salmon steaks, or swigged at room temperature with sausage and mash.

HUNGARIAN WINE WHITE

Chapel Hill Hungarian Irsai Oliver 1994   13.5 B

Gentle, muscat-edged aperitif. Top seventy stores only.

Oaked Chardonnay, Szekszard 1995   13.5 B

Not hugely gripping fruitwise, but clean and freshly finished.

Reka Valley Hungarian Chardonnay, Tesco   8 B

Perfectly dreadful. Might go well with stale baked beans on toast. Not at all stores.

Tokaji Aszu 5 Puttonyos (50cl)   16 D

Brilliant almond and orange marmalade wine with a gorgeous honey polish to the fruit. Wonderful with soft fruits.

ITALIAN WINE RED

Barolo Giacossa Fratelli 1991   14 D

Hints of typicity. Subdued ferocity rather than the full barolo roar. Not at all stores.

Cabernet Sauvignon del Veneto, Tesco   13.5 B

Very attractive with spicy meatballs. Not at all stores.

Calmasino Bardolino Classico 1994   13 C

Light and cherryish. Selected stores.

Cantina del Taburno 1994   13.5 C

Oh so narrowly fails to make 14! I feel mean, cruel and curmudgeonly.

Carignano del Sulcis 1992 (Sardinia)   16.5 D

This wine has made great strides over the past year in bottle. It is the sort of rich, herby, characterful brew which seems as if it was wrenched out of the earth without any intervening chemistry of man. Top sixteen stores only.

Catarratto di Sicilia, Tesco   13.5 C

Rich and good with grilled fish.

Chianti Classico 1994, Tesco   14 C

Richer than the Colli Senesi. More concentrated. Worth the extra 50 pence.

Chianti Classico Riserva 1991, Tesco   14 D

Perhaps a touch expensive but it is more multi-layered than the other chiantis in Tesco's range and more richly complex.

Chianti Colli Senesi 1994, Tesco   14 C

Nice controlled earthy overtones to the fruit.

Chianti Rufina 1994, Tesco   14 C

Nice tannic touch to the fruit: gives it character and food compatibility.

Fontanafredda Barolo 1991   10 E

Lousy value.

Giacosa Fratelli Barolo 1991   14 D

Thrusting tannins and soft licorice-tinged, prune/plum fruit. Expensive but most flavoursome. Selected stores.

Italian Red (1 litre)   11 B

Tetrapak. Fruit juice for red wine beginners.

La Calonica Vino Nobile de Montepulciano 1991   15   D

A most rewardingly fruity quaffing bottle with enough texture and flavour to accompany most food.

La Vis Trentino Merlot 1993   13.5   C

Soft and squashy with a tannic 'ping' dragging itself along in the background. Not at all stores.

Merlot del Piave, Tesco   12   B

Merlot del Trentino, Tesco   14   C

Pity it's not under four quid but it is a most attractive wine in spite of this small hiccup: soft, fruity, deeply flavoured, subtly leathery.

Monica di Sardegna, Tesco   11   B

Might go well with tomato tartlets.

Montepulciano d'Abruzzo, Tesco   12   B

Petit Verdot Casale del Giglio 1994   15   C

A most interesting and attractive wine. Gently earthy, spicy, warm, subtly herby and savoury-edged, it's fruity and most appealing to nose, eye and throat. Selected stores.

Pinot Noir del Veneto, Tesco   12   B

Tastes like cough mixture (mild and soothing). Odd. Not at all stores.

Rosso del Lazio, Tesco   13   B

Rosso del Piemonte, Tesco   12   C

Rosso del Salento, Tesco   15   B

Warm and sunny, simple yet gripping, this is a bargain

fruit-packed bottle. Seductively jammy wine with a serious undertone. Not at all stores.

Rosso di Montalcino 1993, Tesco `13.5` `D`
Attractively fruity but not attractively priced.

Shiraz Casale del Giglio 1994 `14` `C`
More accessibly sweet-natured and fruity than the previous year's vintage. But still a delicious red wine of style.

Sicilian Red, Tesco `13` `B`
Also comes in a useful 3-litre box for under £11 (equalling 45p a glass).

Sorbaiano Rosse delle Miniere
Montescudaio Rosso 1993 `16` `E`
Ripe, ready, bursting with plum/cherry/blackcurrant flavours. Delicious.

Trulle Primitivo del Salento 1994 `15` `C`
A southern Italian answer to pinotage – but no burnt rubber aftertaste! Lovely fruit on parade here. Selected stores.

Valpolicella Amazone 1990 `12` `D`
Top seventy-seven stores only.

Villa Gaida Lambrusco Rosso DOC `12` `B`
Sweet and cherry ripe.

ITALIAN WINE WHITE

Baracco Martina 1995 `15` `B`
This is a delicate, delicious, delightfully fruity and refreshing aperitif wine. Selected stores.

Bianco del Lazio, Tesco
14 | B

A fruit cake in Lazio! Tasty stuff. Not at all stores.

Bianco di Custoza, Barbi 1995
13.5 | C

Chardonnay del Trentino, Tesco
13.5 | C

Selected stores.

Chardonnay del Veneto, Tesco
13 | B

Works softly – like a cat burglar.

Colli Amerini, Tesco
14 | C

Has an edge of near-coriander dryness and spiciness. Excellent with grilled chicken. Not at all stores.

Colli Toscani La Panca, Tesco
13 | C

Selected stores.

Frascati 1995, Tesco
14 | C

Getting pricey at £3.99 but it's worth it. Has more flavour as well as the typical lemony frascatiness. About as good as the genre can get.

Greco di Puglia 1995, Tesco
13.5 | C

Selected stores.

Nuragus di Cagliari, Tesco
12 | B

Not as bright and breezy a wine as it once was. Not at all stores.

Orvieto Classico Abboccato, Tesco
13 | B

Off-dry, but very pleasant fruit. Good aperitif.

Orvieto Classico, Vaselli 1994　　12　C

Pinot Grigio del Veneto, Tesco　　14　B

A pinot grigio with fruit! Alleluja!

Pinot Grigio, Tiefenbrunner 1993　　12　C

Pipoli Chiaro Aglianico Bianco 1995　　13　C

Selected stores.

Prosecco del Veneto, Tesco　　13.5　B

Fresh, nutty, attractive. A pleasurable glug by itself or with fish pie. Not at all stores.

Salice del Salentino Bianco 1995　　12.5　C

Sauvignon Blanc del Veneto, Tesco　　12.5　B

Not at all stores.

Sicilian White, Tesco　　14　B

Warm, sunny, accommodatingly fruity. Great value. Not at all stores.

Soave Classico 1992, Tesco　　11　C

Stowells of Chelsea Chardonnay (3-litre box)　　13.5　G

Some weight to the fruit, and balance. A pleasant glug.

Stowells of Chelsea Chardonnay Trentino (3-litre box)　　13.5　G

Simple, dry, good fruit.

Taburno Flanghia 1994　　11　D

Nothing like a soave or frascati, but a lot pricier.

397

Trulle Chardonnay del Salento 1995 `15` `C`

This is a controlled, gorgeously fluent wine of style, complexity and thirst-quenching crispness yet fruitiness. Not at all stores.

Verdicchio dei Castelli di Jesi Classico 1994, Tesco `13.5` `C`

Tinged with not unpleasant fruit. Not at all stores.

Villa Cerro Soave Recioto 1992 `14` `C`

An interesting sweet aperitif. Good with hard fruit and a slug of cheese and Italian sweetmeats and cakes. Also almond biscuits.

Villa Pigna Chiara `14` `B`

Nutty – yet a suggestion of crispness.

MEXICAN WINE RED

L. A. Cetto Petite Syrah 1993 `15.5` `C`

Characterful and tannic – the edge of wine is almost coarse but it is terrific with rich food.

MOROCCAN WINE RED

Moroccan Red `14` `B`

Raisiny and ripe: excellent with roast vegetables and meats.

NEW ZEALAND WINE RED

Coopers Creek Merlot 1994 `15.5` `D`

Soft, rich, rivetingly fruity depth with a texture which encourages the wine to slip down like brushed velvet. Top fifteen stores only.

New Zealand Cabernet Sauvignon, Tesco `14` `C`

Soft, ripe, juicy, friendly as a teddy bear.

New Zealand Cabernet Sauvignon/Merlot 1992, Tesco `13` `C`

Curious marriage which isn't entirely convincing in spite of its respectable, if not over-exciting, rating.

Riverlea Wines Cabernet Sauvignon/ Merlot, Gisborne 1991, Tesco `15` `C`

Amazingly well-integrated varieties with softness, smoothness and very effective final delivery. Delicious.

NEW ZEALAND WINE WHITE

Brancott Estate Sauvignon Blanc 1994 `12.5` `F`

The finish fails to inspire or provide the basis for a bigger rating. £11 is a lot of money and this is not a lot of wine for the money.

Coopers Creek Chardonnay, Gisborne 1995 `14.5` `E`

New vintage, top seventy stores only. Not cheap at eight quid but a beautifully crafted wine of elegant fruit with balance, youth and invigorating flavour.

Dry White, Tesco

Attractive all-round wine with plenty of rounded fruit. Might be better, in fact, with less fruit and more of that searing New Zealand grassiness.

Jackson Estate Sauvignon Blanc 1995

Not as spectacularly rich and inviting as previous vintages, but, though pricey, still hanging on in. Here is a wine, in this vintage, which will develop better over 1997. Top sixteen stores only.

New Zealand Dry White, Tesco

Simple, fruity, hints at real style rather than flaunts it. Not at all stores.

New Zealand Sauvignon Blanc 1995, Tesco

Crushed grassy undertones lift the wine out of the ordinary – and give it great compatibility with shellfish or smoked eels.

Stoneleigh Marlborough Chardonnay 1993

Top seventy stores only.

Villa Maria Chenin/Chardonnay 1994

Has a rich ribbon of rounded melony fruit running through a delicious lemony acidity. Terrific marriage of grape varieties. Top seventy-seven stores only.

Villa Maria Sauvignon Blanc 1994 (half bottle)

Delightful half bottle for a solo hedonist faced with a plate of smoked salmon or eel. Top seventy-seven stores only.

PORTUGUESE WINE RED

Borba Alentejo 1995 `16` `C`

Lovely, rich, polished, well-textured fruit for the money. Terrific glug and good with food.

Dao 1992, Tesco `12` `B`

Dom Jose, Tesco `12.5` `B`

Not as highly rated as once it was. It's become too civilised. Lost its character.

Douro 1992, Tesco `12` `C`

Garrafeira Fonseca 1984 `12` `C`

I might reduce it to make a basis for a mushroom sauce but I wouldn't drink it without the dish for company. Top seventy stores only.

J.P. Barrel Selection 1991 `15.5` `C`

Has the lot: acid, fruit, tannins, well-structured and properly finished off. Has richness, softness and bramble-fruited depth. Bargain. Not at all stores.

PORTUGUESE WINE WHITE

Bairrada 1993, Tesco `13` `B`

Can't argue with this once fried fish is plonked beside it.

Douro Branco 1993, Tesco `14` `B`

Softness of the fruit makes it plump and giving but there's a lean, lemony quality to the acidity and this gives the wine a two-fisted attack. Excellent value.

Dry Portuguese Rose, Tesco   `12` `B`

Dry Vinho Verde, Tesco   `13` `B`

An amusing aperitif, nothing more.

ROMANIAN WINE   RED

Romanian Cellars Pinot Noir   `15` `B`

Dry cherries with a blackcurrant tang. Lush, fruit-centred glug with a dryness well suited to partner food.

Romanian Cellars Pinot Noir/Merlot   `16` `B`

Enchanting. Brilliant value. The East Europeans seem to make a habit of successfully marrying unlikely grape varieties and this bottle is no exception. Top seventy stores only.

SOUTH AFRICAN WINE   RED

Backsberg Merlot 1993   `14` `C`

Still acidically evolving in bottle. Good with light food but in a couple of years great with rich food. Top fourteen stores only.

Beyers Truter Pinotage 1995, Tesco   `16` `C`

Superb fruit with good spiciness and plum/blackcurrant flavours, baked but not overbaked and wonderfully soft and deep in the throat. A brilliantly versatile wine, good with meats and chilled with fish.

Cape Pinotage 1992, Tesco 14 B

Sweet, elegantly smoky and rubbery fruit, like a drier style of beaujolais but tastier.

Charles Back Gamay 1995 12 C

Runs so quickly over the tongue that you scarcely catch the fruit. But I believe it is delicious – if you can hold on to it.

Clearsprings Cape Red (3-litre box) 14 E

Good cheering glug: bright, breezy, bouncy.

Fairview Merlot Reserve 1992 15 D

Leathery, aromatic, serious yet wonderfully gluggable. Classy, striking yet ineffably modest and self-effacing. Top seventy stores only.

Fairview Shiraz 1992 14 C

Soft, delicious, not over-spicy. Rather pleased-with-myself quality to the fruit. Not available in all stores.

International Winemaker Cabernet Sauvignon/Merlot, Stellenbosch, Tesco 15 C

Compelling structure: soft, rich, deep, balanced (acid, tannins) but overall there is that warm shroud of fruit which speaks of fecund vines cheerfully baking in the sun. Selected stores.

Kanonkop Pinotage 1993 15.5 E

When you drink a wine as character-packed and fruity and softly textured as this you ask yourself: pinotage growers who grubbed up their wines to grow more fashionable varieties need their heads examined. Top seventeen stores only.

Oak Village Vintage Reserve, Stellenbosch 1994 14.5 C

Rich, vigorous, dry, full of flavour. Selected stores.

Paarl Cabernet Sauvignon, Tesco

Enticing blackcurrant aroma, falls apart on the finish.

Rustenberg Pinot Noir 1991

Great pong! Lousy finish! It smells like a very old, classically made volnay. It hits the throat like a wet sock. Top sixteen stores.

Schoone Gevel Merlot 1994

Soft and impressively well-tuned on the finish. But don't pair it with too robust a dish. Selected stores.

South African Red, Tesco

75cl and 1.5L. Has depth of fruit with an edged freshness (not tartness) which gives the subtle, smoky fruit vigour. In the magnum this is a sexy dinner-party red of style and flavour. Easy to drink, yes, but with sufficient complexity and clout to go easily with roast and grilled meats and vegetables.

South African Shiraz/Cabernet Sauvignon 1995, Tesco

Sweet-edged but a dry, plumply developed, fruity wine of sinful quaffability.

Stellenbosch Merlot, Tesco

Terrific fruit here! Glorious softness, exciting richness without blowsiness or overdoneness. It's got a lovely texture and lush, savoury caress-edged ripeness with nary a hint of strain. Selected stores.

Stowells of Chelsea Pinotage (3-litre box)

Soft, not as vivacious – nor with as big a finish – as some, but attractive and well-balanced.

SOUTH AFRICAN WINE WHITE

Barrel Fermented Chenin 1995

A full, rich chenin restrained by subtle lime acidity and a nutty finish. Not dry but far from sweet – just beautifully fruity.

Boschendal Grand Cuvee Sauvignon Blanc 1994

One of the richer-finishing sauvignons. Top seventy-seven stores only.

Cape Bay Semillon/Chardonnay 1995 `14` `C`

Good fish wine with some style and freshness. Drink it young. It won't keep.

Cape Chenin Blanc, Tesco `13` `B`

Cape Colombar, Tesco `15` `B`

Aromatically a marriage of eau de cologne and apple and pear. The fruit is a medley of flavours: pawpaw and ripe melon being the most prominent. Not a serious wine but a joy of gluggability.

Cape Colombar/Chardonnay, Tesco `13.5` `B`

Danie de Wet Chardonnay Green Label 1995 `13.5` `C`

Unusually less-than-exciting chardonnay from Mr de Wet. It may develop better in bottle over the next six months but in doing so it will surely lose its impishly pert freshness and lemonic personality. Not at all stores.

De Wetshof Estate Rhine Riesling 1995

I'd cellar it for at least three years before opening what I would expect to be a richer, more satisfying 15-point wine. Top seventy-seven stores only.

Franschoek Semillon, Tesco

Real flavour here from firm fruit and positive acidity. Delicious aperitif as well as great with oriental food and seafood dishes.

La Motte Sauvignon Blanc 1995 `12.5` `D`

Top sixteen stores only.

Leopard Creek Chardonnay 1994 `14` `C`

Milder than you would expect from a leopard but tasty and attractive.

Oak Village Sauvignon Blanc 1995 `12.5` `C`

Overgaauw Chardonnay 1995 `14` `D`

Hints at exotic richness without going over the brink into blowsiness: controlled, subtly ripe, elegant in the modern mould.

Robertson Chardonnay 1995, Tesco `13.5` `C`

Not at all stores.

Robertson Chardonnay/Colombard 1995, Tesco

Schoone Gevel Chardonnay 1995 `15` `D`

Creaminess, flavour, weight, crispness, depth – from start to finish this is a flavoursome wine. Would suit mild Thai fish dishes and complex vegetable starters.

South African Cape Dry White (3-litre box) `14.5` `E`

Vivid soft fruit with a clear finish. A brilliant crisp solvent to wash away those cares at the end of the day – and an excellent-value box. Has real sunny fruit on the finish.

South African White, Tesco `13` `B`

Simple, fruity glug. Also available in 1.5L size.

Stowells of Chelsea Chenin Blanc (3-litre box) `14` `F`

Comes out bright and clean – here are fruit and zip and real style.

Swartland Sauvignon Blanc 1995, Tesco `12` `C`

Not at all stores.

Van Loveren Blanc de Noirs Muscadel 1995 `14` `B`

Better and more firmly structured than previous vintages. A delightful rose aperitif. Not at all stores.

Van Loveren Special Late Harvest Gewurztraminer 1995 (half bottle) `14` `C`

Delicious floral fruit of gently honeyed sweetness. Personally, I'd cellar it for five years to get a 17-point bombshell.

SPANISH WINE   RED

Berberana Monastrel 1994 `13.5` `B`

Respectable, fruity, all above board.

Campillo Gran Reserva, Rioja 1982 `11` `E`

Fading on the finish – the fruit, that is. The tannins, though soft, are still around. Top fourteen stores only.

Cinco Casas Red, Tesco `14.5` `B`

Lots of fresh young fruit and flavour. Delicious price.

Don Darias   `14` `B`

Brilliant with curry, just brilliant.

Gandia Merlot   `14` `B`

Gran Don Darias   `13` `B`

Marques de Caceres Rioja 1991   `14` `C`

Calm, polished, dry, very attractive. Not a coarse note any-where.

Marquis de Chive Reserva 1989   `14` `C`

Packed with a maturity of flavour which is belied by the vigour and youthfulness of the final flourish as the wine goes down.

Marques de Chive Tempranillo   `13.5` `B`

Fails by a whisker to rate higher. It should shave more closely.

Marquis de Grinon Petit Verdot 1994   `16` `E`

Brilliant texture, weight, balance, fruit and style. Has rich, dusky, almost exotic fruit with a hint of dry allspice and a deep, lingering, tannin-edged finish. Superb price for such all-embracing flavour and sheer chutzpah. Will age well to AD2000. Move over cab sauv! Petit Verdot has arrived! Top fourteen stores only.

Marques de Grinon Rioja 1994   `15.5` `C`

Elegantly delicious and positively balanced for food and quaffing. A modern rioja, not a whit coarse, it has style, depth and flavour. Selected stores.

Marquis de Grinon Syrah 1993   `17.5` `E`

Perfect drinking syrah of mature softness. It's an exciting wine, this, showing what Spain can do with a great French grape –

make it better (tastier, richer, more finely textured) than Rhone equivalents at two and three times the price. Top seventy-seven stores only.

Rioja Vina Mara, Tesco ⟦13.5⟧ ⟦C⟧

Senorio de los Llanos 1989 ⟦13⟧ ⟦C⟧

Spanish Red (1 litre) ⟦14.5⟧ ⟦B⟧

Tetrapak. Great value here for a big, soup-plate of flavours and textured fruitiness.

Stowells of Chelsea Tempranillo (3-litre box) ⟦14⟧ ⟦F⟧

Great glugging flavour and texture.

Torres Coronas 1992 ⟦13⟧ ⟦C⟧

Rather dry and humourless for such exuberant Catalan provenance. Hard to believe Saudi is not related to such wine. The fruit is there but it seems reluctant to smile.

Torres Sangredetoro 1994 ⟦16⟧ ⟦C⟧

Brilliant! Best vintage for ages.

Vina Ardanza Rioja Reserva 1987 ⟦12.5⟧ ⟦E⟧

Needs food like a crutch – it limps without it. And it's an awful lot of money. Top fourteen stores only.

Vina Azabache Rioja 1990 ⟦14⟧ ⟦C⟧

A food rioja – needs a stew with apricots and chorizo and lots of beans. Selected stores.

Vina Mara Rioja Alavesa ⟦16⟧

A new batch of this non-vintage blend and it's the best it has been. Delicious balance of fruit, acid and tannins all working to seductive effect on tastebud and throat. A wonderful glug (sunny and warm) and good with all sorts of casserole and roast vegetable dishes.

Vina Mayor Ribero del Duero 1991 `14.5` `C`
Aromatic, chunky edge to fruit which is elegant and soft.

SPANISH WINE   WHITE

Don Darias `14` `B`
With a spicy fish stew or curry, this is the wine.

Marques de Chive White Wine, Tesco `12` `B`
Vanilla, coconut and fruit which don't quite marry up. But great with Thai food.

Marquis de Grinon Durius Sauvignon Blanc 1994 `13.5` `C`
Grassy, hints at richness, indecisive on the finish. Selected stores.

Moscatel de Valencia, Tesco `15` `B`

Vina Mara Superior Rioja, Tesco `14` `C`
Vanilla-like crispness and flavour. Good food wine – indeed, it needs food to come alive.

Vina Mara White Rioja, Tesco `13` `C`
Modern and somewhat prim.

USA WINE   RED

Californian Cabernet Sauvignon, Tesco `14.5` `C`
Good price for a Californian cabernet. Very smoothly textured

and finely woven – the fruit is as smooth as an LA hotel doorman. Selected stores but little left.

Californian Red, Tesco · 13 · B

Interesting what went through the label designer's mind when (s)he designed this curious blue and somewhat incongruous townscape on the bottle. Maybe too much of this wine perhaps? Very audacious. The wine only surprises by being soft and dry and quiet-mannered.

Californian Zinfandel, Tesco · 14 · C

Only just 14 this close to a fiver. A good introduction to zin – if not a blockbuster one – and it does have positive structure and flavour.

E. & J. Gallo Turning Leaf Cabernet Sauvignon 1994 · 13.5 · D

Warm and possessing some depth but uncompetitively priced compared with Chile or South Africa. But you're getting better, Gallo, so stick at it! You might just make a terrific wine at a dirt-cheap price one day.

E. & J. Gallo Turning Leaf Zinfandel 1994 · 12 · D

Not bad, but very overpriced at nigh on six quid. Anodyne and characterless, it lacks the oomph of real red zin. It fails to finish with £6 worth of vivacity. If it was £3.29 it would be a good buy. A partially turned new leaf.

Gallo Sonoma County Cabernet Sauvignon 1992 · 13.5 · E

Only just fails to make 14. It is expensive – but it is gently impressive, if rather ripe.

Glass Mountain Cabernet Sauvignon 1991 · 16 · D

Delightful pure fruit sweetness. Not a harsh edge anywhere. Available at regional stores only.

Tesco Californian Pinot Noir

Dullest pinot noir I've tasted in ages.

USA WINE WHITE

August Sebastiani's White Zinfandel 1994

Sweetish fruit but fair flavour. Rated at £2.99 only. Not worth £3.99.

Californian Chardonnay 1994, Tesco

A reasonable wine at £2.99 but at £4.99 it sucks. Selected stores.

Californian White, Tesco

E. & J. Gallo Turning Leaf Chardonnay 1994

Classy and rich. Not especially elegant or finely balanced as great Californian chardonnays are, but it's good with chicken.

Gallo Sonoma Chardonnay 1993

This is an extremely classy chardonnay. Good oak/fruit/acid. Very delicate, very fine.

Glass Mountain Californian Chardonnay 1992

Some real elegance here and rich style without blowsiness or intemperance. A delicious bottle to enjoy solo. Divertingly delicious fruit. Available in regional stores only.

Quady Elysium Black Muscat 1993 (half bottle) 15 D

Cassis-like. Try it with blackcurrant fool.

Washington State White 〔13〕〔C〕

This I found hard to dislike but equally difficult to enthuse over. It seems *loose* to me – as if the components weren't knit properly.

FORTIFIED WINE

Australian Aged Tawny Liqueur Wine, Tesco 〔14.5〕〔E〕

Wonderful figgy, raisiny, bottle-softened warrior. To fight with fruit cake.

Dow's 20 Year Old Tawny Port (half bottle) 〔16.5〕〔F〕

A gorgeous, raisiny, ripe, sweet tipple for cheese and biscuits. Top twenty-five stores only.

Finest Madeira, Tesco 〔14〕〔D〕

Brilliant with fruit cake. Not at all stores.

Floc de Gascogne 〔14〕〔D〕

Made from grape juice with armagnac tossed in to bring it up to 17%. A simple peasant recipe and I enjoy its rusticity as a pick-me-up (or should I say as a pull-me-down?) after a hard day's wine tasting. The view of my household is that it is about as toothsome a proposition as old rugby boots pickled in treacle.

Special Reserve Port, Tesco 〔14〕〔D〕

Not at all stores.

Superior Manzanilla, Tesco (half bottle) 〔16〕〔B〕

Brilliant value. Saline, elegant and very dry. A nutty world-class aperitif. Or drink with grilled prawns.

Superior Oloroso Secco, Tesco (half bottle) `16` `B`

Brilliant food for thought.

Superior Palo Cortado, Tesco (half bottle) `17` `C`

Rich, very dry camomile fruit, nutty undertone. For drinking alone with literature – or a superb aperitif. It revives even the most jaded tastebuds – lovely dry fruit.

10 Year Old Tawny Port `13` `E`

Tesco Tawny Port `13.5` `D`

Finishes sweet. Not at all stores.

Warre's 1980 Vintage Port `17` `G`

Just overwhelmingly fruity and rich. Beautiful, round and smooth. Quite exceptional. Top twenty-five stores only.

Warre's Traditional LBV 1981 `15.5` `F`

Rich and ripe. Very smooth and polished.

SPARKLING WINE/CHAMPAGNE

Asti Spumante, Tesco `13` `C`

Sweet as Grandma's tooth. Try it with ice-cream.

Australian Sparkling Brut, Tesco `15` `C`

Lovely feathery feel and terrific fruit and acid balance making it impressively elegant in the mouth. Under a fiver it is outstanding value for money.

Blanc de Blancs Champagne, Tesco `13` `G`

Good solid stuff. Bit pricey.

Blanc de Noirs Champagne, Tesco `13.5` `E`

Has elegance and style.

Blanquette de Limoux, Tesco `13` `D`

Soft attractive bubbly. Only a weak finish prevents it scoring much higher.

Cava, Tesco `15` `C`

Very elegant. Tasty fruit, clean and firm. Not at all stores.

Champagne Brut, Tesco `13.5` `E`

Champagne Nicolas Feuillate Brut Premier Cru `15` `G`

A point for every pound. A beautiful, stylish, quietly haughty bottle of bubbly.

Champagne Premier Cru 1983, Tesco `11` `H`

Champagne, Tesco `13` `F`

Chardonnay Frizzante, Tesco `10` `B`

Chardonnay Spumante `13.5` `D`

Cremant de Bourgogne 1989, Tesco `18` `D`

Deutz (New Zealand) `15.5` `E`

Has much flavour and class. Much better than the Deutz made in France.

Freixenet Brut Rose (Spain) `14.5` `D`

A delicious, summery rose of style and flavour.

Henri Mandois Champagne `12` `F`

Jansz Tasmanian Sparkling 『12』 『E』

Lindauer Brut 『13.5』 『D』

Delicate hint of lemon. A lovely little bubbly at a reasonable price.

Louis Massing Grand Cru Blanc de Blancs 『16』 『E』

Michel Arnould Champagne 『12』 『G』

Moscato Sparkler, Tesco 『12』 『A』

A 5% junior wine for senior tipplers.

Paul de Villeroy Brut Champagne 1989 『14』 『G』

A deliciously light, elegant, subtly lemon-edged bubbly of class. Top seventy stores only.

Premier Cru Brut Champagne, Tesco 『14』 『F』

Classy, delicious and very well made. Knocks many a grande marque into a cocked hat.

Prosecco Spumante, Tesco 『14』 『C』

Delicious peachy/strawberry aperitif. Great fun.

Robertson South African Sparkling, Tesco 『13.5』 『D』

Fresh and perky. A youthful bubbly for youthful occasions (christenings, etc.).

Rose Cava, Tesco 『14.5』 『C』

Delicately delicious. Excellent price for such a bubbly.

Simonsig Kaapse Vonkel Sparkling Brut 1992 (South Africa) 『15』 『E』

Delicious, soothing, classy.

South African Sparkling Sauvignon Blanc (Tesco) `12.5` `C`

Sparkling Chardonnay 1992, Tesco (Australia) `13` `D`

Rather too fat and fruity on the finish. Bubblies should finish freshly. Not at all stores.

Sparkling Chardonnay, Tesco (France) `14` `C`

Very soft. Very, very soft. Certainly not for classicists, but I like it. Top seventy stores only.

Vintage Cava 1991, Tesco `13` `D`

Vintage Champagne 1985, Tesco `13` `G`

Yalumba Pinot Noir/Chardonnay, Australia `16` `E`

Absolutely stunner for the money: rich and biscuity, great balancing acidity and an overall style hinting refinement and class. Rheims quakes in its Gucci boots!

Seppelt Sparkling Shiraz (Australian) `16` `E`

Wonderful bittersweet fruit of emulsion-like thickness and rich, blackberry flavour. Great fun with game birds. Not available in all stores.

Yalumba Cuvee Sparkling Cabernet Sauvignon `15` `E`

Utterly ravishing stuff. Dry fruit, soft to finish. Great fun. Eat? Nothing. Drinks by itself.

WAITROSE

Suspicious minds

The food and drink pages of the *Weekend Guardian* have become a coveted position in the paper for retailers advertising their wines. I would like to feel that the popularity of the *Superplonk* column has contributed in some small but delicious way to the success of these pages, so brilliantly edited by Mr Matthew Fort, but Keith Bailey of Wellingborough suspected a different and altogether more dubious reason after he observed an amusing coincidence involving Waitrose.

On a day when I chose to put the spotlight on Waitrose wines, devoting a whole column to them, a full-page Waitrose advertisement appeared opposite. Mr Bailey's suspicions were justifiably aroused, and he was compelled to write to the *Guardian* on 16 December 1995:

I count myself among Malcolm Gluck's legion of fans, and make straight for his wine column in the *Guardian*'s Weekend supplement each week. This week was no exception and I read with interest his column devoted to Waitrose wines.

I was slightly miffed that I do not have access to a Waitrose, but I was nonplussed by the appearance of a full-page ad opposite the column for, surprise, surprise, Waitrose.

I buy the *Guardian* for its impartial reporting and (generally) obvious integrity and do not expect to be subjected to such an obvious editorial/advertising cross-over.

Was there collaboration over the advert/editorial placement, or was Mr Gluck not party to it? I sincerely hope that his integrity cannot be bought for the price of a full-page colour advert.

Both the *Guardian* and I were keen to put to rest any suggestion of foul play, and it seems appropriate to take this further opportunity here to scotch any suggestion of 'advertorial' collusion. Helen Oldfield, deputy editor of the *Weekend Guardian*, wrote to Mr Bailey on 29 December:

Thank you for your letter. As you know, Malcolm Gluck writes about wine from all the various supermarket chains; in fact he features virtually nothing but supermarket wine. Therefore, it is unsurprising to find he should from time to time concentrate on Waitrose, as he has on Safeway, Tesco, the Co-op, etc. I can assure you, Malcolm Gluck would not write about Waitrose because he knew they were going to place an advertisement with us. Generally speaking, we in the editorial office do not know what ads will be included until a very late stage, and Malcolm, as a freelance, wouldn't know until he saw the magazine in print.

It is possible that Waitrose guessed – because they'd sent out advance samples of wine – that Gluck, and possibly other wine writers, might be writing about what their shops have to offer and therefore decided to place an advertisement. But that happens in several areas of the paper: a new play opens, it is reviewed, ads for the play appear; likewise a new model of car might be advertised in the same issue of the paper that it is road-tested on the motoring page. Our advertising department would not turn down an advertisement on the grounds that we might be running editorial on the same product.

However, I take your point that it is unfortunate if ad and editorial appear side by side. Sadly, we wouldn't know that until late on when it's hard to switch things around.

The letter was duly passed on to me, and early in the new year I was pleased to reassure Mr Bailey that this was an isolated incident and a complete fluke:

Helen Oldfield passed me your letter to the paper about the extraordinary gobsmacking coincidence whereby my *Superplonk* column, which was devoted to Waitrose, appeared cheek by jowl with an advertisement for that very store. I can only tell you that this was a total and utter coincidence. In no way does the advertising department ever know what I write. It was just one of those things. Oddbins, Thresher, Tesco, Sainsbury's, Waitrose – they've all advertised in the *Weekend Guardian* at times. We must be grateful for their support!

Thanks very much for writing and for your kind comments about the column. I shall keep it up for as long as my liver holds out.

Interestingly, this was not the first time that readers had cast aspersions on the marketing techniques of the Waitrose chain, part of the John Lewis Partnership. Back in 1990, a sudden rise in the price of two wines recommended by *Superplonk* led several readers to wonder whether Waitrose had bumped up the price after the wines had received a favourable review. R.H. Ross wrote on 23 September 1990:

I follow your Saturday article in the *Weekend Guardian* with interest, and often with pleasure as well, when I sample some of your recommendations. I was therefore somewhat surprised at the prices of your choices on 22

September bearing in mind the title *Superplonk*.

However, I have in the past been so impressed with your judgement that I gritted my teeth and resolved to meet the expense because of your high praise for all three wines. Imagine my disappointment at the local Waitrose – Saffron Walden, on the same day, when I discovered the price of Henri's marvel was now £18.75 and the Macon had gone up to £4.95. Only the red burgundy was available at the same price.

The only reason offered was that it was new stock, as shown in their current September 1990 price list. However, to my simple mind they have taken advantage of your expertise and the following of your readers.

I realise that your article must take some time to prepare, but the wines were identical in every respect, and I find it difficult to accept that so short a period could account for such increases. Rather, it seems like a little bit of sharp practice on someone's part. Of course, no one forced me to purchase at the new prices, I could easily have walked away from the situation. Perhaps you could pass on my feelings to the director responsible for pricing policy in the wines deparment.

I am sure he will take more notice of your remonstration than he would of mine. But certainly it is not what I would have expected from a branch of John Lewis Partnership, who are renowned for their fair trading practices.

I would not expect such blatant profiteering either, and I replied to Mr Ross that I thought such a policy on the part of Waitrose was most unlikely, and that it was more probably the result of new stock arriving from the wholesaler.

In 1995, a couple more readers, Mr A. Barker of Wargrave and William Blezard of East Sheen, wrote to me reporting pricing discrepancies at Waitrose. William Blezard subsequently received a full explanation from Waitrose regarding the price of the Avontuur Pinotage 1993 which he had bought for £4.79

instead of the £3.99 quoted in the column – apparently there had been errors both on my part and by the retailer – along with a voucher for £10. He was most satisfied with the outcome.

Looking back on this correspondence I was surprised that I had even reviewed a wine at £18.75, some way above the customary *Superplonk* price bracket (unless the wine attached to such a price tag was unequivocally wondrous and worth the outlay – which is exceedingly rare). Of course, the target market and location of many of its stores mean that Waitrose does place more emphasis on the higher price brackets than some other supermarket chains. But these letters and others underline that price-sensitivity and providing value for money are important issues in all areas of the wine market, not just at the end where I prefer to shop.

This is best illustrated by David Rodgers' letter regarding the previously mentioned discrepancy in the prices of Waitrose burgundies which I had reviewed. He wrote in September 1990:

I read your enthusiastic and informative column in the *Weekend Guardian* with considerable interest each week in keen anticipation of bargains and delights in store.

I thought that you might like to know that having drooled over your description of your burgundy finds in Waitrose in this week's issue, I rushed to the excellent Waitrose wine section in Brighton, only to be somewhat disappointed. Firstly, two of the three wines you've recommended were priced higher than you had found; £4.95 for the 1989 Macon Lugny instead of £4.45 and £18.75 for the Puligny Montrachet 1987 instead of £16.50. I did wonder whether Waitrose were so quick on the ball that they thought your accolade deserved a greater price for the product in excess of 10 per cent, but I thought that was rather unlikely.

Then, in seeking 'the most incredible red burgundy for

under a tenner', the Faiveley 1986 Savigny les Beaune at £8.45 was nowhere to be seen either on display or behind the scenes. What was available was the 1987. I decided to buy it, thinking that the 1986 might have been a *Guardian* misprint (perish the thought!). Although very palatable the 1987, for me, did not come up to the delight that you discovered in the 1986.

Coming back to the two whites with increased prices, I felt that £18.75 against £16.50 tipped the balance, so I did not indulge myself and I bought the 1989 Macon at £4.95 and enjoyed it very much.

I thought you might like to know this saga. It shows how your articles bring new happenings and experiences to your readers.

New happenings and experiences indeed. For Mike Staples of Guildford, a trip to Waitrose in search of a *Superplonk* recommendation led to an absorbing afternoon at a Rhone co-operative. Good wines will often have interesting stories behind them, and it is marvellous to hear of readers and customers going out to the regions and discovering the wines where they are grown. I was pleased that one of my recommendations led to this opportunity for Mr Staples who wrote in September 1993:

I thought you might like to hear that having tasted the excellent Cotes du Rhone from Laudun available at Waitrose on your 17-pointer recommendation, I followed it up by dropping in at the Vignerons de Laudun co-operative while on our annual camping holiday at Le Gran du Roi in August.

We spent a pleasant hour or so sampling a range of reds and whites and came away with a selection including an '88 Villages red and a '92 Villages white – Medaille d'Or Paris '93, Rose and Blanc de Blanc mousseux, ranging from 178 francs for the Waitrose to 26F for the white, which we found really excellent.

Altogether a delightful diversion from the sun and sea and I thank you for stimulating this excursion!

I have been aware for some time that my writing on wine inspires readers in search of bargains to trek to places some distance away from their homes, but I think it is fair to hazard a guess that Mr Staples' pilgrimage of several hundred kilometres holds the record for distance covered, bearing in mind both the outward and the return journey.

Waitrose Limited
Customer Service Department
Southern Industrial Area
Bracknell
Berks
RG12 8YA

Tel 01344 424680
Fax 01344 862584

Findlater Mackie Todd & Co Limited (Waitrose Direct)
Freepost London SW19 3YY

Tel 0181 543 0966
Fax 0181 543 2415

ARGENTINIAN WINE RED

Santa Julia Malbec/Cabernet Sauvignon, Mendoza 1994 `14.5` `C`

Hairy but not too frighteningly dark and fruity. X-certificate stuff for robust dishes.

ARGENTINIAN WINE WHITE

Alamos Ridge Chardonnay, Mendoza 1994 `15.5` `C`

Makes meursault appear really lousy value. Lovely texture and fruit here.

Santa Julia Chardonnay 1995 `15` `C`

Has personality, flavour and a knock-'em-dead style where food's concerned. A richly fruity wine, dry but never austere.

Santa Julia Torrontes, Mendoza 1996 `14` `C`

Superb aperitif and fish wine.

AUSTRALIAN WINE RED

Angove's Nanya Malbec/Ruby Cabernet 1994 `14` `C`

Australian Malbec/Ruby Cabernet 1995, Waitrose `13` `C`

Smells of marzipan. Fruity as a candied cherry chocolate bar. Good for beginners intimidated by real wines.

Brown Brothers Tarrango 1995 `13` `C`

Too fruit-juicy to rate higher at this price.

**Browns Padthaway Cabernet Sauvignon
1994** `16` `E`

Stunning concentration of flavour and richness. And, unusually
from Australia, balance of acid and tannin.

Browns Shiraz/Malbec, Padthaway 1994 `12` `D`

**Chateau Reynella Basket Press Shiraz
1994** `16.5` `D`

Classic Australian shiraz.

**Hardys Nottage Hill Cabernet Sauvignon/
Shiraz 1994** `15` `C`

Rich Aussie with an insouciant touch of dry fruit.

**Orlando Jacob's Creek Dry Red, Shiraz/
Cabernet 1994** `13.5` `C`

Old favourite. Or is it – any longer?

Oxford Landing Cabernet/Shiraz 1995 `13` `C`

Penfolds Bin 2 Shiraz/Mourvedre 1994 `15.5` `C`

Pizzazz, potency, purpose and polish. Wonderful savoury depth
and warmth of fruit. Excellent texture and very classy.

**Penfolds Rawson's Retreat Bin 35
Cabernet/Shiraz 1994** `15.5` `C`

Excellent value. Has lovely texture and warm, spicy fruit of
depth, flavour, balance and finish. Great roast food wine.

Peter Lehmann Cabernet Sauvignon 1992 `16.5` `D`

Rosemount Estate Cabernet Sauvignon 1994

`14` `D`

Smooth, perhaps too smooth – it has flavour and polish but lacks character and verve. But it must rate 14 because of its soupy richness.

Yaldara Reserve Grenache, Whitmore Old Vineyard 1995

`16.5` `D`

Beautifully concentrated, ripe, enormously velvety wine. Quite rich enough to spread on brioche.

AUSTRALIAN WINE — WHITE

Arrowfield Show Reserve Botrytis Riesling 1993 (half bottle)

`15.5` `E`

Expensive but remarkable. Will age for ten to fifteen years. Wonderful honey fruit with magnificent smoky acids. Potential complexity is enormous. 19 in AD 2000?

Australian Riesling/Gewurztraminer 1995, Waitrose

`12` `C`

Basedow Barossa Chardonnay 1995

`15` `E`

Good food wine but it is expensive. Scallops make it an entertaining companion – and roast cod with sorrel sauce.

Hardys Nottage Hill Chardonnay 1995

`15.5` `C`

Deep and very rich. Let it breathe for a couple of hours to develop the acidity before serving. Also available via Findlater, Mackie Todd.

Houghton Wildflower Ridge Chenin Blanc 1994

`14` `C`

Great with rich fish dishes.

**Katnook Estate Sauvignon Blanc,
Coonawarra 1995** `13.5` `E`

Lindemans Bin 65 Chardonnay 1995 `15.5` `C`

Rich, satisfying, brooding, gently oily – this is a textbook Aussie chardonnay of elegance and style. Superb with grilled veggies.

Moondah Brook Verdelho 1995 `14` `D`

Unusual and delicious. An expensive aperitif (though it works well as one) but great with a first-course fish salad.

Ninth Island Chardonnay, Tasmania 1995 `14` `E`

Expensive, but not without its charms.

Oxford Landing Chardonnay 1995 `14` `C`

Perfectly delightful balance of fruit and acid.

**Penfolds Bin 202 South Australian
Riesling 1994** `14` `C`

A delicious, dry, off-beat riesling with lots of flavour and soft fruit saved from squashy lushness by lemonic acids. Will age well for a couple of years, but terrific with shellfish now.

Penfolds Koonunga Hill Chardonnay 1994 `14.5` `C`

Still one of the best branded Aussie chardonnays in spite of the fearsome fiver staring it in the face.

**Penfolds Organic Chardonnay/Sauvignon
Blanc, Clare Valley 1994** `13.5` `D`

Tasty, fresh, decent. Touch expensive.

**Penfolds Rawson's Retreat Bin 21
Semillon/Chardonnay/Colombard 1995** `15.5` `C`

Apples, walnuts, pineapple, melon – quite an impressive medley here. The acidity is pure, crisp Golden Delicious.

429

Rosemount Show Reserve Chardonnay 1995 | 17 | E

Utter refinement and elegance. A world-class chardonnay of silky class and beautifully integrated fruit and wood.

Saltram Mamre Brook Chardonnay 1994 | 15 | D

Has a luxurious edge to the fruit which strikes the tongue like a rare product of some exotic orchard. Almost mango-like on the finish.

St Huberts Sauvignon Blanc 1996 | 13 | D

Villa Maria Private Bin Chardonnay, Gisborne 1995 | 14.5 | D

Delicious richness and briskness.

BULGARIAN WINE | RED

Bulgarian Cabernet Sauvignon/Merlot 1991 | 14 | B

Cabernet Sauvignon Russe 1990 | 14 | B

Dry, serious-edged, yet friendly and food-compatible.

Cabernet Sauvignon/Merlot, Iambol 1995 | 15 | B

Light but well-structured, good firm flesh to the bones. Cherry/plum flavour. Good with pasta.

Mavrud Reserve, Assenovgrad 1991 | 15.5 | B

Real classy structure to this wine. Maturing beautifully. Earthy dryness with enough personality and flavour to do food proud. Liver and bacon, kidneys in red wine, oxtail stew – choose your offal.

Merlot/Gamza, Pleven 1995

Light, friendly, fruity, soft, winsome.

Oriachovitza Barrel-aged Merlot 1995

Delicious quaffing plonk. But hark. Is that chicken casserole sizzling in the background? Perfect.

CHILEAN WINE RED

Concha y Toro Merlot 1995

Utterly delicious and so rich and deep for the money it takes your breath away as effortlessly as it lathers the tongue.

Cono Sur Cabernet Sauvignon 1994

Cono Sur Pinot Noir Reserve 1995

More effectively structured than previous vintages.

Isla Negra Chilean Red 1995

Dry and handsome, beautifully muscled and textured.

Las Cumbres Chilean Dry Red 1995

Brilliant value. Dry, fruity, seriously structured.

Santa Carolina Malbec 1994

Hums with vigour, personality and deep savoury richness. Lovely texture and a fabulous finish of lingering depth and polish.

Stowells of Chelsea Chilean Merlot Cabernet (3-litre box) 10 G

This wine is soft yet with an agreeably gentle level of proud tannins. Why don't I rate it higher? I simply find the aroma off-puttingly ripe and rubbery. It really ought to be better put together than this.

Valdivieso Barrel-Fermented Cabernet/ Merlot, Lontue 1994 `15` `C`

Slips down sinfully easily. Masses of fruit elegantly contrived and most deeply expressed. Smooth as a Labour Party PR person.

CHILEAN WINE   WHITE

Caliterra Chardonnay, Curico 1995 `16` `C`

Nuttiness under the fruit gives it an added layer of complexity. The fruit is dry and rich, the structure poised and fine. The texture perfect.

Montenuevo Sauvignon Blanc, Maipo 1996 `15.5` `C`

Lovely freshness coating the rich fruit. Terrific glugging stuff and grilled prawn bottle.

Stowells of Chelsea Chilean Sauvignon Blanc (3-litre box) `15.5` `F`

Brilliantly classy fruit of real sauvignon style: clean, fresh, fruity and gently nutty, this is solid, well-made wine of style and modernity. Yet is sufficiently classic in personality to please the hardened sauvignon fan – especially at 54p a glass.

ENGLISH WINE   RED

Chapel Down Epoch I East Sussex 1994 `10` `C`

ENGLISH WINE   WHITE

Chiltern Valley Medium Dry 1992   11 C

Denbies Surrey Gold 1992   13 C

Tanners Brook   7 B
Dull as ditchwater – not necessarily as fruity.

FRENCH WINE   RED

Beaujolais 1995, Waitrose   12 C

Beaune 1er Cru, E. Delaunay 1993   10 E

Bergerac Rouge 1995   14 B
Good country wine glugging.

Cahors Cuvee Reserve 1994   13.5 C

Chateau Carignan Premieres Cotes de Bordeaux 1988   13 E

Chateau Chicane, Graves 1994   14 E
No chicanery here – good honest fruit. Bit unexciting a response? Perhaps . . .

Chateau de Nages Costieres de Nimes 1995   15 C
Rich, dry, herby, deeply fruity and most accommodating with grilled meat and vegetables.

433

Chateau des Deduits, Fleurie Duboeuf 1995 `12` `E`

Chateau Haut d'Allard Cotes de Bourg 1994 `15` `D`

Lovely charred edge to the rich, dark fruit. Cherries, blackcurrant plus texture. Delicious stuff.

Chateau La Faviere, Bordeaux Superieur 1994 `14` `D`

Must have roast lamb drenched in herbs with it.

Chateau Saint-Maurice Cotes du Rhone 1994 `15` `C`

A most humane, clean-shaven specimen from an oft barbaric bearded breed. Great glugging tipple (with character).

Chateau Segonzac Premieres Cotes de Blaye 1994 `14.5` `D`

Stridently burnt edge to the savoury fruit. Great food claret.

Chateau Sergant Lalande de Pomerol 1990 `14.5` `E`

Expensive but mature. Firm, balanced, rich-edged, classy.

Chateau St Auriol, Corbieres 1993 `14.5` `C`

Classy, concentrated, dry, herby, warm.

Chateauneuf-du-Pape, Delas Freres 1993 `13` `E`

Chorey-les-Beaune, Domaine Maillard Pere et Fils 1993 `12` `E`

Some meat. Some flavour.

Clos Saint Michel Chateauneuf-du-Pape 1994 `16` `E`

Expensive but exquisite. Superb charcoal-grilled fruit with wonderful depth of flavour. Big, meaty, savoury as a gravy.

Cotes de Ventoux 1995 `15` `B`

Has surprising polish and high-stepping style. Delicious. No earth but lots of insidiously lap-up-able fruit.

Cotes du Rhone 1995, Waitrose `14` `B`

A soft, easy-to-glug wine with strong hints of class.

Cotes du Roussillon 1995 `14` `B`

A quaffer with the style and muscularity to take on food.

Domaine de Cantemerle, Cotes du Rhone Villages 1994 `14.5` `C`

Bright soft fruit with a meaty edge. Dry but mellow.

Domaine de Rose Merlot/Syrah, VdP d'Oc 1995 `14.5` `B`

Lots of inviting fruit here, dry and most savourily tasty.

Domaine des Fontaines Merlot, Vin de Pays d'Oc 1995 `15` `B`

Very dry and rather wrinkled to begin with, then it softens, lingers and chuckles as it descends.

Domaine Fontaine de Cathala Syrah/ Cabernet Cuvee Prestige VdP d'Oc 1994 (half bottle) `15` `A`

Brilliant half for solo carnivores. Lovely firm fruit.

Domaine Sainte Lucie Gigondas 1994 `15.5` `D`

This has improved considerably since last tasted in October 1995. Lovely herby stuff. All the scented warmth of Provence is in this bottle.

Ermitage du Pic St Loup, Coteaux du Languedoc 1995

Only just makes this rating. It should be 50p cheaper, by rights.

Foncalieu Cabernet Sauvignon Vin de Pays de l'Aude 1994

Likes food and fast company.

Good Ordinary Claret Bordeaux, Waitrose

Better than ever and at a terrific price – especially in the sexy magnum at a bit over seven quid. If only basic claret was always this extraordinarily good, Bordeaux would again be top dog.

Graves Cordier 1995

Authentic, well priced.

Hautes Cotes de Beaune, Tete de Cuvee, Caves des Hautes Cotes 1992

James Herrick Cuvee Simone VdP d'Oc 1995

Superb classy stuff. Has texture, weight, balance, length and an overall feel of great natural rich hedgerow fruitiness.

L'Enclos Domeque Mourvedre/Syrah VdP d'Oc 1995

A vegan and vegetarian wine of softness, richness, smoothness and flavoursome fruitiness. On the dry side but has warmth and a controlled potency.

La Roseraie de Gruaud Larose, St Julien 1992

Good stink. Pity about the finish on the fruit.

Les Granges des Domaines Edmond de Rothschild, Haut-Medoc 1993 `13.5` `E`

Vegetal and firm. Touch overpriced.

Les Tuguets Madiran 1993 `13.5` `C`

I'd put this wine down for another two years before opening it. Will score higher then. Exclusive to Waitrose.

Macon Superieur Les Epillets, Cave de Lugny 1995 `13.5` `C`

Mercurey La Framboisiere, Faiveley 1993 `12.5` `E`

Expensive.

Merlot/Cabernet Sauvignon, VdP d'Oc 1995 `15` `B`

Delicious serious-sided fun. Like hearing Bertrand Russell telling a dirty joke. A dry, deep, naughtily exciting wine.

Minervois 1995 `14.5` `B`

Soft yet with enough rough to go with casseroles.

Prieure de Fonclaire Grande Reserve, Buzet 1994 `14` `C`

Rattling good with bangers 'n' mash – great in the half bottle for the solo bangerist.

Red Burgundy JC Boisset 1994 `10` `C`

Saint Joseph, Caves de Saint-Desirat, 1991 `14` `E`

A big, juicy, lovely glug – touch pricey – but great with mushroom risotto.

Special Reserve Claret, Cotes de Castillon 1994, Waitrose
`14` `C`

Brisk, dry, vigorous, stylish typicity and wonderful with roast meat and vegetation.

St Aubin 1er Cru 'Les Combes', Domaine Prunier 1993
`12` `E`

Not unpleasant fruit but a very unpleasant price.

Syrah Domaines des Salices, Lurton 1995
`15` `C`

Lovely lush softness, dryness and flavour. Yummy fruit.

Syrah Galet Vineyards 1994
`14.5` `C`

Rhone style fruit but not price. Terrific herby warmth of fruit. Easy drinking yet serious.

Winter Hill VdP de l'Aude 1995
`15` `B`

Brilliant-value rich, dry red which will make even claret fans purse their lips and pat their purses.

FRENCH WINE WHITE

Beblenheim Gewurztraminer d'Alsace Cuvee 1993 (half bottle)
`15` `B`

Delicious hedonistic fruit in the half bottle for the solo tippler. Rose petals crushed and vinified.

Bordeaux Blanc Medium Dry
`11` `B`

Bordeaux Sauvignon 1995, Waitrose
`12.5` `B`

Boulder Creek VdP de Vaucluse 1995
`13` `B`

Cheap and cheerful with fish stew.

Chablis Gaec des Reugnis 1995 `12` `E`

Chablis Premier Cru Beauroy 1993 `11` `E`

Chardonnay (Matured in French Oak) VdP d'Oc 1995 `14` `C`

Rich and flavourful. Good with robust fish dishes.

Chardonnay Vin de Pays du Jardin de la France 1995 `13` `B`

Chateau Carsin Cuvee Prestige 1994 `14` `E`

Classy stuff. Delicate wood and fruit.

Chateau de La Chartreuse, Sauternes 1989 (half bottle) `14` `E`

Superb fruit here for extreme, richly heeled hedonists.

Chateau la Caussade Ste Croix du Mont 1992 `15` `E`

Try it as an aperitif before you try it with blue cheese. Stunningly rich fruit.

Cotes du Luberon 1995 `13.5` `C`

Great fish 'n' chips plonk.

Cuckoo Hill Viognier VdP d'Oc 1995 `15.5` `C`

Classic viognier with clean apricot fruit and fresh finish. Delicious tippling here.

Cuvee d'Alban Barrique Fermented, Bordeaux 1995 `13` `C`

Domaine de Planterieu VdP des Cotes de Gascogne 1995 `14` `C`

Bite, backbone and flesh – a well-bodied, fresh, fruity wine.

Domaine des Fontanelles Sauvignon Vin de Pays d'Oc 1995

`14` `C`

Satisfyingly subtle.

Domaine du Bousquet Chardonnay/ Sauvignon Blanc 1995

`15` `C`

Most insistently fruity. Quite delicious. More melony than lemony.

Domaine Petit Chateau Chardonnay, Vin de Pays du Jardin de la France 1995

`14` `C`

Most agreeably fruity in a classic white burgundy mould.

Gewurztraminer d'Alsace 1993, Waitrose

`14` `D`

Lovely rich fruit for grilled duck breasts or prawns with ginger.

James Herrick Chardonnay VdP d'Oc 1995

`15` `C`

Very elegant, well-shaped, delicately fruity and classy.

Le Pujalet Vin de Pays du Gers 1995

`14` `B`

Delightfully fruity aperitif.

Le Voyageur Sauvignon, Bordeaux 1995

`14` `C`

Packaged like cheap cologne but not fruited. Fun to look at, fun to drink with grilled sole.

Macon Lugny, Les Charmes 1994

`13.5` `D`

Has charm, yes (fruitwise) but nearly six quid is a lot to ask.

Macon Solutre, Auvigue 1995

`13.5` `D`

Macon-Villages Chardonnay 1995

`13.5` `C`

Muscadet 1995, Waitrose 11 B

Pinot Blanc d'Alsace Blanck Freres 1995 13 C

Pouilly Fume, Masson-Blondelet 1995 12 E

Premieres Cotes de Bordeaux 13 C
A pud wine. But the pud needs to be very light.

Puligny Montrachet Bernard Grapin 1993 10 G

Roussanne Ryman VdP d'Oc 1995 13.5 C
Amusing.

Sancerre La Vraignonette 1995 11 D

Sauvignon de Touraine 1995 14 C
A delicious fish wine or aperitif. Class, fruit, freshness and style.
An Aussie wine made in France.

**Terret/Chardonnay, VdP des Cotes de
Thau, J. & F. Lurton 1995** 12 C

**Tokay Pinot Gris d'Alsace, Cave de
Beblenheim 1995 (half bottle)** 14 B
Lay it down for three years. It'll improve immeasurably.

Vouvray, Domaine de la Robiniere, 1994 13 C
Needs five years more to blossom brilliantly.

White Burgundy Chardonnay, Boisset 1994 12 C

**Winter Hill Semillon/Chardonnay, VdP
d'Oc 1995** 13 C

Winter Hill VdP de l'Aude 1995 13.5 B
Clean, fresh, cheap.

GERMAN WINE WHITE

Avelsbacher Hammerstein Riesling Spatlese, 1989

Lovely conversation-enhancing aperitif. Lemon-tinged perfection.

Bacharacher Schloss Stahleck Riesling Kabinett 1992

Brilliant aperitif. Lovely, slowly developing fruit and vivid acids. Great with smoked fish.

Devil's Rock Riesling, St Ursula, Pfalz 1994/5

Delicate true-riesling aroma, delicate acidity and good fruit, and fresh, mineral-edged finish. Excellent smoked fish wine. Developing very subtle petrolly undertones. Will improve for eighteen months or more.

Erdener Treppchen Riesling, Monchhof 1991

Delicious aperitif. Petrolly, lemony, racy.

Hochheimer Reichestal Riesling Kabinett 1993

10 points now but it will rate 15 in five years' time.

Kirchheimer Schwarzerde Beerenauslese, Pfalz 1994 (half bottle)

Brilliant acids under the rich honeyed fruit. Great with soft fruits.

Longuicher Probstberg Riesling Spatlese, Moselland 1988 `14` `C`

Good price for such maturity of fruit.

Morio Muskat, Pfalz 1995 `12.5` `B`

Ockfener Bockstein Riesling, Dr Wagner 1995 `12` `D`

Schumann-Nagler Geisenheimer Monchspfad Riesling Spatlese 1990 `13.5` `D`

Ungsteiner Honigsackel Gewurztraminer Spatlese, Pfalz 1994 `15.5` `E`

Turns dry and deep once the soft lychee fruit has become becalmed by the acidity. Delicious curiosity. Needs sweet sauces. Chicken dishes kill its mellowness. Great with Peking duck.

Urziger Wurzgarten Riesling Spatlese, Monchhof 1993 `12` `D`

GREEK WINE RED

Vin de Crete Red, Kourtaki 1995 `13` `B`

Pleasant brew which might work with pickled boar's snout.

GREEK WINE WHITE

Kouros Patras 1994 `13` `C`

HUNGARIAN WINE RED

Deer Leap Sauvignon/Cabernet Franc 1995 `14` `B`

Has some style to it: dry, gently earthy, some flavour.

HUNGARIAN WINE WHITE

Chapel Hill Irsai Oliver 1995 `14` `B`

Brilliant aperitif.

Deer Leap Dry White 1995 `13` `B`

Clean, not hugely exciting.

Deer Leap Gewurztraminer, Mor 1995 `12` `C`

Deer Leap Pinot Gris 1995 `15` `B`

Delicious aperitif wine with a soft apricot subtlety and a gently nutty finish.

Deer Leap Sauvignon Blanc 1995 `14` `C`

Gently spritzig, fresh, gently fruity – not a class sauvignon, but a good one.

Hungarian Cabernet Sauvignon Rose, Nagyrede 1995 `15` `B`

One of the most fragrant and deliciously fruity roses around. Excellent value for money.

Lakeside Oak Chardonnay 1995 `13.5` `B`

Orchard Hill Dry Country Wine 1994 `12` `B`

Tokaji Aszu 5 Puttonyos 1989 (50cl)

Raisins and honey. Try it with fruit cake or goose liver pate.

Tokaji Disznoko Dry Furmint 1994 13.5 C

The first vintage of this wine I've found able to rate well.

ITALIAN WINE RED

**Amarone Classico della Valpolicella,
Ca'Fornari 1990**

Spiced prunes, aniseed and tannin. An acquired taste – especially at nine quid.

Barolo Nicolello 1991

Pleasant licorice edge. Satisfying tannins. But ten quid!!?

Campo ai Sassi, Rosso di Montalcino 1994

Tannin, fruit, acidity, all deftly knitted together with style.

**Castello di Fonterutoli Chianti Classico
1993** 14.5 D

Lots of personality plus loads of baked, dry-edged fruit.

Chianti 1995, Waitrose 13.5 C

Simple soft stuff.

**Chianti Classico Riserva, Poggio a'
Fratti 1985** 13 E

Gripping, earthy stuff. Pricey.

Fiordaliso Sangiovese di Toscana, 1994

Utterly delicious. Combines fruit of a cherry/plum style with a dry edge and a lingering, faintly tannic finish. A serious glug.

Le Pergole Torte, Montevertine 1987 | 12.5 | E

Le Trulle Negroamaro del Salento 1995 | 14.5 | C

Soft, savoury, ripe, flavoursome. Delicious glug, great with food.

Monica di Sardegna 1993, Waitrose | 14 | C

Lovely rich fruit here of surprising vibrancy for such a price. Has a curious light cherry side (fruity) and a brisk savoury side (dry).

Montepulciano d'Abruzzo, Umani Ronchi 1995 | 13 | C

Salice Salentino Riserva, Taurino 1993 | 14.5 | D

A cross between a balsamic medicine and an invalid's broth. Will revive any palate – especially under rich food.

Teroldego Rotaliano, Ca'Vit 1995 | 13 | C

Like beaujolais in feel.

Vino Nobile di Montepulciano, Avignonesi 1992 | 13 | E

Delicious but too pricey.

Waitrose Carafe Red Wine (1 litre) | 13 | C

Party popper.

ITALIAN WINE   WHITE

Chardonnay delle Tre Venezie, Pasqua 1994 | 13.5 | C

Chardonnay, Vino da Tavola delle Tre Venezie, Vallade 1995 `13` `B`

Frascati Superiore, Villa Rufinella 1995 `11` `C`

Lugana DOC Villa Flora, Zenato 1995 `15.5` `C`
A wine of considerable class and wit. Lovely fruit, balance, freshness and depth.

Nuragus di Cagliari DOC, Sardegna 1995, Waitrose `14.5` `C`
Back to form with a vengeance. Fruity, clean, nutty and fresh.

Pinot Grigio VdT delle Tre Venezie, Fiordaliso 1995 `12.5` `C`

Sauvignon Friuli Grave, San Simone 1995 `13` `C`

Soave Classico Vigneto Colombara, Zeneto 1995 `15` `C`
The most delicious soave I've tasted.

Stowells of Chelsea Chardonnay Trentino (3-litre box) `13.5` `G`
Simple, dry, good fruit.

Verdicchio dei Casteli Jesi, Moncaro 1995 `12` `C`

Waitrose Carafe White Wine (1 litre) `10` `C`

LEBANESE WINE RED

Chateau Musar 1988 `13` `E`
Hot, heady, pruney, expensive and too ripely arthritic for my taste. Has to have food with it.

NEW ZEALAND WINE RED

Montana Cabernet Sauvignon 1994 `14` `C`

Is it my imagination or is this wine beginning to taste more like old-style claret?

NEW ZEALAND WINE WHITE

Cooks Chardonnay, Gisborne 1995 `16` `C`

Great stuff. Has style, richness and elegance.

Lawson Dry Hills Sauvignon Blanc, Marlborough 1995 `14.5` `E`

Classic richness.

New Zealand Dry White Wine, Gisborne 1996 `14` `C`

Terrific depth of flavour here.

PORTUGUESE WINE RED

Ramada Tinto 1994 `13.5` `B`

Vale do Bomfim Reserva, Douro 1990 `14` `D`

This is quietly impressive but at over a fiver the finish needs to be more competitive to rate higher.

ROMANIAN WINE RED

Samburesti Pinot Noir 1994

Juicy with an edge of dry rusticity. First-class pasta plonk or chilled for salmon and eel.

Vat 4 Cabernet Sauvignon, Samburesti
1994

Dry, jammy hints but firm and fruity enough to go with light meat and cheese dishes.

SOUTH AFRICAN WINE RED

Athlone Pinot Noir 1995
Rich stuff.

Cabernet Sauvignon/Shiraz Du Toitskloof,
Worcester 1995

Plums and cherries which turn vigorous and biting on the finish. Good glugging stuff.

Cape Dry Red 1995

A most agreeably drinkable party wine. Which party I'm not prepared to reveal.

Clos Malverne Pinotage Reserve,
Stellenbosch 1995

Rich and dry and as warm and colourful on the tongue as beautiful to the eye.

Culemborg Pinotage, Paarl 1995 `15` `C`

Rich as the Christmas stuffing. Delicious thick fruit.

Delheim Cabernet Sauvignon, Stellenbosch 1994 `14` `D`

Needs a lamb chop to spring into vibrant life.

Diamond Hills Pinotage/Cabernet Sauvignon 1995 `16` `C`

Brilliant richness and softness held sympathetically by textured tannins. Lovely stuff.

Fairview Shiraz Reserve, Paarl 1994 `15` `D`

Not a hint of Australian spice or muscle – but more tannic velvetiness. Waitrose exclusive.

Klein Constantia Cabernet Sauvignon, Constantia 1993 `14` `D`

Hums with richness and savouriness. Almost too sinfully drinkable.

Merwida Winery Ruby Cabernet 1995 `15` `C`

So rich and sweet to finish – it's disarming.

Warwick Estate Cabernet Franc 1993 `15` `E`

Bourgeuil meets the Medoc and creates a new star.

Warwick Estate Merlot 1994 `13.5` `E`

SOUTH AFRICAN WINE WHITE

Avontuur Chardonnay, Stellenbosch 1995 `14.5` `D`

Gently lemonic chardonnay perfectly suited to shellfish and fish dishes.

Bellingham Sauvignon Blanc, Paarl 1996 `14` `C`

Excellent fish wine.

Cape Dry White, Paarl 1996 `13.5` `B`

Cape Release 1996 `13.5` `C`

Tasty party wine at 66p more than it should be.

Culemborg Blanc de Noirs 1996 `14` `C`

Delicious rose aperitif.

Culemborg Chardonnay, Western Cape 1995 `13.5` `C`

Ripe, full, fruity. Waitrose exclusive.

Culemborg Chenin Blanc, Paarl 1995 `14` `B`

Brilliant cuttle fish and calamares wine.

Delheim Chardonnay 1994 `14` `D`

Rich, creamy, woody and seemingly assertive, this wine is described as (sic) 'voluptious' on its back label – this can only be an amalgam of voluptuous and meretricious for it flatters to deceive. It is rich but this richness is superficial. It will not take to highly flavoured foods. Getting mature now, this wine.

Diamond Hills Chenin Blanc/Chardonnay 1995 `14.5` `C`

A deliciously fruity aperitif wine which offers whistle-clean freshness, a hint of smoked melon depth and gooseberry-edged finish of some style.

Klein Constantia Chardonnay 1995 `14.5` `D`

Woody, ripe, rich. Elegant fulsomeness.

Kumala Colombard/Chardonnay 1996 `13.5` `C`

Springfield Estate Chardonnay, Robertson 1995 `15.5` `C`

Soft, highly flavoured. A gorgeous treat at the end of the day.

SPANISH WINE   RED

Agramont Navarra 1992 `14.5` `C`

Delicious with tarragon chicken.

Campillo Rioja Gran Reserva 1986 `14.5` `E`

Old war horse with very couth manners.

Cosme Palacio Rioja 1993 `15` `D`

Classic rioja – rich and beautifully structured.

Fuente del Ritmo, Tempranillo La Mancha 1994 `13.5` `C`

Not half as rich and thrilling as previous vintages, or as well priced.

Las Lomas Tempranillo/Cabernet Sauvignon, Valencia 1995 `15` `B`

Soft, full of flavour and richness, and a rolling flourish on the finish. Great value.

Ribera del Duero, Callejo 1994 `14` `C`

Rioja Crianza 1993, Waitrose `13.5` `C`

Stowells of Chelsea Tempranillo (3-litre box) `14` `F`

Great glugging flavour and texture.

SPANISH WINE   WHITE

Agramont Viura/Chardonnay, Navarra 1995   `13.5`   `C`

Banda Oro Rioja Blanco 1992   `11`   `D`

Rather misshapen but, unlike Quasimodo, not good value.

Castillo de Liria Moscatel, Valencia   `16`   `C`

Brilliant honey-rich fruit of treacly texture.

Don Hugo Rosado   `12`   `B`

USA WINE   RED

Bel Arbors Cabernet Sauvignon, California 1992   `14`   `C`

Rather a hit and miss affair with the fruit in fine fettle up to the last minute, then it turns juicy, then the tannins finally strike.

Canyon Springs Gamay/Zinfandel   `12`   `C`

So juicy it dribbles down the chin more agreeably than it slides down the throat. The marriage of grapes is not entirely happy.

Cartlidge & Browne Zinfandel 1993   `13`   `C`

Simple, juicy stuff.

Fetzer Valley Oaks Cabernet 1993   `13.5`   `D`

USA WINE   WHITE

**Canyon Springs Pinot Noir Rose, California
1995**   `10` `C`

**Cartlidge & Browne Chardonnay, California
1995**   `15` `C`

Classy, restrained (yet with a rich-edged finish), extremely
charming. A classic Californian for little money.

Fetzer Sundial Chardonnay, California 1994   `14.5` `D`

Just about deserves its points but I wish it was a quid cheaper
considering the quality of fruit on offer.

**Stowells of Chelsea California Blush
(3-litre box)**   `12.5` `F`

FORTIFIED WINE

Churchill's Dry White Port   `14` `E`

An interesting aperitif for honey-dentured drinkers.

**Passito di Pantelleria, Pellegrino 1994
(half bottle)**   `14` `D`

Soft fruits accompaniment.

Red Muscadel 1975   `14.5` `D`

Great with Christmas pudding. A stunning oldie with fruit like
diesel oil.

Solera Jerezana Dry Oloroso, Waitrose   `16.5` `D`

Fantastic! Rich old classic dry sherry! Uniquely dry, rich, deep, textured and very puzzling – when do you drink it? Bedtime with a book.

Starboard Batch 88 `12` `E`

Joke wine. Starboard is the other side to port. Geddit? At eight quid you may prefer not to.

White Jerepigo 1979 `15` `D`

Delicious with fruit tart at the end of the meal. Thick and honey-rich with a classical cherry centre.

SPARKLING WINE/CHAMPAGNE

Angas Brut Rose (Australian) `15.5` `D`

Like pleasantly acidic raspberries – dry ones.

BB Club Sparkling Chardonnay (Hungary) `13.5` `C`

Blanc de Blancs, Waitrose `14` `G`

Expensive, but it is lean, lissom and roller-blade smooth.

Blanquette de Limoux, Waitrose `13.5` `D`

**Bohemia Regal Demi-Sec, Czech Republic
Red Sparkling Wine** `10` `D`

Cava Brut, Waitrose `16` `D`

Superb! Clean, nutty, fresh, elegant, brilliantly priced.

Champagne Bredon Brut `14` `F`

Bredon the label, bread on the fruit. A most attractively biscuity champagne for the money. Exclusive to Waitrose.

Champagne Brut Blanc de Noirs, Waitrose `14` `F`

Classic; expensive but classic.

Champagne Brut Rose, Waitrose `13` `G`

Champagne Brut Vintage 1989, Waitrose `14` `G`

Surprising, such a decent rating for such an expensive wine. But it is very beautiful.

Champagne Brut, Waitrose `13.5` `F`

Champagne Rose, Waitrose `15` `F`

The closest the poor teetotaller can come to grasping the flavour of this scrumptious article is by chewing a digestive biscuit spread thickly with crushed rose petals and drinking Perrier water with a microscopically thin slice of lime zest.

Champagne, Waitrose `14` `F`

One of the best supermarket champagnes you can buy.

Chapel Down Century NV (England) `12` `D`

Like home-made, well-made, wine. Has a teasing apricot edge.

Clairette de Die Tradition (France) `13.5` `D`

Great fun. A peachy bubbly!

Cremant de Bourgogne Blanc de Noirs, Lugny `14` `D`

An impressively classically styled bubbly at a good price.

Cremant de Bourgogne Brut Rose, Cave de Lugny `13` `D`

Mildly fruity.

Duc de Marre Champagne   13   G

Rich biscuity fruit – delicious with smoked fish but expensive and too hearty, perhaps, for most bubbly fans. Also available through mail order.

Duc de Marre Grand Cru Brut   17   G

A real treat which is not absurdly priced. Has old wine in the blend (at least a dozen years old) and this gives biscuity aroma and chewiness to the fruit almost as pervasive as a fresh-baked croissant. Yet it finishes with vigour and purpose. Only via Findlater, Mackie Todd.

Green Point Vineyards Brut, Australian 1993   13.5   F

Krone Borealis Brut 1992 (South African)   13.5   D

Le Baron de Beaumont Chardonnay Brut (France)   15   C

Brilliant-value tippling.

Santi Chardonnay Brut (Italy)   11   D

Saumur Brut, Waitrose   14   D

An inexpensive alternative to more expensive bubblies. Has a classic dry shape to the fruit.

Seaview Brut   14   D

Seppelt Great Western Brut   15   C

I've said it all before about this wine. Let its rating say it all now.

STOP PRESS

ASDA

ARGENTINIAN WINE RED

Asda Argentinian Red 1996

This has improved considerably in bottle since I tasted it last time. It's great value with a lovely touch of dry richness and depth to the vigorously stylish fruit.

ARGENTINIAN WINE WHITE

La Rural Mendoza Pinot Blanc/Chardonnay 1996

Rich, smoky-melon fruit with a hint of grapefruit on the acidity. Great for fish dishes.

AUSTRALIAN WINE RED

Chateau Reynella Basket Press Shiraz 1994

The richness of this wine is not superficial but committed and deep. It is an outstanding Aussie.

Penfolds Bin 2 Shiraz/Mourvedre 1994 `15.5` `D`

Manages to combine the best Aussie characteristics: softness and flavour with characterful depth and strength of personality.

CHILEAN WINE — RED

Chilean Cabernet/Merlot 1995, Asda — `16.5` `C`

The new vintage has a gorgeous lingering flavour of coffee, walnuts and plum. The texture and depth of fruit is extraordinary for the money.

Valdivieso Malbec 1996 — `17.5` `C`

Wonderful wine! Quite wonderful! The texture is the softest velvet, the fruit is exquisite plum and blackberry, the balance is poised.

CHILEAN WINE — WHITE

Valdivieso Chardonnay 1996 — `16.5` `C`

Wonderful richness of complexity and length of flavour. Balanced, elegant, vivid (yet soft and ripe), hugely stylish and totally captivating.

FRENCH WINE — RED

Domaine de la Baume Merlot VdP d'Oc 1994 — `17` `D`

One of the greatest merlots on sale. World-class. Almost perfect.

FRENCH WINE WHITE

Cotes de Bergerac 'Confit de la Colline' 1995 (half bottle)　15　D

Richly honeyed and waxy and very deep. Not a lot of balancing acidity but with blue cheese or fresh fruit this hiccup will not cause alarm.

Cotes du Rhone Blanc Chateau du Trignon 1995　15.5　D

Beautiful muted richness and soft earthiness which hits the back palate perfectly.

Phillipe de Baudin Sauvignon Blanc VdP d'Oc 1995　15　C

Utterly delicious, balanced, clean, classically Cos-lettuce crisp, and with a finely wrought price-tag. It's as subtle but as positive as a Wildean epigram.

GREEK WINE RED

Marble Mountain St George/Cabernet 1995　

Brilliant flavour and texture. A new grape begorrah! St George – what a name. It comes across like a soft, spicy Barolo.

Temple Ruins Greek Red 1995　

Possibly the best Greek wine for the money on sale. Has a wonderful claret-like quality to rich dry fruit.

SOUTH AFRICAN WINE   RED

Fairview Estate Shiraz 1995   `17.5` `C`

Dazzling layers of fruit to this new vintage – like a cake. Lovely richness, flavour and haunting style.

Landskroon Pinotage 1995   `15` `C`

This new vintage seems civilised and polite at first, then it suddenly whacks flavour at you like an old leather glove. Great!

SOUTH AFRICAN WINE   WHITE

Muscat Frontignan Blanc Danie de Wet   `17` `C`

Brilliant and can only deepen its depth and honey fruit over the next three years (19 points then).

SPARKLING WINE/CHAMPAGNE

Cava Rosado, Asda   `15` `C`

Brilliant for the money. Simply terrific style for under a fiver.

Cranswick Pinot/Chardonnay Brut   `15` `D`

This is tasting much better than it was in the spring of 1996. Beautifully crafted stuff. Fruity yet refreshing, it's bold, classic, stylish and very ripe.

Hardys Ebenezer Pinot Noir Brut

Don't hold your breath – it probably won't be in store until January 1997. But it's definitely one for the millennium when it will be a 19 point wine of even greater complexity than it is already.

CO-OP

BULGARIAN WINE RED

Sliven Merlot/Pinot Noir, Bulgarian Vintners

Brilliant value. Has soft initial attack of fruit (blackcurrant yawn yawn) but then something delicious and sinister happens – dry cherries seize the throat like balsam.

FRENCH WINE RED

La Baume Syrah Grenache 1995

GREEK WINE RED

Vin de Crete Red, Kourtaki 1995 `13` `B`

PORTUGUESE WINE RED

Quinta da Pancas 1995 `16` `D`

Best vintage for some years. Certainly the vintage most fulfilling of the estate's potential to grow really stylish, warm, complex cabernets without a hint of coarseness. Great tannins, superb fruit, lovely balance and all round compactness.

Ramada, Estremadura 1994 `14.5` `B`

A simple fruit glug? Not a flawless thesis but . . . what about the hot sunny edge to the fruit? What about the smoothness? What about the sheer pleasure of it?

SPARKLING WINE/CHAMPAGNE

Cordoniu Premier Cuvee Brut (Spain) `14` `D`

MORRISONS

CHILEAN WINE   WHITE

Gato Blanco Sauvignon Blanc 1995   14 B

Some flavour here based on savoury fruit. Not a lot of freshness
to it – needs food. Roast chicken is my bet.

FRENCH WINE   WHITE

Domaine de Cray Touraine 1992   15 B

Brilliant mature bargain. The fruit is deep, rich, highly aromatic
and very satisfying to drink with a chicken stew.

La Source Chardonnay d'Oc 1995   14.5 C

Fantastic! The Frogs floor the Roos with one sip! It's sealed
with a plastic cork – and this ensures the fruit will never be
contaminated (as it might be with natural cork). This fruit is
warm, nutty, full and delicious.

HUNGARIAN WINE   WHITE

Chapel Hill Irsai Oliver 1995   14 B

Pleasing and brilliantly priced aperitif. Tickles the tastebuds
delightfully.

SAFEWAY

AUSTRALIAN WINE RED

**Penfolds Clare Valley Shiraz/Cabernet
Sauvignon 1994**

As good, and as classy, an organic red as it's possible to find.

ITALIAN WINE RED

Casa di Giovanni 1994, Safeway

New vintage. Gripping stuff, dry and personality-packed.

SAINSBURY'S

FRENCH WINE RED

Pavillon Rouge, Margaux 1993

Overpriced, overrated and over here – but only at the top six stores on the chain.

FRENCH WINE WHITE

Chateau Romer du Hayot Sauternes 1981 (half bottle)

This is treacle-textured and very rich. But it is only marginally more a complex sweet wine than the Muscat de Valencia which costs six times less money. Value? Forget it. (Top forty-four stores only.)

VdP de l'Agenais Semillon/Sauvignon 1995

Brilliant value-for-money fish 'n' chip wine.

SOMERFIELD/ GATEWAY

FRENCH WINE   RED

Somerfield VdP de l'Ardeche   `14` `B`

This has improved since I tasted it earlier this year. It is earthy, soft, agreeably drinkable.

ITALIAN WINE   RED

Vignetti Casterna Valpolicella, Pasqua 1993 `15` `C`

This new vintage is great, juicy, fruity fun.

PORTUGUESE WINE   RED

Leziria Vinho de Mesa Ribatejo NV   `14` `B`

Hints of richness, pace and positive fun-seeking intentions. It's the last attribute which wins the day.

Quinta da Pancas 1995   `16` `D`

Best vintage for some years. Certainly the vintage most fulfilling of the estate's potential to grow really stylish, warm, complex cabernets without a hint of coarseness. Great tannins, superb fruit, lovely balance and all round compactness.

TESCO

FRENCH WINE — RED

Chateau Bessan Segur, Medoc 1995 `14` `D`
Needs food to show what it can do. It's brisk, savoury, dry and moody.

Chateau Robert Cotes de Bourg 1993 `14` `D`
Curious sloppy edge to the fruit which is intentionally well-dressed and most proper. Has classic claret touches otherwise. Selected stores.

ITALIAN WINE — RED

Marchese del Casa Sicilian Red, Tesco `10` `B`
Delicious simplicity and food friendliness.

SPANISH WINE — RED

Agramont Garnacha 1995 `14.5` `C`
Superb food wine. The fruit and acidity are in perfect step to deal with anything from a roast chicken to cheese. Top seventy-seven stores only.

STOP PRESS

SPANISH WINE WHITE

Agramont Navarra Viura Chardonnay 1995

Lemony, classy, stylish and great with fish. Selected stores.

USA WINE WHITE

Weston Estate Californian Chardonnay 1995

Aromatic, rich, oily, opulent. It's a bottle to guzzle.

SPARKLING WINE/CHAMPAGNE

La Marca Prosecco Spumante (Italy)

Elegant, incisive, delicately priced.

Villa Pigna Reserva Brut (Italy)

Brilliant steal! Not classic in shape but for a bit over a fiver this bubbly is great with mild food and pre-prandial pottering. Top seventy-seven stores only.

NOTES

NOTES

NOTES

NOTES

NOTES

NOTES

Summerplonk 1997

Malcolm Gluck

In the summer of 1997, for the very first time, Britain's bestselling wine scribe will give his verdict on the best-value summer wines available through our top supermarket chains in a brand new guide, SUMMERPLONK 1997.

From now on, Malcolm Gluck will pass judgement twice annually on bargain bottles from Asda, Budgens, Co-op, Kwik Save, Marks & Spencer, Morrisons, Safeway, Sainsbury's, Somerfield/Gateway, Tesco and Waitrose.

SUMMERPLONK 1997 will be available from bookshops and supermarkets from 19th June 1997. Price £4.99.